Case Studies
in Criminal Procedure

Case Studies
in Criminal Procedure

Susan Jacobs, J.D., Ph.D.

University of Nebraska at Omaha

PEARSON
Prentice
Hall

Upper Saddle River, New Jersey 07458

Library of Congress Cataloging-in-Publication Data

Jacobs, Susan
  Case studies in criminal procedure / Susan Jacobs.
    p. cm.
  Includes bibliographical references and index.
  ISBN 0-13-170044-8
  1. Criminal procedure—United States—Cases. I. Title.

  KF9618.J33 2006
  345.73'05—dc22

                          2005015073

Executive Editor: Frank Mortimer, Jr.
Associate Editor: Sarah Holle
Editorial Assistant: Kelly Krug
Production Editor: Stephanie Levy, nSight, Inc.
Production Liaison: Barbara Marttine Cappuccio
Director of Manufacturing and Production:
  Bruce Johnson
Managing Editor: Mary Carnis

Manufacturing Manager: Ilene Sanford
Manufacturing Buyer: Cathleen Petersen
Senior Design Coordinator: Miguel Ortiz
Cover Designer: Marianne Frasco
Cover Image: Richard Cummins/CORBIS
Composition: LaserWords
Printing and Binding: R.R. Donnelley & Sons

Pearson Education LTD.
Pearson Education Australia PTY, Limited
Pearson Education Singapore, Pte. Ltd
Pearson Education North Asia Ltd
Pearson Education, Canada, Ltd
Pearson Educación de Mexico, S.A. de C.V.
Pearson Education–Japan
Pearson Education Malaysia, Pte. Ltd

10 9 8 7 6 5 4 3 2 1
ISBN 0-13-170044-8

Contents

CHAPTER 5   Search and Search Warrants   54

CHAPTER 7   Stop and Frisk Exception   90

CHAPTER 10   Plain View Exception   137

CHAPTER 11   Automobile Exception   142

CHAPTER 14   Pretrial Identification   179

CHAPTER 15   Effective Assistance of Counsel   185

Preface

The study of criminal procedure is the study of the constitutional requirements governing criminal prosecution. The Bill of Rights in the U.S. Constitution sets out guaranteed rights that citizens have relative to the government; 4 of those first 10 amendments deal specifically with rights people have during the course of criminal prosecution. The 4th Amendment protects us from the police, mandating procedures for lawful searches and seizures. The 5th Amendment contains the guarantee of due process, a cornerstone of freedom. The 6th Amendment protects us from the prosecutor, guaranteeing standards for trial. The 8th Amendment protects us from the courts, mandating reasonable bail and fines and prohibiting cruel and unusual punishment. Each of these is a critical component of criminal prosecution, with study of the 4th Amendment surely the most important and the most complex.

This book is not designed as a text. It presumes students are studying criminal procedure and are using a text that sets out the basic constitutional rules that govern the investigation and prosecution of alleged criminal behavior. This collection of cases is designed to help students understand how the constitutional rules work.

This book has been successfully used in classroom settings, where students are placed in groups of four to six people, groups that are small enough to ensure that each student will participate and large enough to give students the benefits of others' thinking. The students begin by discussing the questions posed at the end of a selected fact pattern. The thinking is this: If the student can clearly articulate the constitutional rule and the student's analysis of how that rule applies to the facts at hand, the student demonstrates understanding of the material. Sometimes students think they understand the material, but they cannot articulate or explain how the principle applies. These exercises force that articulation and illustrate for the student where the "soft spots" remain. After students have completed their analyses, they read the court's opinion in the case and understand how that court thought the reasoning should proceed. These are nonthreatening exercises because students are working with one another in an ungraded atmosphere. They might make mistakes and they will help others who make mistakes. In so doing, they will learn. Students report that they enjoy working with these cases and find them instructive.

Some cases raise a number of issues related to a single subject or related to a number of different subjects. Those cases were selected to illustrate how the various constitutional principles governing criminal procedure influence one another and how a decision with respect to one can impact another. Especially when we are working with exceptions to 4th Amendment protections, we discover that one exception can "feed" on another.

In some of these cases the courts rely on U.S. Supreme Court precedent. The Supreme Court cases relied on are cited. Sometimes the courts rely on other lower court opinions. Those lower court opinions are not cited; the text here simply notes an omitted citation with [*].

I begin with some introductory material, reviewing the concepts of federalism and privacy. Federalism offers citizens constitutional protection in both the federal and state constitutions, and offers the unique opportunity for a defendant to find constitutional protection in the state constitution when that protection is not available under the federal constitution. Privacy is not specifically guaranteed in the Constitution, but it is an important principle in search and seizure law and it is important for students to understand how to determine when a reasonable expectation of privacy exists.

I then move to examination of the 4th Amendment protections. The 4th Amendment guarantees that "The right of the people to be secure in their persons, houses, papers, and effects, against unreasonable searches and seizures, shall not be violated, and no Warrants shall issue, but upon probable cause, supported by Oath or affirmation, and particularly describing the place to be searched, and the persons or things to be seized." In this amendment, the government promises that arrests and searches will be premised on probable cause and (preferably) will be accompanied by a warrant. This section examines the constitutional meaning of probable cause for arrest and for search. Cases on warrants focus here on search warrants because that is the arena in which the constitutional questions most frequently arise.

With the protections of the 4th Amendment in mind, we begin our exploration of how those protections are enforced and the exceptions to those 4th Amendment protections.

Chapter 6 examines the Exclusionary Rule and its general application. The Exclusionary Rule is the mechanism created by the Supreme Court to hold the government to its constitutional promises. It declares that if the government obtains evidence unconstitutionally, that evidence will be excluded from the trial. That is, the penalty for unconstitutional discovery of evidence on the part of the government is that the government will not profit from its misdeed. Cases on the good faith exception, hot pursuit, exigent circumstances, fruit of the poisonous tree, attenuation, independent source, and inevitable discovery exceptions are included in this section.

The next six chapters deal with exceptions to the 4th Amendment that are the real meat of understanding search and seizure. The 4th Amendment guarantees that the government will not search us or our property, nor will it seize us or our property, unless the government has probable cause and (preferably) a warrant. Exceptions have been created that restrict those protections:

- The search incident to arrest exception allows the government to search us, without any search probable cause and without a search warrant, if the police have made a lawful, custodial arrest.

- The consent exception allows the government to search us without any search probable cause and without a warrant if we have consented to that search.

- The stop and frisk exception allows the government to stop us if police have reasonable suspicion that we are engaged in criminal activity, and it allows them to frisk us if they have reasonable suspicion to believe we are armed and dangerous.

- The plain view exception allows the government to observe things in plain view (if the police are lawfully in a place from which that observation is made) and to seize evidence without a warrant if the police have observed it in plain view.

- The automobile exception allows the government to stop and search our automobile if police have probable cause to believe evidence of a crime will be found in the vehicle.

- The open fields exception allows the government to trespass on our property and seize evidence of crime if that trespass and seizure of evidence occurs outside the curtilage of the home.

The final section of the book examines constitutional protections at trial, beginning with constitutional protections that come into play during interrogation and those that govern admissions and confessions. This examination focuses primarily on *Miranda* cases that are designed to protect the 5th Amendment right to be free from self-incrimination and the 6th Amendment right to counsel. We then move to the law that has developed in the arena of eyewitness identification, focusing primarily on the constitutional entitlements to counsel and to due process that come into play here. Finally, we examine the constitutional right to assistance of counsel and the corresponding issue of effectiveness of counsel.

Throughout the book we focus on federal constitutional provisions and seek to understand how they actually work. Students discover quickly that constitutional rules are easily stated. The challenging part comes in applying them in light of the facts in real cases. This book is designed to meet that challenge. Cases are included here to illustrate each of the important rules in criminal procedure. Cases have been selected primarily on the grounds that they illustrate a specific constitutional principle, and that the court explains its reasoning and tries to show how the principle actually works. The cases in this collection are all lower court opinions; that is, no U.S. Supreme Court opinions are included. That is purposeful. Students are invited to understand and question the reasoning the courts lead us through in these cases. In some instances, conflicting opinions on the same point are included to illustrate how these constitutional rules can be interpreted toward different ends. Indeed, reasonable minds can differ; students are invited to understand some of these differences. Because these are all lower court opinions, students must understand that they are not definitive, and they are subject to reversal. Nonetheless, they are illustrative of thoughtful analyses of the constitutional principles raised.

All but one of these cases has been drawn, with permission, from the *Criminal Law Reporter*, published by the Bureau of National Affairs. This is the best source of abbreviated case material available for students and professors of criminal procedure. The *Criminal Law*

Reporter is published approximately twice a month and each issue contains scores of cases covering virtually every important topic in criminal law and criminal procedure. The Bureau of National Affairs was enormously generous in allowing this use of their materials. Without doubt, students of criminal procedure will benefit from their willingness to contribute to this educational effort.

ACKNOWLEDGMENTS

Much of the content of this book was adapted, with permission, from the *Criminal Law Reporter*. Copyright by The Bureau of National Affairs, Inc. (800-372-1033). http://www.bna.com

I am enormously grateful to the Bureau of National Affairs for its permission to use its materials, in this adapted format, toward the end of further enhancing students' understanding of criminal procedure.

Students in undergraduate criminal procedure classes have used these materials and have offered suggestions as to how they are best used. Their thoughtful comments have been helpful and I am appreciative. Robert Lockwood of Portland State University, Patricia Parke of East Carolina University, and Kay Henrikson of MacMurray College who reviewed the manuscript and made valuable suggestions for additions and clarifications and I have tried to incorporate those ideas. Shortcomings that remain are entirely my own.

Finally, I extend my thanks to my colleagues, Lori Hughes and Colleen Kadleck, for their tutorials and inordinate patience. I will be especially grateful if they do not tell people what they did to help.

chapter 1

Federalism

When the Federal constitution was presented to the states for ratification, people objected because there was nothing in it that protected individuals from their government. We had already experienced what we considered abuse of governmental power and we had fought and won the Revolutionary War to free ourselves from England's power. After the Revolution, we set up our own government that made each state virtually autonomous. Before long, we realized we needed more than what the Articles of Confederation called a "firm league of friendship" to bind these states together. We needed a single monetary system, for example; we needed some common laws to govern trade between the states. In short, we needed a national government. However, creating a national government was hard because, by definition, it meant taking power away from states and giving that power to a new national government.

We succeeded in doing that by creating a national government and, at the same time, allowing each state to maintain a good deal of sovereign autonomy. Therefore, we have a national government and each state has its own government. We have a federal constitution and each state has its own constitution.

In criminal prosecution, we are protected by constitutional guarantees set out in both the federal and state constitutions. The U.S. Supreme Court interprets the federal constitution. Each state's Supreme Court is authorized to interpret its own state constitution.

If the U.S. Supreme Court declares that the federal constitution grants a particular right to individuals, no state can take that right away. However, a state can give its citizens more rights than the federal government has given, and that is true even if the constitutional language being interpreted by the federal and state courts is exactly the same. When the

---

When the appellate court has cited and relied upon a U.S. Supreme Court opinion in reaching its decision, those citations are set out in full so you will know what Supreme Court authority the court relied upon. When you see an asterisk [*] in the court's opinion, that means the appellate court has referenced and relied upon a lower court case in reaching its decision. Those case citations are not included here.

U.S. Supreme Court interprets the federal constitution and declares that an individual had some constitutional right that the government had infringed on, we all have that right and no state can take it away. When the U.S. Supreme Court interprets the federal constitution and declares that an individual did not have the constitutional right claimed and the government acted properly in not giving that right, we all do not have that right under the federal constitution. However, a state Supreme Court, interpreting its own state constitution, could still find that we have that right under the provisions of its state constitution.

This is not a mistake, or some clever end-run that states created to avoid some Supreme Court decisions. This is precisely the way our system was designed to work when we abandoned each state's entire sovereignty as set out in the Articles of Confederation, in favor of a system that has a national government, with powers defined by the U.S. Constitution, as well as state governments with their own governmental structures defined in their own state constitutions.

In this federalist system, individuals are protected from their governments by state and federal constitutions. This has interesting implications for criminal prosecution because it means states can hold police to a higher standard than they are held to under the federal constitution. That is, individuals might have more rights under a state constitution than under the federal constitution, which means that police are not entitled to do some things under a state constitution that they are allowed to do under the federal constitution.

The argument for this constitutional "state's rights" movement was forcefully made by Justices Brennan and Marshall in their dissent in *Michigan v. Mosley,* 423 U.S. 96:120–21 (1975):

> In light of today's erosion of *Miranda* standards as a matter of federal constitutional law, it is appropriate to observe that no State is precluded by the decision from adhering to higher standards under state law. Each State has power to impose higher standards governing police practices under state law than is required by the Federal Constitution .... Understandably, state courts and legislatures are, as matters of state law, increasingly according protections once provided as federal rights but now increasingly deprecated by decisions of this Court [citations omitted].

To make sure the point was not lost, Justices Brennan and Marshall concluded their dissent with the citation to the state constitutional counterpart to the federal constitution that, in their opinions, had been restrictively interpreted.

Justice Brennan pursued the point further in an article published in the *Harvard Law Review* in which he suggested, in essence, that one way to commit legal malpractice is to raise only federal constitutional issues in state court, rather than to raise both federal and state constitutional issues (Brennan, 1977).

Each state is free to interpret its own state constitution. That means a state can hold its police to a higher standard than they are held to under the federal constitution, but it means something else as well: Because each state interprets its own constitution, state constitutional interpretations can (and do) vary from state to state. This is important for our purposes here. State courts interpreting their own state constitutions decided many of the cases in this book. When a state court is deciding a case based on its state constitution, that state court can consider cases decided in other jurisdictions, but the state court is not required to follow precedent from any other state. Indeed, that is one of the principles illustrated in these cases on federalism.

1.1   STATE v. CUNTAPAY (HAW. 2004): 74 CRL 454
(*Federalism/Privacy*)

The defendant was playing cards in the garage of a friend's house when police entered. The police saw the defendant walk to the washroom attached to the garage and reach behind the washing machine. When he emerged, his hands were empty. The police searched behind the washing machine and found a magnetic "hide-a-key" box, protruding from which was a bit of plastic bag with methamphetamine in it. An officer arrested the defendant and recovered drug paraphernalia from his fanny pack.

The defendant was a short-term social guest at his friend's house.

- *Did he have a reasonable expectation of privacy that was protected by the federal constitution? Explain.*
- *Presume the Hawaii constitution has a provision that is virtually identical to the federal provision. Is the state Supreme Court required to interpret its state constitution in the same way the U.S. Supreme Court interprets its federal counterpart? Why?*

State v. Cuntapay (Haw. 2004): 74 CrL 454.

Short-term guests have expectations of privacy in their hosts' homes that are protected by the Hawaii Constitution's counterpart to the 4th Amendment. The Hawaii Supreme Court followed the reasoning of Justice Ruth Bader Ginsburg's dissent in *Minnesota v. Carter*, 525 U.S. 83 (1998) and held that when a host chooses to share the privacy of his or her home with a guest, that guest's expectation of privacy in the home is one that society deems reasonable.

In *Minnesota v. Olson*, 495 U.S. 91 (1990), the U.S. Supreme Court recognized that an overnight guest has a reasonable expectation of privacy in his host's home that is protected by the 4th Amendment. In *Carter*, however, the Court held that a short-term guest, who was in the host's residence for the first time and was there for the sole purpose of packaging cocaine, did not have a legitimate expectation of privacy in the host's house. Relying on the purely commercial nature of the transaction, the relatively short time period, and lack of any previous connection between guest and host, the court held that the guest's situation was closer to that of someone simply permitted on the premises than that of an overnight guest.

Justice Ginsburg, dissenting in *Carter*, stated that she would have held that "when a homeowner or lessor personally invites a guest into her home to share in a common endeavor, whether it be for conversation, to engage in leisure activities, or for business purposes licit or illicit, that guest should share his host's shelter against unreasonable searches and seizures." She reasoned that "[t]hrough the host's invitation, the guest gains a reasonable expectation of privacy in the home." The *Olson* opinion relied in part on the longstanding social custom of spending the night at the home of another. Extending this logic to shorter-term guests, Justice Ginsburg said "[v]isiting the home of a friend, relative, or business associate, whatever the time of day, serves functions recognized as valuable by society."

The Hawaii Supreme Court, interpreting the state constitution's counterpart to the federal 4th Amendment, agreed with Justice Ginsburg that short-term guests have a reasonable privacy expectation in their hosts' homes.

The Hawaii Supreme Court [*] held, similarly to *Olson,* that an overnight guest has a reasonable expectation of privacy in his host's home. The court said that "a person has a 'halo' of privacy wherever he goes and can invoke a protectable right to privacy wherever he may legitimately be and reasonably expect freedom from government intrusion." In the instant case, the defendant was not a one-time visitor, but visited the garage once or twice a week to play cards and darts, always at the invitation of the homeowner. Following Justice Ginsburg's reasoning in *Carter,* the court held that the fact that the defendant was not an overnight guest "did not detract from the 'halo' of privacy that protected him wherever he might 'legitimately be and reasonably expect freedom from government intrusion.'"

Two judges dissented, arguing that the defendant's testimony did not show that he was a friend, relative, business associate, or invitee of the home dweller, as required to establish a reasonable expectation of privacy in the garage.

Courts in Minnesota and the District of Columbia [*] have held that a short-term social guest has a reasonable expectation of privacy in a host's home that is protected by the 4th Amendment. These courts reasoned, in part, that the *Carter* decision is based on a distinction between social and commercial guests, not a distinction between overnight and short-term guests.

1.2 STATE v. MARTINEZ (MONT. 2003): 73 CRL 85
(*Stop and Frisk/Federalism/Probable Cause*)

A woman met with a Billings, Montana police detective and informed him that, within 3 days, a man named "Ricky" would be driving a load of marijuana to a Billings motel from Oregon in a particular vehicle. Police confirmed that the vehicle described by the informer was registered in Oregon to one of the defendants in this case, Jesus Martinez, and that Martinez had registered at the motel several times in previous weeks. The informer said that she was the girlfriend of the other defendant, Daniel Olson. She said she had been in prison but that she "wanted to do what she thought was right."

A few weeks later, Martinez registered again at the motel but was driving a vehicle registered to another Oregon resident. Later that day, the informer called police and told them that "Ricky" had checked in and that her boyfriend had stolen a flatbed truck in Great Falls, Montana, and had driven it to an area of Billings. The police then located a truck that had been stolen in Great Falls the previous day. The police placed Martinez under surveillance for the next $2\frac{1}{2}$ days, but they did not observe him engaging in any activity they associated with drug dealing. During surveillance, however, police had pulled Martinez over for a traffic violation and found a 0.4-gram bud of marijuana in the borrowed car. Unable to link the bud to Martinez, the police released him.

The next day, the informer reported that Martinez and Olson were going to leave Billings at 1:00 p.m., probably in a different vehicle, to drive to Bozeman, Montana, to sell the remaining marijuana. Police corroborated that the defendants left Billings on the highway to Bozeman at 1:00 p.m. in a pickup. Officers stopped the pickup a few miles outside of town, and the stop led to the discovery of marijuana, which was used to convict the defendants.

- *Relying on the U.S. Constitution, was the stop of the defendants' car as it left Billings constitutional? Explain.*
- *Could a court, applying the state constitution, reach any other conclusion? Explain.*

State v. Martinez (Mont. 2003). 73 CrL 85

Montana relies on its state constitution to require more in tip cases than the 4th Amendment as interpreted in *Alabama v. White.*

In *Alabama v. White,* 496 U.S. 325 (1990) and *Florida v. J.L.,* 529 U.S. 266 (2000), the U.S. Supreme Court dealt with the value of corroborating the innocent but predictive details in a tip from an anonymous informer. In *White,* an anonymous informer alleged that the defendant was going to leave a certain apartment building with a small quantity of drugs and drive in a certain car to a certain hotel. The officers stopped the defendant after she left the apartment building, got into the car described, and started driving by the most direct route to the hotel. The *White* court upheld the stop, explaining that an anonymous tipster's accurate predictions about a suspect's future conduct—even innocent conduct—suggests that the informer has inside information and demonstrates a basis of knowledge that establishes the reliability of the tipster.

In *J.L.,* the Supreme Court held that corroboration of innocent, readily observable facts in a tip from an anonymous caller that a described man had a gun was not enough to justify a stop. The court emphasized the predictive nature of the innocent facts corroborated in *White,* and it reiterated its concern that allowing stops based on corroboration of innocent, readily observable information would lead to abusive invasions of privacy.

In this case, the Montana Supreme Court held that police officers' corroboration of an informer's predictions about alleged drug traffickers' movements was not enough to justify an investigative stop of their vehicle. It also held that an informer's registration with police did not, by itself, qualify her for the presumption of trustworthiness afforded to citizen informers.

The Montana Supreme Court's rulings in this case regarding the nature of the informer and the sufficiency of the corroboration are noteworthy when placed against the backdrop of a trend in other jurisdictions of paring back on the corroboration requirement. Before *J.L.,* some courts had allowed stops based on corroboration of innocent, nonpredictive details in anonymous tips about firearms and drunk drivers. The exceptions were based, in part, on the idea that the risks presented by such tips justified immediate stops. *J.L.* rejected the motion of a firearm exception, but many courts after *J.L.* have continued to hold that officers who receive a tip about drunk driving do not have to observe erratic driving or other suspicious facts before making a stop [*]. Other courts have extended the presumption of reliability afforded to "citizen informers" to tipsters who communicate with police in such a way as to potentially subject them to being held accountable for making a false police report [*].

Here, prosecutors argued that police corroboration of the innocent details about the defendant's movement was enough to justify a stop. The Montana Supreme Court disagreed.

The court said that when an officer receives an informer's tip, the officer must evaluate the veracity, reliability, and basis of knowledge of the informer to determine whether the report supports reasonable suspicion. Here the court concluded the informer did not qualify as a citizen informer of presumed reliability. The detective testified that the informer had been in prison but that she "wanted to do what she thought was right." The majority found this explanation insufficient to establish the informer's motives. It also commented that, although she had registered with police as an informer, the way in which she conveyed her information only through the detective handling her might not have exposed her to criminal or civil liability for making false reports.

The majority also decided that the tip in this case was less reliable than those in the drunk driving cases because the basis for the informer's knowledge was not shown.

The prosecution urged the court to follow the reasoning of the U.S. Supreme Court in *White* and hold that, even if the informer's trustworthiness could not be presumed, her accurate predictions of the defendants' future conduct were enough to establish her reliability. The Montana Supreme Court declined that invitation and explained:

> This court recognizes that the *quantum* of information regarding suspected criminal activity needed to justify an investigative stop is lower than that required for an arrest or a search based on probable cause. However, we do not agree with the *White* Court that information of a lesser *quality* will support particularized suspicion. Regarding the use of informant tips in the context of investigative stop, we stated in [*]—although concededly in dicta—that a 'tip that has not been shown to be reliable or trustworthy for purposes of establishing probable cause to procure a search warrant is also unreliable for purposes of providing an officer with particularized suspicion' [emphasis in original].

The majority added that "[w]hile corroboration of a tip with innocent information may lend an unknown or untested tipster some credibility, such indicia of reliability does not obviate the relevance of the tipster's basis of knowledge as a factor in the evaluation."

The majority decided that the record in the instant case contained no information as to the source and circumstances under which the informer came by the information she conveyed to the detective. It said the lower court and the dissenters erred by inferring from the informer's relationship with one of the defendants that she was privy to conversations about their illegal plans. It stressed that the officers knew the informer had never personally witnessed any drugs or drug deals. "[W]here an informant's tip is anonymous and lacks any indication of the basis for the informant's opinion, the officer must corroborate the tip by observing suspicious behavior that alerts the officer to the existence of a possible violation."

Emphasizing that the police were unable to corroborate any of the informer's allegations that the defendants were involved in the criminal activity she reported, the majority held that the officers did not have the reasonable suspicion required by the Montana constitution to conduct an investigative detention.

Two judges dissented. One argued that the informer qualified as a citizen informer and that the events leading up to the stop established her reliability. The other argued that there was enough for the police to infer that the source of the information provided by the informer was from her personal observations.

chapter 2

Privacy

The right to privacy is not guaranteed in the Bill of Rights, but the 4th Amendment requires that searches and seizures be "reasonable." The reasonableness requirement is often associated with exploration of whether a citizen's reasonable expectation of privacy has been violated by a governmental search or seizure.

The United States Supreme Court made it clear in *Katz v. United States,* 389 U.S. 347 (1967) that the 4th Amendment protects people, not places. That notwithstanding, some of the cases selected here focus on whether one's expectation of privacy is enhanced in some places, especially one's home or office or a home in which one is an invited guest.

As is always the case, it is important to know what the constitutional standard is to determine whether police are behaving constitutionally. The constitutional standard for privacy, as set out in *Katz,* is a simply stated two-part test: The first part is subjective, determining whether the person had an actual expectation of privacy; the second part is objective, determining whether that expectation of privacy is reasonable.

2.1 UNITED STATES v. LONGORIA (TENTH CIR. 1999) (*Privacy*)

The defendant was accused of being a member of a drug ring that transported drugs from Mexico to metropolitan Kansas City. He and his codefendants allegedly carried on some of their illegal conduct at commercial premises owned by the informer. The informer, acting

---

When the appellate court has cited and relied upon a U.S. Supreme Court opinion in reaching its decision, those citations are set out in full so you will know what Supreme Court authority the court relied upon. When you see an asterisk [*] in the court's opinion, that means the appellate court has referenced and relied upon a lower court case in reaching its decision. Those case citations are not included here.

under government supervision, surreptitiously made video and audio recordings of conversations that occurred there. He recorded not only his own conversations with the defendant, but also conversations between the defendant and the codefendants. The latter conversations were conducted in Spanish, which the informer did not understand.

To come within the protection of an "oral communication" under Title III, a conversation must be one in which a party had a subjective expectation of privacy that is objectively reasonable.

- *Did the defendant have a reasonable expectation of privacy? Explain.*

United States v. Longoria (Tenth Cir. 1999): 65 CrL 153

The court was willing to assume that the defendant had a subjective expectation of privacy on the basis of his knowledge that the informer did not understand Spanish. However, the defendant's expectation that the informer would not disclose the substance of the conversations is not an expectation that society would consider to be objectively reasonable.

Despite the language factor, this case is governed by the principle that the 4th Amendment does not protect what is knowingly exposed to others. A person assumes the risk that persons who hear what he or she says will betray his or her confidence and repeat those words to law enforcement authorities, according to *Hoffa v. United States,* 385 U.S. 293 (1966).

No prior decisions have recognized an exception to this rule for conversations conducted in a language the informer did not understand. One reason for not recognizing such an exception is that "comprehension is a malleable concept not easily measured by either the defendant or the court." No workable standard based on subjective evaluations of linguistic capabilities could be defined.

A more important reason for rejecting the defendant's argument is that "[i]n our increasingly multilingual society, one exposing conversations to others must necessarily assume the risk his statements will be overheard and understood." The informer may have concealed his ability to understand Spanish, just as he concealed the recording equipment and his informer status.

2.2   STATE v. TORGRIMSON (MN.CT.APP. 2002)
(*Stop and Frisk/Probable Cause*)

Police surreptitiously taped a conversation between suspects who had been confined in a police car.

- *Does that violate the 4th Amendment? Explain.*

State v. Torgrimson (Minn.Ct.App. 2002): 70 CrL 301

Surreptitious taping of a conversation between suspects who have been confined in a police car does not violate the 4th Amendment.

The court said that after taking careful note that the 4th Amendment protects people and not places, it was not prepared to accept the proposition that there is a reasonable expectation of privacy inside a police vehicle. Comparing the case to *Katz v. United States,* 389 U.S. 347 (1967), the court observed: "A phone booth is fully accessible to the public as a place to engage in private conversations. A police vehicle, however, is not freely accessible. It is owned and operated by the state and/or the local government. It is used for the purpose of responding to and preventing crime. For all practical purposes, the vehicle serves as the police officer's office. Further, in some instances, the back seat of the vehicle can act as the equivalent of a temporary jail cell."

The court noted that several state and federal courts have come to the same conclusion [*].

2.3   RANDOLPH v. STATE (GA.CT.APP. 2003)
(*Privacy*)

Police officers responding to a domestic disturbance at the defendant's home found his wife alone and upset. She stated that her husband had taken their child from the house, and she accused him of impoverishing the family with his cocaine use. The defendant returned to the house, explained he had taken the child to a neighbor for safety, and accused his wife of being an alcoholic.

Following up on the wife's comment about cocaine use, an officer requested permission to search the house. When the defendant refused consent, the officer turned to the wife and asked her. She readily agreed, led the officer to an upstairs bedroom, and pointed out a piece of cut straw with white powder residue. The trial court held that the wife's consent superseded the defendant's refusal, and it denied his motion to suppress.

This is a problem often encountered when one cohabitant gives consent and another cohabitant refuses. We can deal with it strictly as a consent issue or we can deal with the broader question of privacy as well. Think about privacy here. This is a difficult question, on which courts are divided.

- *Both spouses' positions cannot be satisfied. Which should prevail? Why?*

Randolph v. State (Ga.Ct.App. 2003): 74 CrL 167

When both spouses are present at the time police request permission to search their home, one spouse's consent may not override the other spouse's refusal to give consent according to a divided court in this case. This was a case of first impression in Georgia, although courts in other states have grappled with the same issue. The court here concluded that it is reasonable for one cohabitant to believe that his or her stated desire for privacy will be honored even in the face of another cohabitant's consent to a search.

It is clear, under *United States v. Matlock,* 415 U.S. 164 (1974), that a third party with common authority over a home, such as the wife in this case, may consent to a search and that the consent is valid against an absent, nonconsenting resident with whom the home is shared. The inquiry in this case was whether a cohabitant's consent is valid when the non-consenting cohabitant is present at the time consent is requested and the search is performed.

Ruling that consent given in these circumstances is invalid, the court took guidance from the *Matlock* court's explanation of its holding. The consent of one who possesses common authority over premises or effects is valid as against the absent, nonconsenting person with whom that authority is shared, the Supreme Court said, because it is reasonable to expect that a cohabitant with the authority to give consent might, in fact, exercise that authority.

In this case, the Georgia Court of Appeals said it was "reasonable for one occupant to believe that his stated desire for privacy will be honored, even if there is another occupant who could consent to a search." Generally speaking, cohabitants accommodate each other by not admitting persons over another's objections while the objecting person is present, thus making the expectation of that courtesy reasonable, the court observed. It cited [*] holding that one cohabitant's consent to search was vitiated by the police's failure to obtain the consent of another cohabitant who was home at the time.

Moreover, "we find it inherently reasonable that police honor a present occupant's express objection to a search of his dwelling, shared or otherwise," the court said. A person who grants consent to a search may subsequently withdraw consent; by the same token, an objecting cohabitant should be permitted to exercise his competing right to be free from a search. The "right involved is the right to be free from police intrusion, not the right to invite police into one's home," the court explained. It quoted with approval from a Florida District Court of Appeals case [*] that "constitutional rights may not be defeated by the expedient of soliciting several persons successively until the sought-after consent is obtained."

Accordingly, *Matlock's* presumption that a cohabitant waives his right of privacy as to other cohabitants cannot apply here, the court decided. Given the defendant's "unequivocal assertion of that right, it seems disingenuous to conclude that he waived it."

The court observed that the facts of this case, involving counteraccusations by quarreling spouses and "dueling responses," raise issues concerning the motive for consent in the instant case, while illustrating the difficulties of case-by-case determinations in general. "[I]t is preferable," the court said, "that a neutral magistrate determine whether [the consenting cohabitant's] accusations were founded or whether they stemmed from the ongoing altercation." A bright-line rule requiring police to obtain a warrant in the face of competing responses to requests for consent provides greater guidance for law enforcement without unduly hampering crime investigation, the court concluded.

In a concurring opinion, one judge opposed the bright-line rule, believing that a reasonableness inquiry under the 4th Amendment must be made on a case-by-case basis. Three other judges concurred separately, supporting the bright-line rule because they thought that rule serves the additional function of safeguarding citizens' privacy rights.

Two judges dissented, arguing that the court's holding is inconsistent with *Matlock*. That precedent stands for the proposition, according to the dissenters, that a third party who shares control of a premises with another may authorize a search over the entire area regardless of the other party's agreement, relationship, or proximity.

Other courts have struggled with this question in opinions that commentators categorize into two groups. One view is that the *Matlock* court intended to leave the cohabitant with freedom to act in his own or the public's interest even if the other cohabitant is present and objecting [*].

The contrary view is that, like the court here, the objecting cohabitant reasonably expects his cohabitant to accommodate his wishes. Courts adopting this position seldom do so as boldly as the Georgia court did here; instead, they offer supporting reasons that must also be taken into account—for example, respecting the wishes of the nonconsenting cohabitant in part as a means to deter violence [*]. Police should not ignore the objecting party when police are aware that the person objecting is the one whose property is the object of the search [*].

2.4   UNITED STATES v. HAQQ (SECOND CIR. 2002)
(*Privacy*)

Police officers entered the home the defendant shared with several other individuals to arrest him on outstanding warrants. During a protective sweep of the premises, they entered a bedroom used by another resident and found a suitcase on the bed. An officer opened the suitcase and discovered, along with several pairs of shoes, firearms that led to federal charges against the defendant.

According to testimony adduced at a suppression hearing, the suitcase belonged to the person who used the bedroom. The defendant had used it on a recent trip. He claimed he had the owner's permission to use the suitcase, but the owner gave contrary testimony.

The district court ruled that under *Arizona v. Hicks,* 480 U.S. 321 (1987), the defendant's expectation of privacy in his home permitted him to object to the seizure of objects—such as the guns—that were not in plain view. Accordingly, it suppressed the guns as well as a confession and additional physical evidence obtained after the guns were discovered.

- *Was this evidence properly found during a protective sweep? Explain.*
- *Did the defendant have a reasonable expectation of privacy in his home? If so, did that expectation of privacy extend to the suitcase in the home? Explain.*
- *Should the evidence be suppressed? Why?*

United States v. Haqq (Second Cir. 2002): 70 CrL 380

Before ruling that a police search of an object found in a defendant's home violated the defendant's 4th Amendment rights, a court must find that the defendant had a reasonable expectation of privacy in the object according to a majority of the Second Circuit Court of Appeals. Contrary to the reasoning of the district court, this case is about the search or seizure of an object, rather than about an impermissibly broad search of a home. The U.S.

Supreme Court's decision in *Arizona v. Hicks,* 480 U.S. 321 (1987), does not mean that a defendant's reasonable expectation of privacy in his home provides a basis for challenging searches of items within the home.

In *Hicks,* officers lawfully entered the defendant's apartment under exigent circumstances after a shooting. One officer, thinking that an expensive-looking stereo system seemed "out of place" in the otherwise shabby apartment, turned over some of the system's components and recorded their serial numbers. The items turned out to be stolen. The Supreme Court held that the officer's moving of the equipment was unrelated to the reasons for the lawful entry and, therefore, was a search separate and apart from the search for the shooter, victims, and weapons. That search was not justified by the exigent circumstances that made the officer's presence in the apartment lawful, and the search was therefore unconstitutional, the *Hicks* court said.

The justices who decided *Hicks* treated the search at issue as a search of the stereo equipment, not of the apartment. Subsequent U.S. Supreme Court decisions confirm that *Hicks* was about the search or seizure of an object, rather than about an impermissibly broad search of a home.

The district court read *Hicks* to support the broad proposition that a defendant's "reasonable expectation of privacy in his home [is] sufficient to permit him to object to the seizure of objects [within the home] which [are] not in fact in plain view." If this were so, however, the majority pointed out, then *Hicks,* as applied to a dwelling shared by multiple persons, would be contrary to the principle laid down in *Katz v. United States,* 389 U.S. 347 (1967), that a person cannot claim 4th Amendment protection without having a legitimate expectation of privacy in the place or thing that has been searched. The majority refused to say that *Hicks* meant to create an exception to the well-established principle.

In *Hicks,* the defendant was the sole occupant of the apartment, and there was thus no question about who had custody and control of the stereo equipment. In this case, in contrast, there was a factual question as to whether the defendant had custody and control of the suitcase.

The majority sent the case back to the district court for resolution of that question and others bearing on whether the defendant had a privacy expectation in the suitcase and, if so, whether that expectation was reasonable.

One judge concurred but warned that the majority's decision had a "potential to facilitate government intrusion into what we think of as private space." He suggested that the court should recognize a presumption of privacy for every item within a home and not in plain view.

2.5   UNITED STATES v. BERRYHILL (SIXTH CIR. 2003)
(Privacy)

The defendant was invited to an apartment by a friend who was the houseguest of the tenant. The defendant later sought to suppress evidence obtained by police in a search of the apartment. The defendant argued that modern social custom of "crashing" at the residence of a friend of a friend demonstrates societal acceptance of his expectation of privacy. He maintained that the U.S. Supreme Court, in *Minnesota v. Olson*, 495 U.S. 91 (1990), recognized the reasonable privacy expectation of a guest, invited by a houseguest, without the knowledge of the tenant or owner of the premises. In support of that proposition, the defendant emphasized the last sentence of this passage from *Olson:*

> The houseguest is there with the permission of his host, who is willing to share his house and his privacy with his guest. It is unlikely that the guest will be confined to a restricted area of the house, and when the host is away or asleep, the guest will have a measure of control over the premises. The host may admit or exclude from the house as he prefers, but it is unlikely that he will admit someone who wants to see or meet with the guest over the objection of the guest. On the other hand, few houseguests will invite others to visit them while they are guests without consulting their hosts, but the latter, who have the authority to exclude despite the wishes of the guest, will often be accommodating.

The district court held that the defendant failed to prove that he intended to stay at the apartment overnight and concluded that he lacked an expectation of privacy in the apartment under *Olson*.

- *Does the defendant have to prove that he intended to stay overnight to have a reasonable expectation of privacy?*
- *Does it matter that the defendant here was not the houseguest, but was a guest of the houseguest? Explain your reasoning.*
- *Does the defendant have a reasonable expectation of privacy in this case? Why?*

United States v. Berryhill (Sixth Cir. 2003): 74 CrL 213

A houseguest's own guest, who was in the host's residence without the host's knowledge or permission, does not have a reasonable expectation of privacy in the residence that was protected by the 4th Amendment. The court explained that the Supreme Court's holding in *Minnesota v. Olson*, 495 U.S. 92 (1990), that an invited overnight houseguest has a reasonable privacy expectation in the host's home, was based in part on an invited guest's knowledge that his host will respect his privacy after granting permission to be at the residence.

Under *Katz v. United States*, 389 U.S. 347 (1967), the question of whether an individual is protected by the 4th Amendment is answered by looking at whether the defendant exhibited a subjective expectation of privacy and whether that expectation is one that society would accept as reasonable. In *Olson*, the U.S. Supreme Court ruled that a defendant's status as an overnight guest was by itself enough to show that the defendant had a reasonable expectation of privacy in the home. The *Olson* court reasoned that "[s]taying overnight in another's home is a longstanding social custom that serves functions recognized as valuable by society."

In contrast, in *Minnesota v. Carter*, 525 U.S. 83 (1998), the court held that short-term visitors on a premises who were there for the sole purpose of conducting a commercial transaction and who had no previous connection to the householder had no privacy expectation in the host's home that was protected by the 4th Amendment. The Supreme Court, however, has not addressed whether the uninvited guest of a houseguest has a reasonable expectation of privacy in the host's residence.

The court did not accept the defendant's invitation to extend the holding of *Olson* to uninvited houseguests. The passage from *Olson* relied on by the defendant, when taken as a whole, "indicates that the reason a houseguest has a reasonable expectation of privacy is because he knows that the host would respect his privacy, having obtained the host's permission to be at the residence," the court said. "*Olson* cannot be taken for the proposition that guests' visitors can be assured that their privacy will be respected by the lawful owners or tenants of the residence," the court held.

In addition, the court affirmed the district court's finding that the defendant did not actually intend to spend the night at the apartment. The fact that the defendant did not have any "overnight" items with him—such as a toothbrush or clothes—and instead was carrying only materials to manufacture methamphetamine, did not support his claim, the court held.

2.6   PEOPLE v. STEWART (CAL.CT.APP. 2003)
(*Privacy*)

Police went to a house to conduct a probation search of the resident. The resident was not at home, but police found the defendant on the premises with methamphetamine and drug paraphernalia. The defendant lived in a mobile home on the property and had known the owners of the house for 4 years. During that time, he possessed a copy of their house key and had unlimited access to the premises. He went to the house on a daily basis to socialize and to use the shower, laundry, and cooking facilities. While the owners were away, he had permission to spend the night on the premises to prevent others from entering.

- *Did the defendant have a reasonable expectation of privacy that was violated by this search and seizure? Explain.*

People v. Stewart (Cal.Ct.App. 2003): 74 CrL 141

A frequent guest at a search residence who had not stayed over the night immediately preceding the search nonetheless had a reasonable expectation of privacy in the residence at the time of the search on the basis of a 4-year-long intimate social connection with the owners of the premises.

The defendant's conviction was reversed. The court found that the defendant had a reasonable expectation of privacy in the premises protected by the 4th Amendment. In *Minnesota v. Olson*, 495 U.S. 92 (1990), the U.S. Supreme Court ruled that a defendant's status as an overnight guest was, by itself, enough to show that the defendant had an expectation of privacy in the home that society is prepared to recognize as reasonable.

By contrast, in *Minnesota v. Carter,* 525 U.S. 83 (1998), the court held that visitors on a premises who stayed 2.5 hours for the sole purpose of conducting a commercial transaction and who had no previous connection to the householder had no privacy expectation in the host's home that was protected by the 4th Amendment's requirements for police searches.

The court found that the facts of this case put it closer to *Olson* than to *Carter* on the privacy continuum. In light of the indicators of the defendant's close relationship with the owners of the premises, the fact that he had not stayed overnight was not controlling.

2.7   UNITED STATES v. MIRAVALLES (ELEVENTH CIR. 2002) (*Privacy*)

Law enforcement officers suspected that the defendant had cigars with counterfeit labels in his apartment. Hoping to develop probable cause for a search warrant, they entered his building through the front door, the electronic locking system of which was not working that day, and knocked at the apartment door. The ensuing conversation with the defendant's wife did not result in the consensual entry the officers sought, but it apparently prompted the defendant's wife to throw several plastic garbage bags down a trash chute located in the common area. An officer hiding in the hallway observed this activity. Officers recovered the bags from a bin on the ground floor and verified that they contained counterfeit cigar labels.

- *Did the defendant have a reasonable expectation of privacy in his apartment?*
- *Did the fact that the door lock was inoperable matter? Explain.*

United States v. Miravalles (Eleventh Cir. 2002): 70 CrL 434

A defendant who lived in an apartment building with a front door that could not be locked had no reasonable expectation of privacy, protected by the 4th Amendment, in the common areas of the building.

The court said the question of "whether the tenants of a large, multiunit apartment building have a reasonable expectation of privacy in the common areas of the building" was one of first impression for the Eleventh Circuit. The court said the answer is no, "at least where the lock on the door of the building is not functioning and anyone may enter."

At least four federal courts of appeals have given the same answer even when the door is locked, the court noted. They reasoned that tenants have little control over common areas, which are available for the use of other tenants, landlords, and persons such as repair workers who other tenants and landlords may decide to admit. Privacy expectations in this context are inversely proportional to the number of units in the building.

The court disagreed with the idea in the only contrary federal appellate court decision [*] that it is reasonable for apartment tenants to expect that the general public or trespassers will be excluded from the building's common areas.

2.8   UNITED STATES v. SLANINA (FIFTH CIR. 2002)
UNITED STATES v. ANGEVINE (TENTH CIR. 2002)
(*Privacy*)

Here are two fact patterns that are very similar, in that they raise the same legal question.
[Fifth Circuit]

A public employee's supervisor, who had criminal law enforcement responsibilities, searched his office computer without a warrant as part of an investigation into both workplace misconduct and criminal activity. The defendant was a firefighter who had downloaded illegal images onto his office computer. A city information systems worker, while connecting the computer to the city hall network, discovered files with names suggesting that they contained images of child pornography. He alerted the fire chief, who, in turn, alerted the city supervisor with authority over both the fire and police departments. The supervisor searched the defendant's computer and saw numerous illegal images. The supervisor called in FBI agents who conducted a more thorough search and obtained images that were used to convict the defendant.
[Tenth Circuit]

In the second case, the defendant was a public university professor who downloaded images of child pornography from the Internet onto his office computer and then later deleted them. University employees were warned that system administrators kept records of who deleted files and when. Police officers obtained a warrant to search the defendant's computer and employed software to recover the deleted images, which were eventually used to convict him.

   ■ *Do these employees have a reasonable expectation of privacy that has been violated here? Explain fully.*

United States v. Slanina (Fifth Cir. 2002): 70 CrL 474
United States v. Angevine (Tenth Cir. 2002): 70 CrL 474

The Fifth Circuit found a reasonable expectation of privacy, but applied an employer-search exception. The Tenth Circuit said there is no reasonable expectation of privacy.

The Fifth Circuit first rejected the government's contention that the defendant lacked a constitutionally protected expectation of privacy in the computer. The government pointed out that the defendant knew he was not allowed to use his city computer to access pornography and that network administrators and computer technicians had access to his computer.

The court decided that although the computer administrators and technicians "necessarily had some access to [the defendant's] computer, there is no evidence that such access was routine." Moreover, the city did not disseminate any policy that prevented the storage of personal information on city computers and did not inform its employees that computer usage and Internet access would be monitored. "Accordingly, given that absence of a city policy placing [the defendant] on notice that his computer usage would be monitored and the lack of any indication that other employees had routine access to his computer, we hold that [the defendant's] expectation of privacy was reasonable," the court concluded.

In *O'Connor v. Ortega,* 480 U.S. 709 (1987), a plurality of the U.S. Supreme Court concluded that a doctor at a state hospital had a reasonable expectation of privacy in his office's desk and file cabinets but that the 4th Amendment's warrant requirement did not apply to a hospital administrator's search as part of an investigation into noncriminal work-related misconduct. Relying on the special needs doctrine, the plurality held "that public employer intrusions on the constitutionally protected privacy interests of government employees for noninvestigatory, work-related purposes, as well as for investigations of work-related misconduct, should be judged by the standard of reasonableness under all the circumstances."

The Fifth Circuit acknowledged that the search in the instant case was distinguishable from the one in *O'Connor* on a couple of points, including the fact that the search here was for evidence of not only workplace misconduct, but also criminal offenses. However, the court agreed with the reasoning in a Fourth Circuit case [*] that government employers do not lose their special need for the efficient and proper operation of the workplace merely because "the same misconduct that violates a government employer's policy also happens to be illegal."

Unlike the searches in *O'Connor* and [*], the search here was conducted by a law enforcement officer. Nevertheless, the court agreed with a line of Seventh Circuit case law that has held that law enforcement personnel may also rely on the *O'Connor* exception so long as the investigation is, at least in part, an investigation into workplace misconduct [*]. "To hold that a warrant is necessary any time a law enforcement official recognizes the possibility that an investigation into work-related misconduct will yield evidence of criminal acts would frustrate the government employer's interest in 'the efficient and proper operation of the workplace,'" the court said, quoting *O'Connor.*

The court also made clear that, under one of its recent decisions [*], the FBI's search of the defendant's computer was not rendered unconstitutional by the fact that it was more thorough than the supervisor's search. The court, however, did endeavor to limit the reach of its ruling in the instant case by emphasizing that it was not addressing "the constitutionality of a search of a government employee by a law enforcement officer who is not also the employee's supervisor," or "the situation where the criminal acts of a government employee do not also violate workplace employment policy."

The Tenth Circuit sidestepped the defendant's claims that the warrant was invalid. The Tenth Circuit said that the officers did not need a warrant. The court pointed out that in *O'Connor,* the Supreme Court recognized that public employees' expectations of privacy in their workplace can be reduced by virtue of "office practices and procedures." The university's computer policies prevented university employees from having a reasonable expectation of privacy in data downloaded from the Internet onto university computers, the court decided.

The university's computer-use policy expressly prohibited employees from accessing or storing obscene material. Unlike the computer policy at issue in the Fifth Circuit case, the university's policy reserved the right to randomly audit Internet use and to monitor specific individuals suspected of misusing university computers. The policy explicitly cautioned computer users that information flowing through the university network was not confidential either in transit or in storage on a university computer. Under this policy, reasonable computer users should have been aware that network administrators and others were free to view data downloaded from the Internet, the court said.

The court also pointed out that every time the defendant logged onto his office computer, the university displayed a splash screen that warned of "criminal penalties" for misuse and the university's right to conduct inspections to protect business-related concerns. "These office practices and procedures should have warned reasonable employees not to access child pornography with university computers," the court said.

In a previous case [*], the Tenth Circuit identified a list of additional factors to consider when determining expectations of privacy in the workplace: "(1) the employee's relationship to the item seized; (2) whether the item was in the immediate control of the employee when it was seized; and (3) whether the employee took actions to maintain his privacy in the item."

In the instant case, the court noted that the university issued the computer to the defendant for only work-related purposes and explicitly reserved ownership of the computer hardware as well as data stored on it. Moreover, the pornographic images seized by police were not within the defendant's immediate control.

Although the defendant had deleted the pornographic files, the court decided that this was not sufficient to maintain private access to the seized pornography. Noting that the defendant had downloaded child pornography through a monitored computer network that warned users that system administrators kept file logs of when and by whom files were deleted, the court said it was "reluctant to find a reasonable expectation of privacy where the circumstances reveal a careless effort to maintain a privacy interest."

2.9   UNITED STATES v. GILL (NINTH CIR. 2002)
(*Privacy*)

On a Thursday, a U.S. postal police officer at a Los Angeles post office was watching a video monitor when he observed the defendant approach the counter with a suspicious heavily taped package. The defendant appeared nervous, turned sideways in an apparent attempt to avoid surveillance cameras, and sent the package by Express Mail to an address in a town near Seattle. Examination of the package revealed that the names of both the sender and the recipient were misspelled, leading the officer to conclude that they were aliases. Using a license plate check to learn the defendant's identity, the officer determined that the defendant's name and address did not match the return address on the package but his photo did match the person the officer had observed. Further checking showed that the defendant had a prior firearms arrest and gang connections.

The officer forwarded the package to another postal officer in Seattle who received it the next day and observed the following suspicious-package profile characteristics: excessive tape, use of handwritten labels, a significant distance between the sender's address and the post office from which it was mailed, use of aliases, the size and shape of the package, and the fact that it was mailed from a "source city" for drugs. The officer also determined that the address to which the package was to be delivered had been vacant for several months. He knew from past experience that packages were sometimes sent to vacant houses for later pickup by recipients. The officer drafted a search warrant affidavit and faxed it to a prosecutor, who said he would review it over the weekend.

The following Monday, the Los Angeles officer reported that a person claiming to be the sender had inquired about the package and gave a telephone number that turned out to be disconnected. The officer in Seattle learned that the individual who subscribed to the utilities for the address to which the package was sent had prior narcotics convictions and gang affiliation. That officer completed his affidavit and warrant on Tuesday, but the magistrate was unable to sign it until the next day.

After the warrant was issued, the officer opened the package and found a bottle of liquid that field-tested positive for PCP. The defendant was arrested in Los Angeles, and a search of his abode turned up more of the substance. A controlled delivery of the package led to the discovery of narcotics paraphernalia.

The defendant moved to suppress the PCP.

- *Make the argument(s) for the defendant that the evidence should be suppressed.*
- *Make the argument(s) for the government that seizure of the evidence did not violate the 4th Amendment.*
- *What do you conclude?*

United States v. Gill (Ninth Cir. 2002): 70 CrL 422

A 5-day delay of an Express Mail package while postal authorities investigated the sender and recipient was not an unreasonable seizure under the 4th Amendment. The court stressed that the predominant interest of the defendant, the sender of the package, was in the privacy of the package, not in its prompt delivery.

Beginning with basics, the court noted that under *United States v. Van Leeuwen*, 397 U.S. 249 (1970), first-class mail is protected by the 4th Amendment from unreasonable searches and seizures. Ninth Circuit precedent allows the seizure and detention of mail on the basis of a reasonable and articulable suspicion of criminal activity [*].

By the time the officer in Los Angeles sent the package to his colleague in Seattle, reasonable suspicion existed, the court said. The excessive wrapping, the sender's "furtive movements," the use of aliases, and the fact that the sender resided at a different address than the return address "all contributed to a suspicion for detention of the package."

The defendant also argued that the lengthy delay before the search warrant was obtained was unreasonable, given the fact that the package was sent Express Mail. Disagreeing, the court cited a case [*] for the proposition that the main 4th Amendment interest in a mailed package is in the privacy of its contents, not the speed with which it is delivered. "Even with Express Mail, [the defendant's] predominant interest was in the privacy of the package and not merely prompt delivery," the court said. The delay in [*] was 9 hours, but longer delays— 29 hours in *Van Leeuwen* and 5 days in [*]—have been held to be reasonable.

The court distinguished the facts in this case from those in another case [*], where the court ruled that delays of packages ranging from 7 to 23 days were unreasonable on the ground that the delays would have been much shorter had the police acted diligently. Here, the court emphasized, the investigation began at the end of one work week and ended in the middle of the next, and much of the delay involved review of the affidavit over a weekend and the unavailability of the magistrate.

One judge concurred but wrote separately to argue that postal authorities do not need reasonable suspicion to detain mail "where the detention is unintrusive and does not significantly delay delivery." In such a case, he said, no "seizure" occurs. He also said that postal authorities should not be forbidden to take "reasonable and nonintrusive" steps to protect the public from the use of the mails for the transmission of hazardous chemical and biological substances.

In a footnote to the majority opinion, the court observed that it was not rejecting this concurring analysis.

c h a p t e r   3

Probable Cause

The 4th Amendment requires probable cause before people or things may be searched or seized.

The kind of probable cause that is required is fairly commonsensical. If police want to *arrest* someone, they need probable cause to believe a crime has been committed and the person they want to arrest has committed the crime. If police want to *search,* they need probable cause to believe a crime has been committed and evidence of the crime will be found in the place they want to search. If police want to *seize* something as evidence, they need probable cause to believe a crime has been committed and the property they want to take is evidence of that crime.

How much factual support is required to establish probable cause is a little more difficult. The rule is easy enough to state: To establish probable cause, police must have facts sufficient to persuade a person of reasonable caution that there is a fair probability that (if, for example, they want to search for and seize evidence) a crime has been committed and evidence of the crime can be found in the particular place police want to search. It takes some time and thought and reading of cases to understand what will persuade a person of reasonable caution that a fair probability exists.

Although this might require some time and attention, the concept of probable cause is not especially difficult and the amount of evidence required to establish it is certainly not very high. It is a long way from most other standards of proof required in trials, as detailed in Table 3–1.

Probable cause—a fair probability—requires less evidence than any of these.

When the appellate court has cited and relied upon a U.S. Supreme Court opinion in reaching its decision, those citations are set out in full so you will know what Supreme Court authority the court relied upon. When you see an asterisk [*] in the court's opinion, that means the appellate court has referenced and relied upon a lower court case in reaching its decision. Those case citations are not included here.

Table 3–1   Standards of Proof

Beyond a reasonable doubt	The highest standard of proof, required for criminal conviction.
Clear and convincing	Statutorily required for some things.
Preponderance of the evidence	Required for winning a civil suit.

3.1   UNITED STATES V. SPARKS (TENTH CIR. 2002)
(*Probable Cause: Search*)

A 911 caller reported a suspicious package wrapped in plastic at a particular point along a roadside. Testing indicated that the package contained a pound of methamphetamine. A police detective replaced the package with a decoy package and kept the area under surveillance.

The defendant was arrested when he drove to the spot, picked up the package, and began to drive away.

After the defendant was arrested, police sought to search his home. An officer filed an affidavit for a search warrant. In that affidavit he said that, in his experience, it is common for drug dealers to keep paraphernalia and records of their illegal activity in their residences. A warrant was issued.

- *Was the defendant's act of picking up a package on the roadside probable cause to arrest him? Explain.*
- *Was the officer's general experience with drug dealers probable cause to search the defendant's home? Explain.*

United States v. Sparks (Tenth Cir. 2002): 71 CrL 273

The court decided that the detective's observation of the defendant retrieving the decoy package was enough to provide probable cause for his arrest. "Although [the defendant's] actions could theoretically have been innocent, we believe a prudent, cautious and trained police officer more likely would have construed those actions as indicating [the defendant] was familiar with and had some connection to the original bag containing methamphetamine." The court pointed out that the defendant had walked directly to the package, picked it up without making any attempt to examine it, returned immediately to his truck, and started to drive away. "Considered in their entirety, we conclude these circumstances would have led a reasonable person to believe that [the defendant] was engaged in, or otherwise connected to, the trafficking of methamphetamine (given the large quantity of methamphetamine found in the bag). Thus, we conclude that probable cause existed for [the detective] to arrest [the defendant]."

The events leading up to the defendant's arrest, when combined with the officer's experience and the fact that the defendant's residence was within eyesight of the location where the package was found, also provided probable cause for the search warrant. Hence, the Tenth Circuit in this case held that an officer's statement in a warrant affidavit that, in his experience, it is common for drug dealers to keep paraphernalia and records of their illegal activity in their residences was enough to justify a search of the home of someone arrested in possession of drugs.

The court acknowledged that other courts have held that an officer's general experience with drug investigations is not enough to supply the requisite link between a defendant's residence and his drug activities elsewhere. The Tenth Circuit rejected this approach, however, explaining: "Given the large quantity of methamphetamine found in the bag, and given [the defendant's] apparent connection with the bag (in light of his actions in retrieving the decoy package), it was reasonable for [the detective] to conclude that [the defendant] was involved in the distribution of methamphetamine. In turn, it was reasonable for [the detective] to believe there was a fair probability that additional evidence of crime (e.g., drug paraphernalia and/or sales records) would be found in [the defendant's] nearby residence."

One judge dissented, arguing that the defendant's arrest, and hence the search of his home, was not supported by probable cause. She concluded that the defendant's singular act of picking up a package lying on the roadside in broad daylight does not, in the absence of any other information connecting the defendant with drug dealing or the package, provide probable cause to believe that he knew what the package contained.

3.2   UNITED STATES V. JACKSON (SEVENTH CIR. 2002)
(*Probable Cause: Search/Hearsay*)

A police officer, accompanied by a confidential informer, went before a magistrate to seek a warrant to search the defendant's residence. The underlying affidavit was based almost entirely on the informer's representations that he knew the defendant and had observed him in possession of a quantity of cocaine that the defendant intended to sell. The affidavit also recounted the informer's assertion that he knew what cocaine looked and smelled like because in the past he had used, packaged, and sold it. The only information provided by the informer that the officer was able to corroborate was the defendant's race and birth date and the fact that a vehicle parked in front of the residence was registered to the defendant.

- ■ *What is the test for evaluating sufficiency of hearsay information to establish probable cause?*
  - ● *What are the state's arguments that this informant's information is sufficient to establish probable cause?*
  - ● *What are the defendant's arguments that this informant's information is not sufficient to establish probable cause?*
    - ▲ *What do you conclude?*

United States v. Jackson (Seventh Cir. 2002): 71 CrL 214

The Seventh Circuit considered this a close case. It decided that the informer's appearance before the judge supported probable cause for issuance of the warrant. The opportunity for the magistrate to question the informant helped support the affidavit that was short on detail; the mere presence of the informant before the magistrate was, in itself, a strong indicator of the informant's reliability.

The defendant's argument focused on the reliability and veracity of the informer. The court acknowledged that the information offered by the informant was not especially detailed. Nevertheless, the totality of the circumstances was sufficient to support a finding of probable cause.

Considerations relating to establishing credibility of an informant include his or her personal observations, the degree of details given, independent police corroboration of the informer's information, and whether the informer testified at the probable cause hearing [*]. Deficiency in one factor can be compensated for by a strong showing in another or by some other indication of reliability.

"It is true that the [confidential informant] did not provide the level of specificity and detail that would have removed all ambiguity from the probable cause inquiry, but we cannot examine the facts provided by the [confidential informant] in isolation." According to the court, the most important factor was that the informer provided firsthand observations of illegal activity. The facts provided by the informer were "somewhat cursory," but they established the basis of knowledge and supported his reliability. The informer's personal observations formed "a direct link" between the defendant's criminal conduct and the place to be searched.

The informant's admissions of his own past criminal conduct carried their own indicia of credibility. In addition, the investigating officer corroborated the informer's assertion that one of the vehicles parked outside the place to be searched belonged to the defendant.

In this case, the magistrate apparently did not actually question the informer; nonetheless, his presence distinguishes this case from those in which an officer seeks a warrant on the strength of allegations by an absent informer. The court agreed with the defendant that "an on-the-record exchange between [the confidential informer] and issuing magistrate would further buttress a finding that a [confidential informant] is reliable" but declined to mandate that in every case. Citing [*], the court said that "the presence of the [confidential informant] and the opportunity to be questioned are themselves indicia of reliability because they eliminate some of the ambiguity that accompanies an unknown hearsay declarant. The mere presence of the [confidential informant] allows the issuing judge to confront the [confidential informant] if necessary."

3.3   STATE V. WALLACE (MD. 2002)
(*Probable Cause: Search*)

The defendant was among several passengers in a vehicle stopped for traffic offenses. While one officer was running a computer check on the driver's license and registration, another officer scanned the vehicle with a drug-detection dog. The dog indicated there were drugs in the car. The officers searched the passengers and found cocaine on the defendant.

- *Was this a constitutional search?*
- *If so, what was the probable cause? Or, was no probable cause needed?*
- *If not, why was it unconstitutional?*
  - *If it was unconstitutional, what could officers have done differently to change the result?*

State v. Wallace (Md. 2002): 72 CrL 232

A narcotics-detection canine's alert to the exterior of a vehicle does not, by itself, provide police officers with probable cause to search all the passengers in the vehicle. Officers should have had the dog sniff each passenger individually before searching them.

The majority found that a passenger's presence in a car involved in criminal activity does not, by itself, provide probable cause for a search of the passenger's person. In *United States v. DiRe,* 332 U.S. 581 (1948), the U.S. Supreme Court struck down a search of a passenger in a car in which the driver had sold counterfeit gasoline ration coupons. In [*] a state court held that a defendant's presence in the front passenger seat of a car in which a police officer had found cash in the glove compartment and drugs behind a back-seat armrest did not give the officer probable cause to arrest him.

Even closer to the instant case, according to the majority, was an Illinois case [*] holding that a canine's alert to a car did not provide probable cause to search all of the passengers. In this case, as in the Illinois case, the only connection between the defendant and drugs was the dog's positive alert to the entire passenger compartment of a vehicle driven by someone else; this link is insufficient to provide probable cause. The court agreed with the Illinois court that the officers could have avoided the constitutional violation in this case by having the dog sniff each occupant of the car before searching the occupants' persons.

The majority said that distinguishing between drivers and passengers makes sense in this context because passengers cannot be presumed to have the same control over the contents of vehicles as drivers.

Although the court found support for its position in cases from other jurisdictions, it noted that there are cases to the contrary as well, in which courts find a positive alert by a drug-detection dog provides probable cause to search drivers as well as passengers [*].

Two judges dissented, finding the dog alert to be sufficient probable cause to search the passenger.

Note: In 2003, the U.S. Supreme Court decided *Maryland v. Pringle,* 538 U.S. 921 (2003) [74 CrL 196], a case in which an officer stopped a car for speeding and, in the course of a consent search of the car, found $763 in the glove compartment and five glassine baggies of cocaine between the back-seat armrest and the back seat. All three men in the car denied knowledge or ownership of the drugs or money. Pringle, the front-seat passenger, was arrested and convicted of possession of cocaine and possession with intent to deliver.

On appeal, Pringle said he was in the same position as DiRe, a simple passenger in the car; that, Pringle said, was not enough to establish probable cause to arrest him.

However, the Supreme Court distinguished *DiRe* because, in *DiRe,* the police had information implicating another person in the car and no information implicating DiRe. In *Pringle,* the police had no information directly implicating anyone, but the cash and drugs clearly belonged to someone. Pringle's arrest was not unconstitutional, the Court explained, because "we think it an entirely reasonable inference from these facts that any or all three of the occupants had knowledge of, and exercised dominion and control over, the cocaine. Thus a reasonable officer could conclude that there was probable cause to believe Pringle committed the crime of possession of cocaine, either solely or jointly."

- *Make the argument that* Pringle *changes the result in this case.*
- *Make the argument that the Maryland Supreme Court's decision in* Wallace *would not be changed by* Pringle.

3.4   STATE v. NORDLUND (WASH.CT.APP. 2002) (*Probable Cause: Search*)

The defendant was arrested as a suspect in sexual assaults on two teenaged girls. Officers from the county where one of the crimes occurred sought a warrant to seize and search the defendant's home computer. The affidavits supporting the warrant asserted that the "computer or similar electronic storage device will provide data that will assist in establishing dates and times in which [the defendant] was at his residence which given the number of assaults and the locations, will provide necessary information that may serve to establish [the defendant's] location at critical times relevant to the alleged crimes." The affidavits also stated that the defendant used a computer to access pornography and to communicate by e-mail and asserted on this basis that the computer "could likely provide important evidence in this case regarding intent, dates, and locations."

An officer from another county incorporated these averments into a second warrant application and added what the court described as "generalized statements about the habits of sex offenders." For example, the application stated that in the affiant's "experience and training[,] sex offenders often keep notes, newspaper clippings, diaries and other memorabilia of their crimes" and that such items had been found on suspects' computers in other sexual assault cases.

The warrants were issued, and a search of the computer turned up a file in which the defendant described his whereabouts on the day of one of the assaults. The file was used at trial to impeach the credibility of the defendant and his alibi witnesses.

- *Did the affidavits supply sufficient factual information to establish probable cause to search? Explain.*
- *Was the search warrant constitutional? Explain.*
- *Should the file discovered in the search be used against the defendant?*

State v. Nordlund (Wash.Ct.App. 2002): 71 CrL 679

The affidavits failed to show the required nexus for search of the personal computer. The state was engaged in a fishing expedition.

The court approved the trial court's description of a personal computer as "the modern day repository of a man's records, reflections, and conversations." A search of a personal computer is thus comparable to a search of an individual's personal documents and, as such, may bring 1st and 4th Amendment considerations into conflict.

In such a situation, the 4th Amendment requires careful scrutiny of whether the warrant application supports a factual nexus between the search authorized and the assertion that evidence of a crime is likely to be found as a result of the search.

In this case, the court concluded that warrants were not sufficient to demonstrate probable cause for the seizure and search of the personal computer. There was "no factual nexus" between the information alleged to be stored on the computer and the crimes being investigated.

Describing the first set of affidavits as "conclusory," the court said they did not contain any factual support for the assertion that the computer would establish the defendant's location at the relevant times. Indeed, the computer could only provide relevant information to prove that the defendant was not at the scene of the crime at the relevant times; it could not provide evidence to show where he might have been otherwise.

Likewise, the statement that the defendant used the computer to access pornography and communicate by e-mail did not establish a nexus with any criminal activity. It appears, the court concluded, that the state "was fishing for some incriminating document, which is precisely what the first and fourth amendments prohibit."

The affidavit for the second warrant was no better. The averments copied from the other officers were insufficient, and the generalized statements about sex offenders' habits were inadequate, standing alone, to supply probable cause. The court noted that the Washington Supreme Court had reached the same conclusion [*] in a case about a warrant affidavit describing the habits of drug dealers.

3.5   STATE v. MARKS (MONT. 2002)
(*Probable Cause: Search*)

The defendants, husband and wife, were convicted of arson. The case began when firefighters were called to the defendants' home and observed flames coming from the windows and roof. The wife stated she had left the premises for 20 minutes and returned to find it ablaze.

After the fire was contained, investigators entered and observed that the house contained few items of furniture or clothing, as if some of the contents had been removed before the fire. They also noticed heavy fire and smoke damage that seemed inconsistent with the wife's asserted absence of only 20 minutes.

When investigators asked the husband for consent to a search for evidence of the cause of the fire, he asked if he was suspected of "torching [his] own house," and had his brother call an attorney. Although both defendants ultimately signed consents, the husband continued to object to the search and the wife seemed too upset for her consent to be valid. Accordingly, the investigators put the consents aside and obtained a warrant.

The warrant application recited the paucity of personal belongings in the house, the wife's apparently false statement about her length of absence, and the husband's reluctance to allow a search. The warrant authorized a search for objects and substances used in arson, insurance and financial documents, phone records, and evidence of items removed prior to the fire. Items obtained in the search and through subsequent investigative subpoenas implicated the defendants in the arson of their home.

After losing a suppression motion, the defendants pleaded guilty while maintaining their innocence. On appeal, they challenged the adequacy of the probable cause showing.

- *Was there sufficient probable cause for a search warrant in this case?*
  - *If so, specify the facts that establish probable cause.*
  - *If not, detail what additional facts would have supplied probable cause here.*

State v. Marks (Mont. 2002): 72 CrL 197

The meager amount of personal property found by firefighters in a burned residence, the homeowners' reluctance to allow police to search the premises, and an apparent discrepancy between the extent of the fire damage and what one of the homeowners said about her movements on the day of the fire established probable cause for a warrant to search for evidence of arson.

A determination of probable cause requires only that the facts in the warrant affidavit be sufficient to indicate a fair probability that an offense has been committed and that the evidence sought will be found at the place designated. The majority here eschewed a "sentence-by-sentence" review of the warrant application, saying that such a process would be inconsistent with the totality-of-the-circumstances test prescribed by *Illinois v. Gates*, 462 U.S. 213 (1983).

The probable cause standard was met. The majority stressed the following averments in the affidavit: "facts demonstrating that furniture and clothing were removed from the Markses' home prior to the fire; Mrs. Marks' statements regarding her length of absence conflicted with the time the fire was reported and the extent of fire damage; and the behavior of Mr. Marks was atypical of a fire victim."

The majority also said there was a fair probability that evidence of arson would be found at the place where the fire occurred, and that the items sought in the warrant application were connected to the crime of arson. Insurance and financial documents, for example, tend to establish whether or not an individual had a motive to commit arson, the majority said. Giving credence to the detective's training and experience, the majority ruled that he had provided reasonable justification for his conclusion that evidence connected to the crime of arson would be found at the home.

Two judges dissented. One of them argued that the warrant application was long on suspicion and too short on facts to support a probable cause finding. He complained of the lack of foundation to show that the home's furnishings at the time of the fire were different than they normally would be for this couple. He also objected to the emphasis the majority placed on the wife's statement about how long she had been away, and to the implicit criticism of the husband for declining to have his home searched by police. This judge worried that the majority's opinion "places in serious doubt" the continued viability of prior search and seizure case law.

The other dissenting judge agreed that the finding of probable cause was erroneous.

Note that many states refuse to recognize the good faith exception, declaring instead that their state constitutions hold police to a higher standard than the U.S. Supreme Court has established under the federal constitution. States that do not have a good faith exception in their state constitutional law include Connecticut, Idaho, New Jersey, New Mexico, New York, Pennsylvania, and Vermont.

3.6   MCKAY v. STATE (MD.CT.SPEC.APP. 2002)
(*Probable Cause: Search*)

Narcotics officers acting on a tip made several undercover purchases of cocaine from the defendant's mother. When the officers revealed themselves, the mother admitted that her son was her supplier and agreed to arrange for him to deliver drugs to her at work. The officers stopped the defendant for a traffic offense as he was driving toward his mother's place of employment. A narcotics-detection dog was brought to the scene but failed to alert to the defendant's car. The officers searched the car anyway and found drugs.

The dog's handler testified that the dog was on medication.

- *Is there still probable cause?*
- *Did the dog's failure to alert to drugs eliminate the probable cause, or at least reduce it to something less than probable? Explain your reasoning.*

McKay v. State (Md.Ct.Spec.App. 2002): 72 CrL 320

Narcotics investigators' probable cause to believe that there were drugs in a defendant's car was not negated by a narcotics dog's failure to alert to the vehicle. The court agreed with a First Circuit case [*] that held that drug traffickers' efforts to mask the odor of their wares, variations in dogs' abilities, and other considerations provide reasonable explanations for a nonalert. In this case, there was testimony by the dog's handler that the dog was on medication.

Rather than automatically negating probable cause, a nonalert should be considered as one of the facts in the totality of the circumstances being evaluated for probable cause. Noting that the existence of probable cause in this case was not a close call, the court decided that "the dog's nonalert—particularly in view of the reasonable explanation for it— did not negate the probable cause necessary for the search of the car."

3.7 COMMONWEALTH v. SMITH (MASS.APP.CT. 2003)
(*Probable Cause: Search*)

The warrant affidavit described three controlled purchases of drugs from the defendant. All occurred away from his home; however, police officers conducting surveillance saw the defendant driving his car directly to his home after one buy, and directly from his home to one of the other buys. The first purchase was executed with the aid of a confidential source who professed familiarity with the defendant and his vehicle. The affidavit also contained an assertion that police saw marijuana in the defendant's home while investigating a domestic disturbance, but the assertion was found to be false and was excised from the affidavit.

- *Was there probable cause to search the defendant's home?*
  - *If so, be specific in the facts that lead you to that conclusion.*
  - *If not, explain why you are not persuaded by these facts, as corrected in the affidavit.*

Commonwealth v. Smith (Mass.App.Ct. 2003): 72 CrL 407

A search warrant authorizing a search of a drug suspect's home was deficient for failing to establish a nexus between the home and the defendant's observed drug activities.

The problem with the affidavit, as redacted, was "that it does not explain why there was probable cause to believe that drugs or related evidence would be found at [the place to be searched] other than it being the residence of the defendant," the court said. The confidential source did not claim to have been inside the house or, indeed, even to know exactly where it was. Nor did the source allege that the defendant conducted drug transactions from his home or kept drugs there, the court noted. What the police surveillance revealed about the defendant's driving around the time of two of the drug transactions added little to the probable cause equation. Without more, those observations "established no connection between [the defendant's] home and the controlled buys."

3.8 BALL v. UNITED STATES (D.C. 2002)
(*Probable Cause: Search/Plain Feel*)

The defendant was a passenger in a vehicle stopped for a traffic violation. The officer noticed that the defendant seemed very nervous and repeatedly reached toward his sweatshirt's center pocket despite the officer's admonitions not to do so. The officer decided to frisk the defendant. Touching the pocket, the officer, according to his testimony, "felt a large cylinder container which [he] thought to be a large medicine bottle," and he immediately thought that "it was some kind of contraband or narcotics" on the basis of the defendant's behavior. The officer removed the medicine bottle, opened it, and saw a large number of plastic bags containing a white rock-like substance. This discovery led to the defendant's arrest.

At the suppression hearing, the officer testified that he had been involved in more than 100 drug-related arrests, that he was familiar with the ways that drugs are packaged and hidden, and that he had arrested numerous people who had hidden narcotics in medicine bottles.

- *Was the frisk proper? Why?*
- *What are the arguments that there is no probable cause to seize the medicine bottle in this case? Explain fully.*
- *What are the arguments that there is probable cause to seize the medicine bottle in this case? Explain fully.*

Ball v. United States (D.C. 2002): 71 CrL 574

Perception of a neutral object can create probable cause in light of an officer's experience. The circumstances surrounding a pat-down can justify an officer's "plain feel" seizure of an object that is not itself contraband and does not conform to the shape of contraband. Therefore, an officer's detection of a large medicine bottle in a defendant's pocket, considered in light of the defendant's conduct and the officer's experience with the practices of drug traffickers, gave the officer probable cause to seize and search the bottle.

Under the "plain feel" doctrine recognized in *Minnesota v. Dickerson,* 508 U.S. 366 (1993), an officer can seize contraband without a warrant if, during a valid pat-down under *Terry v. Ohio,* 392 U.S. 1 (1968), the officer detects an object the incriminating nature of which is "immediately apparent" to the officer. "Immediately apparent" does not mean that the officer must be certain that the item felt is contraband; further, the doctrine requires only "that there is probable cause to associate the item with criminal activity."

In this case, there was no claim that the pat-down was impermissible or that the officer exceeded the lawful bounds of the pat-down by manipulating the medicine bottle before deciding that it likely contained contraband. The issue instead was whether the officer's tactile perception of the medicine bottle while patting the outer surface of the defendant's sweatshirt, combined with the attendant circumstances known to the officer at the time, provided probable cause for a belief that the bottle contained contraband before the officer seized it.

The issue was one of first impression in the jurisdiction. Other courts are split on the issue of whether an object can be seized under the "plain feel" doctrine if it is not shaped like contraband but is recognizable as an object that is known to be routinely used to contain or package drugs, the court reported. Looking at the competing lines of case law, the court said the outcome depends on whether the court considers not only the officer's tactile perceptions but also "other attendant circumstances which may inform the officer's belief of what he is touching." Courts that allow other circumstances to be considered find probable cause [*]; if other circumstances cannot be considered, courts find probable cause is lacking [*].

The court here allowed consideration of not only the officer's perceptions but also the context in which they were made. The court looked at its prior 4th Amendment cases: [*] did not involve an object that, like a pill bottle, has innocent uses, but it did recognize that the tactile perception of an object can be informed by the officer's training and experience and other attendant circumstances. The court also deemed it significant that in a case applying the related doctrine of plain view to a pill bottle, a finding of no probable cause was based on the lack of special training or experience on the part of the officer and the lack of testimony that bottles of the type seized were used to transport narcotics [*]. That kind of testimony made the difference in [*], a case that upheld an experienced vice officer's seizure of a plastic bag.

The court said that the common feature among these and other cases that found probable cause on the basis of officers' observations is that the officers recognized distinctive packaging used in the drug trade on the basis of personal experience with that particular packaging. Consideration of such experience in the context of plain feel is consistent with the reasoning in *Dickerson,* that a plain feel seizure is permissible when it does not increase the "invasion of the suspect's privacy beyond that already authorized" for a limited pat-down. To require more certainty from the feel of the object alone would be to expect more from the "immediately apparent" requirement than the probable cause required by the 4th Amendment.

Although there was no evidence presented that the traffic stop took place in a high-crime area, as was the case in many of the decisions cited by the court, the officer had more than the mere tactile identification of a pill bottle to support his action. The defendant's furtive gestures were significant because "they related to the medicine bottle in his jacket pocket," the court noted. The defendant acted as though he wished to conceal something in the pocket, put his hands in the pocket on exiting the vehicle, and repeatedly reached for the pocket despite numerous requests that he keep his hands away from it.

The court acknowledged that there were not as many "attendant circumstances" in this case as in some others in which probable cause was found. Nevertheless, it concluded that the defendant's behavior, particularly his repeated efforts to reach into the pocket, "added enough information to cross the threshold" from reasonable belief that he might be going for a weapon to probable cause to believe the bottle contained drugs.

3.9   PEOPLE v. PRESSY (CAL.CT.APP. 2002)
(Probable Cause: Search/Good Faith)

Police pulled the defendant over after observing him driving erratically. When the officers approached the car, they smelled marijuana and determined that he was driving under the influence of that substance and a controlled nervous stimulant. Searches of the defendant and his car incident to his arrest turned up 1.5 grams of methamphetamine and one marijuana cigarette.

One officer then applied for a warrant to search the defendant's residence for drugs and related items. The officer's affidavit described his background in drug enforcement and included statements that his training and experience as an undercover narcotics agent indicated that drug users keep additional quantities of contraband at their residences. The warrant was issued, and the police found drugs and drug paraphernalia at the defendant's residence.

The defendant moved to suppress the evidence at trial, arguing that the affidavit did not establish probable cause to search his home.

- *Was the warrant good? Explain.*
- *Are the drugs found at the defendant's house admissible as evidence against him? Explain.*

People v. Pressey (Cal.Ct.App. 2002): 72 CrL 79

Illegal drug use does not necessarily provide probable cause to search a user's residence. However, the officer could rely on the warrant and the evidence was thus admissible under the good faith exception to the 4th Amendment exclusionary rule.

Probable Cause

The arrest for simple possession and the opinion expressed in the officer's affidavit did not establish probable cause to search the defendant's residence.

The state relied on decisions that have approved the inference that drug evidence is likely to be found in the residences of drug dealers. Although not all courts agree, California appellate courts and the Ninth Circuit have held that the combination of evidence of drug dealing, such as the discovery on a defendant's person of drugs packaged for sale, and an experienced officer's opinion that more drugs would be found at the defendant's home provide probable cause to search the home [*].

The court declined the state's request to expand the reasoning of those cases to drug users by adopting a per se rule that if a magistrate determines that a person is likely a drug user, then probable cause to search the person's residence follows automatically. The court gave several reasons for its decision.

First, it said, such a rule would be contrary to cases from other jurisdictions that have drawn a sharp distinction, in this context, between drug dealers and individuals possessing drugs for personal use. For example, the Nebraska Supreme Court [*] refused to extend the dealer cases to a mere user, holding that the discovery of a use-sized amount of drugs on a defendant did not permit an inference that there was incriminating evidence at the defendant's home. The California court said that "while the issue has seldom been squarely presented, there is a significant body of reasoning to the effect that suspected drug use does not alone provide probable cause to search the user's residence." It added that it found no authority supporting the state's position.

The dealer cases on which the per se rule is based are distinguishable. Drug dealing is a greater evil than drug use, and the state's justification for searching is thus greater in the dealing context. Moreover, the prospect of uncovering drugs is significant in a trafficker's residence but merely speculative in the case of a user's residence.

In addition, because there are more drug users than drug traffickers, searching the users' homes would result in a much greater invasion of what the U.S. Supreme Court called the "right of residential privacy at the core of the 4th Amendment," in *Wilson v. Layne*, 526 U.S. 603 (1999). The court here said that "little argument and no persuasive justification has been offered ... for a new rule that would potentially open the door to a vast number of residential intrusions."

Finally, substitution of a bright-line rule for case-specific analysis would be contrary to 4th Amendment precedent that generally rejects such standards. The court cited the Supreme Court's comment in *Illinois v. Gates,* 462 U.S. 213 (1983) that the concept of probable cause is "not readily, or even usefully, reduced to a neat set of legal rules."

Summing up, the court declared that "probable cause to search the residence of some-one suspected of using illegal drugs requires more than an opinion or inference, available in every case, that drugs are likely to be present." The court cautioned that it was holding only that such cases must be decided on a case-by-case basis, not that probable cause to search a drug user's home could never arise from the particularized suspicions of an experienced narcotics officer.

Good Faith

The court went on to rule that suppression of the evidence obtained from the defendant's home was not required here. Inferring the presence of contraband in a drug user's home is "arguably analogous" to the accepted inference that is drawn with respect to dealers. "Given the dearth of authority directly on point and the existence of potentially supportive precedent, the issue of probable cause was 'debatable' when the warrant herein was sought, even though the issue, upon examination, is not a particularly close one."

3.10   STATE v. STEELMAN (TEX.CRIM.APP. 2002)
(*Probable Cause: Arrest*)

Police got an anonymous tip reporting drug dealing. When officers arrived at the residence described in the tip, they peeked between the window blinds and saw four men sitting in the living room. They knocked on the door, and the defendant exited and closed the door behind him. The officers testified that they then smelled marijuana in the air, not coming from the defendant's clothes.

When the defendant tried to re-enter the house to fetch identification for the officers, the officers kept him from closing the door and entered. They arrested the occupants and requested permission for a search. The defendant refused. A later search pursuant to a warrant turned up marijuana inside the house, but the state did not rely on the warrant to justify the officers' actions in this case.

- *Did the police have probable cause to arrest? Explain.*
  - *If so, which defendant(s) did the police have probable cause to arrest? Explain.*

State v. Steelman (Tex.Crim.App. 2002): 72 CrL 121

The anonymous tip and odor of marijuana did not provide probable cause for the arrest or entry. Officers who did not know which of the four suspects was smoking did not have probable cause as to any of them.

The tip that someone at the residence was dealing drugs "did not amount to anything." "The tip was never substantiated, and none of the occupants were ever charged with drug dealing."

In that same vein, "the mere odor of burning marijuana did not give the officers probable cause to believe that [the defendant] had committed the offense of possession of marijuana in their presence." In describing the facts, the majority pointed out that the officers smelled the odor of marijuana in the air but not on the defendant himself. Given these circumstances, the officers had "probable cause to believe that someone, somewhere, was or had been smoking marijuana," but the mere smell of marijuana in the air did not give the officers probable cause to believe that the defendant possessed marijuana.

Officers who detect the odor of burning marijuana coming from a particular place but lack specific information as to which of multiple occupants of that place is smoking do not have probable cause to arrest and search the occupants. "[T]he officers in this case had no idea who was smoking or possessing marijuana, and they certainly had no particular reason to believe that [the defendant] was smoking or possessing marijuana." Accordingly, the court upheld the trial court's suppression order.

Three judges concurred in the decision but stated that although the officers had probable cause to detain the defendant outside of his home, the odor of burning marijuana did not provide the officers with probable cause to believe that the defendant had committed a crime in their presence. One of those judges stressed that established 4th Amendment case law requires officers to have probable cause and exigent circumstances to enter a home without a warrant or consent.

Three judges dissented. One argued that the officers had the probable cause required to arrest the defendant and search his home. The other two argued that the odor of burning marijuana corroborated the tip about drug dealing and provided the officers with probable cause to believe that each of the occupants in the house possessed marijuana and would destroy the evidence if given the time to do so. One of those judges also pointed out that the majority's analysis of the officers' lack of specific information as to which of the multiple occupants was smoking marijuana was out of step with decisions by courts in other states [*].

3.11   STATE v. HILLS (LA. 2002)
(*Probable Cause: Arrest*)

Acting on a tip, officers arrested a man for selling drugs on the street. While the officers were handcuffing him and warning him of his rights, the man apparently decided to become an informer on the spot. He stated that he did not want to go to jail and that the cocaine that the officers found had been given to him by the defendant. The arrested man identified the defendant by name, described him, and indicated that the defendant lived upstairs in the building in front of which they were standing.

The officers did not know the arrested man or the defendant, but one of the officers noticed in an upstairs doorway a person, the defendant, who matched the description given by the arrestee and was monitoring the goings-on out front. The officers subsequently seized the defendant as he tried to leave the building. The seizure led to the officers' discovery of cocaine used to convict the defendant of a drug crime.

■ *Did the officers have probable cause to arrest the defendant? Explain.*

State v. Hills (La. 2002): 72 CrL 138

A statement of an informer of unknown credibility that inculpates both himself and another person can be reliable enough to provide probable cause for the arrest of the person fingered by the informer. In the circumstances presented in this case, an arrestee's accusation of a nearby person was enough to provide probable cause for an arrest.

The majority of the court assumed for purposes of deciding this case that the seizure of the defendant amounted to a de facto arrest requiring probable cause. It also agreed with the general proposition that "[a] statement made by an individual caught red-handed in possession of contraband narcotics, acknowledging possession of the drugs but also identifying his or her supplier ... does not possess intrinsic reliability simply because the declarant provides the information in the context of admitting damning facts already known to the police." Nevertheless, the majority continued, the fact that an informer's self-serving accusation of another in a confession is not intrinsically reliable does not demonstrate that there are no circumstances in which an arrestee's accusation of another will bear sufficient indicia of reliability to establish probable cause.

The majority stressed that the informer in this case had reason to believe things would go badly for him if he led the officers on a wild goose chase. In [*] the court had said that this consideration was not particularly significant because the informer might have calculated that "the risk incurred in fabricating the basis for his information may have seemed small, difficult to distinguish from a genuine effort to cooperate and worth the chance of having the charges dropped against him." In contrast, in this case, the informer named a source who was only feet away, and he could reasonably assume that the police would immediately proceed to try to verify the information. He "had little or no time to fabricate a story falsely implicating someone else and he spoke spontaneously in the hope, however misguided, that he could help out his own case by trading off information expanding the scope of the police investigation 'up the chain' of street-level drug trafficking."

One judge dissented, emphasizing that the informer was unknown to the officers, that he was endeavoring to curry favor with them, and that the officers did not observe any activity by the defendant that would suggest he was involved in drug dealing.

3.12   STATE v. COMER (UTAH CT.APP. 2002)
(*Probable Cause: Arrest/Exigent Circumstances*)

A tipster characterized by the court as "an identified citizen informant" reported to police that there was a "family fight" in progress at the home of the defendants, a married couple. When police responded to the scene, the wife opened the door a few inches and stepped out onto the porch. The officers explained that they were there to investigate a report of a family fight and asked her if anyone else was at home. She said her husband was inside; then, without further explanation, she turned around and went indoors.

Officers followed the wife inside and down a hall, where she leaned into a bedroom and told her husband of the officers' presence. Both defendants and the officers then went back to the living room. The wife admitted that she had scratched her husband in a fight. In the course of arresting her for domestic violence assault, the officers found drugs and drug paraphernalia.

Both defendants were charged with a drug offense. They sought suppression of the evidence. The trial court ruled that the combination of the tip and the wife's behavior on the porch triggered the emergency aid doctrine. As set out in [*] that doctrine permits a warrantless search if (1) police have an objectively reasonable basis for believing that an emergency exists and believe there is an immediate need for assistance for the protection of life, (2) the search is not primarily motivated by an intent to arrest and seize evidence, and (3) there is some reasonable basis to associate the emergency with the place to be searched.

- *Would the elements of the emergency aid doctrine be satisfied by these facts? Explain.*
- *If not or if this case occurred in a state that did not have that doctrine, what arguments could the state make to justify the officers' behavior?*
  - *What result and why?*

State v. Comer (Utah Ct.App. 2002): 71 CrL 515

An identified citizen's report of domestic violence at a dwelling does not, without more, justify a police entry into the dwelling under the emergency aid exception to the 4th Amendment's warrant and probable cause requirements. However, the report in this case, coupled with events that occurred when police responded to the report, provided probable cause to believe that a crime had been committed, and that exigent circumstances supported officers' entry of the home.

Because the emergency aid doctrine dispenses with both the warrant and probable cause requirements of the 4th Amendment, it must be carefully limited. The doctrine requires an objectively reasonable belief that an unconscious or semiconscious person, or a person who is missing and feared injured or dead, is in the place to be searched, according to the court. "[T]here must be some reliable and specific indication of the probability that a person is suffering from a serious physical injury before application of the medical emergency doctrine is justified." The wife's suspicious activities at the threshold of the home did not add enough to the report to pass this test.

On the other hand, the court continued, the facts were adequate to justify the entry under the warrant clause exception that relies on probable cause and exigent circumstances.

The report of domestic violence, coming as it did from an "ordinary citizen informant," was presumptively reliable. Furthermore, the wife did nothing to dispel the suspicions raised by the report; instead, she added to the level of suspicion by suddenly retreating inside after saying that her husband was home. Even if a scenario could be imagined in which "such an abrupt withdrawal in the middle of an encounter with police may not appear highly suspicious," such conduct would be suspicious in light of the initial tip, the court said. The officers had probable cause to believe that some sort of domestic violence crime had been or was being committed in the home.

Turning to the exigency prong, the court acknowledged that the case was a close one. However, it pointed out that a domestic violence complaint poses a volatile, dangerous situation for police. Furthermore, the officers could reasonably have feared that the wife was going inside because the husband made a threat against her, she intended to resume the fight, or she intended to cover up evidence of domestic violence that had already occurred.

Under any of these scenarios, the officers could reasonably believe either that there was no time to get a warrant or that their presence was necessary to prevent physical harm to persons or destruction of evidence.

Arrest

The main issue here, of course, is knowing at what point an "arrest" has occurred. It matters because if a person was unconstitutionally arrested and evidence was found as a result of that arrest, that evidence can be excluded from the trial. However, if the police contact did not amount to an "arrest" and evidence was found, that evidence can be used against the defendant at trial. Therefore, the question of whether the individual was actually under arrest becomes a contentious one with serious evidentiary consequences.

The U.S. Supreme Court has narrowed the definition of arrest, a move that works to the advantage of the police and to the disadvantage of the defendant. The traditional conceptualization was simply stated: A person is under arrest when a reasonable person in these circumstances would not feel free to leave, as stated in *United States v. Mendenhall*, 446 U.S. 544 (1980). Then came the bus cases, where police boarded buses and sought to search for drugs; passengers contended they were under arrest at that point because a reasonable person would not feel free to leave a bus in transit. The court explained in *Florida v. Bostick*, 501 U.S. 429 (1991), that an arrest does not occur unless a reasonable person would not feel free to leave or otherwise terminate the encounter. In *California v. Hodari D.*, 499 U.S. 621 (1991), we encountered a case in which the defendant ran from the police, who then chased him. In that case, the government did not contend that there was probable cause to arrest Hodari; the government contended that Hodari was never under arrest. Hodari threw away something (later identified as crack cocaine) during the chase and, after he was caught and charged with possession of cocaine, he contended that the cocaine should be suppressed because he was under arrest at the time he threw it. Hodari argued

---

When the appellate court has cited and relied upon a U.S. Supreme Court opinion in reaching its decision, those citations are set out in full so you will know what Supreme Court authority the court relied upon. When you see an asterisk [*] in the court's opinion, that means the appellate court has referenced and relied upon a lower court case in reaching its decision. Those case citations are not included here.

that, under the circumstances of being chased by the police, a reasonable person would not feel free to leave (that, after all, was what Hodari was trying to do), nor would a reasonable person feel free to terminate the encounter. The court explained that an arrest does not occur until the individual is actually caught or submits to the authority of the police.

We have therefore seen some significant transformation in the definition of arrest. The evolution favors the government in that it makes it more difficult to find an arrest that will require exclusion of evidence. If Hodari had persuaded the court that he was under arrest when he was being pursued by police and when he discarded the cocaine, the government would not have been able to use that evidence against him because it would have been seized as a result of an unconstitutional arrest. However, because Hodari was not under arrest when he was being pursued by police and when he discarded the cocaine, the exclusionary rule did not come into play. The evidence was admissible against him in the prosecution for possession of a controlled substance.

It is important to understand when an arrest occurs because that point in time has enormous implications for operation of the exclusionary rule with respect to the discovery of physical evidence and admissions and confessions the defendant might make to the police.

4.1   UNITED STATES v. AXSOM (EIGHTH CIR. 2002)
(*Arrest*)

Federal agents executed a warrant to search the defendant's home for child pornography and interrogated the defendant in his home. The agents told the defendant that he was not under arrest; they did not give him *Miranda* warnings. The defendant had collections of swords and firearms on display throughout his home and, during the course of the search, federal agents went with him wherever he went, including the bathroom. At one point during the interrogation, the defendant got up to get a glass of water and agents told him to sit down while an agent got the water for him.

The defendant made statements that incriminated him and these statements were used against him at trial. He argued that his statements should have been suppressed because he was in custody at the time they were made and he had not been Mirandized.

- ■ *Was the defendant under arrest?*
  - • *If so, what facts lead to that conclusion? When did the arrest occur?*
  - • *If not, why not?*
- ■ *Must the defendant's incriminatory comments be suppressed? Why?*

United States v. Axsom (Eighth Cir. 2002): 71 CrL 164

A defendant who was not allowed to get his own glass of water and was followed wherever he went inside his home by federal agents executing a search warrant was not "in custody" for purposes of *Miranda v. Arizona,* 384 U.S. 436 (1966).

Whether a person is "in custody" for *Miranda* purposes depends on whether a reasonable person in the same circumstances would believe that his freedom of movement was restricted to the degree associated with a formal arrest. In [*] the Eighth Circuit outlined six common indicia that can point toward or away from a finding of custody:

1. Whether the suspect was informed at the time of questioning that the questioning was voluntary, that he was free to leave or to request the officers to leave, or that he was not considered to be under arrest.
2. Whether the suspect possessed unrestrained freedom of movement during questioning.
3. Whether the suspect initiated contact with authorities or voluntarily acquiesced to official requests to respond to questions.
4. Whether "strong-arm" tactics or deceptive strategies were employed during questioning.
5. Whether the atmosphere of the questioning was police dominated.
6. Whether the suspect was placed under arrest at the termination of the questioning.

[1] The first finding mitigating against a finding of custody was established.

[2] The court understood the agents' caution in escorting the defendant around his home and not allowing him to get his own drink, in light of the fact that the home was a veritable arsenal of weapons. Although the restrictions on the defendant's movement meant that the second "mitigating factor" was absent, a reasonable person in the defendant's shoes would have realized that the agents stayed with him not to restrict his movement, but to protect themselves and the integrity of the search.

[3] Although the defendant did not initiate or arrange for the questioning, he testified at the suppression hearing that he would have answered any questions because he believed it was in his own best interest to appear friendly and cooperative during the search. He even offered to show the agents which of his two computers contained child pornography. Therefore, the third mitigating factor was present.

[4] The agents did not employ strong-arm tactics or deceptive strategies. In fact, after the search, the defendant commended the agents for their professionalism.

[5] Although the execution of the search warrant was certainly police dominated, the interview was not. During the interview the defendant sat on an easy chair and smoked his pipe while the two agents sat across from him on a small sofa. The agents asked questions of the defendant, but the defendant also asked the agents questions about search procedures. Given the presumption that questioning at a suspect's home is less coercive than questioning at a police station, the court found that there was not a police-dominated atmosphere.

[6] Finally, the court noted that the defendant was not arrested at the termination of the questioning.

Viewing the totality of the circumstances, the court said they tipped in favor of a finding that the defendant was not in custody. Given the extensive arsenal of weapons inside the defendant's house, the fact that the defendant was accompanied wherever he went was much less significant than it otherwise would have been.

4.2   STATE v. RANDOLPH (TENN. 2002)
(*Arrest/Federalism*)

A police officer responding to a report of a burglary in progress observed the defendant riding a bicycle about a block from the scene. The officer activated the emergency lights on his patrol car and ordered the defendant to stop, but the defendant kept riding. The officer lost sight of the defendant when he turned a corner but saw him moments later in a ditch removing a shotgun from his pants. The officer ordered the defendant, at gunpoint, to disarm himself and lie down. The defendant complied, and the officer arrested him. It was later determined that the shotgun and other items the defendant had in his possession had been stolen in the burglary.

- *Applying the standard established by the U.S. Supreme Court in* California v. Hodari D., *499 U.S. 621 (1991), was the defendant seized when the officer saw him remove a shotgun from his pants?*
- *Why does it matter whether he was arrested at that point?*
- *Is the Tennessee Supreme Court required to follow the rule established in* Hodari? *Explain.*

State v. Randolph (Tenn. 2002): 71 CrL 218

The Tennessee Supreme Court rejected, as a matter of state constitutional law, the rule from *Hodari* that a suspect is not seized for 4th Amendment purposes until he submits to an officer's show of authority or is physically restrained.

The Tennessee court cited ten other jurisdictions that rejected *Hodari* on state constitutional grounds. The court noted that, in interpreting the state constitution's counterpart to the 4th Amendment, it followed the totality of the circumstances approach. The rule in *Hodari* departs from the totality of the circumstances approach and does not comport with the requirements of the Tennessee Constitution.

In the circumstances of this case, a reasonable person would have felt that he or she was not free to leave when the officer activated the blue lights on his patrol car, and at that point the officer did not have the articulable suspicion required for an investigative detention.

4.3   PEOPLE v. HEILMAN (COLO. 2002)
(*Arrest*)

A police officer observed the defendant with two other men sitting in a van parked in a pull-off near a lake. The officer approached the van in his patrol car at a higher than normal speed, parked approximately 10 feet from the van in a "T" formation, and hurried to the van on foot. As the officer approached, he saw the defendant widen his eyes and throw something to the floor of the van. The officer said he wanted to see everyone's hands and asked the defendant whether he needed any assistance, what he was doing, and what he had thrown down. The officer ordered them out of the car, directed them to put their hands behind their heads, and patted them down. The encounter led to the defendant's consent for a search that turned up drugs.

- *Was the defendant under arrest?*
  - *If so, when did the arrest occur?*
    - ▲ *What facts support probable cause for arrest?*
  - *If the defendant was not under arrest, explain why no arrest had occurred.*
- *Are the drugs admissible? Explain.*

People v. Heilman (Colo. 2002): 71 CrL 130

A police officer's "unfriendly" tone while questioning the occupants of a parked vehicle was among the factors that convinced the Colorado Supreme Court that the encounter amounted to a "seizure" for which the 4th Amendment required articulable suspicion.

The court decided that a reasonable person in the intimidating circumstances in this case would not have felt free to ignore the officer's requests for information and go about his business. The court pointed out that it previously relied on an officer's casual or friendly tone in concluding that no seizure occurred. The opposite was true here, it said. "Reasonable persons would not feel free to disobey the order to raise their hands to plain view while a uniformed officer approached them with a weapon displayed on his hip, ordered them out of their vehicle, directed them to put their hands behind their heads, patted them down, and commenced to search their vehicle."

The encounter in this case occurred in broad daylight and was not supported by reasonable suspicion according to the court.

4.4   PEOPLE v. GHERNA (ILL. 2003)
(*Arrest*)

Two officers on bicycle patrol rolled up on either side of the defendant's parked pickup truck to investigate a bottle of beer they had seen in the cab. The bottle turned out to be unopened and the defendant turned out not to be underage, but the encounter led to the officers' discovery of rock cocaine in the defendant's possession.

The defendant argued that evidence of the cocaine should be suppressed because he was seized for 4th Amendment purposes. The state argued that this was not a seizure because officers on bicycle patrol are "less threatening."

- *What do you think? Justify your answer.*

People v. Gherna (Ill. 2003): 72 CrL 387

The Illinois Supreme Court rejected the prosecutors' argument that an encounter with police officers on bicycle patrol did not amount to a "seizure" for 4th Amendment purposes because such officers are "less threatening."

The court was not persuaded by the state's reliance on the fact that officers on bicycle patrol are outfitted in short pants and short-sleeved shirts. The court pointed out that the officers displayed badges on their shirts and "were equipped with a full complement of police gear, including weapons, radios, handcuffs, and flashlights." The fact that the officers were assigned to bicycle patrol "did not diminish their apparent authority as law enforcement officers."

4.5 KEENOM v. STATE (ARK. 2002)
(*Arrest*)

While shopping at a Wal-Mart, an off-duty narcotics detective became suspicious of a long-haired, bearded shopper with a cart containing items used in the manufacture of methamphetamine—acetone, rubbing alcohol, and coffee filters. The detective later observed the defendant return to the store and speak to another long-haired man who was buying fuel cleaner and camping fuel, which are also associated with methamphetamine production.

The detective contacted a fellow drug task force member and uniformed officers from a nearby town, and they proceeded to the defendant's rural trailer home to conduct a knock and talk at 11:30 p.m. The defendant was awakened by the headlights in his trailer windows and stepped outside barefoot and wearing only a pair of jeans.

The detective explained why the officers were there, and the defendant refused a request for permission to search his home. The officers then questioned the defendant for 20 to 45 minutes. During this questioning, the defendant told the officers to leave and come back in 10 minutes. It was a cold and stormy night, and the defendant also asked to be allowed to fetch a jacket. The police denied both requests. The defendant eventually admitted that he had drugs in the trailer and made other statements that the police relied on to obtain a search warrant. The warrant turned up evidence used to convict the defendant of drug and firearms offenses.

- *What is the standard for determining at what point an arrest occurs?*
  - *Given these facts, was the defendant ever arrested? Explain fully.*
  - *If the defendant was arrested, when did that arrest occur?*
- *Why does it matter if the defendant was arrested prior to the execution of the search warrant?*

Keenom v. State (Ark. 2002): 71 CrL 449

A defendant was "seized" for purposes of the 4th Amendment when a large group of officers conducted a "knock and talk" at his home at night. The court emphasized the defendant's testimony that the police refused to allow him to go back inside his home during the encounter.

The Arkansas Supreme Court previously held in [*] that the 4th Amendment does not require police to have reasonable suspicion to knock on a suspect's door and request permission for a search unless the circumstances and the officers' conduct would have conveyed to a reasonable, innocent person that he or she was not free to ignore the officer's presence and go about his or her business. This line was crossed in the instant case according to the majority: "[The officer's] testimony does not controvert [the defendant's] statement that he was not allowed to go inside to retrieve some clothing. Similarly, his request that the officers leave and come back in ten minutes was ignored. Instead, these officers continued to question him while he stood in the weather, partially clothed, under the glare of the headlights of the officers' cars. This persistence by the officers would strongly convey to a reasonable person the officers' intention not to desist."

This persistent conduct was "the functional equivalent of a physical restraint," and"[s]uch prolonged questioning, leading as it did to [the defendant's] unsuccessful attempts to return to the safety and solitude of his house, would surely lead a reasonable person to believe that he could not ignore the officers."

The majority stressed the difference between the seizure that occurred in this case and less intrusive investigative detentions:

> [T]here is insufficient evidence to hold that the officer had reasonable suspicion to do more than stop appellant simultaneously with his observation of the "suspicious" seeming [defendant] .... There certainly were no grounds for the officer to witness suspicious behavior [at the Wal-Mart] in Bentonville, ascertain the [defendant's] identity, obtain the assistance of other officers, caravan to the [defendant's] rural residence six miles outside Decatur, attempt to obtain the [defendant's] consent to a search of his residence, and, finally, after being refused consent, engage in a twenty to forty-five minute detention of [defendant] on the theory of an investigatory stop.

One judge dissented because he found the facts supported the conclusion that a reasonable person in defendant's situation would have felt free to terminate the encounter.

Another judge also dissented, arguing that even if the defendant was seized, the officers had sufficient information to justify the seizure.

4.6 STATE v. BENTLEY (IDAHO 1999)
(*Arrest*)

Police wanted to arrest the defendant, but the warrant they had for him limited their authority to arresting him in a public place.

Police pretended to be investigating the defendant's report of a car burglary. They came to his house and asked him to come outside to get his vehicle registration and show them the direction in which the burglars had fled. Once the defendant agreed, reluctantly, to come outside, he was arrested pursuant to the misdemeanor warrant, and a search incident to the arrest revealed drugs on his person.

The defendant was then arrested on the misdemeanor.

- *Was this arrest constitutional? Explain fully.*
- *Was the discovery of drugs constitutional? Explain.*

State v. Bentley (Idaho 1999): 65 CrL 69

The court distinguished between cases in which police arrest a defendant who emerges from his house as a result of police compulsion (those arrests are unconstitutional), and cases in which police arrest a defendant who emerges from his house as a result of police trickery. Here, the court concluded the defendant "came outside because he was tricked, not because he was compelled." The distinction is significant. The U.S. Supreme Court has approved police trickery in a number of circumstances and other courts have specifically approved the use of a subterfuge to trick a defendant into leaving his home for the purpose of arresting him. Police officers did not violate the 4th Amendment by tricking a defendant into exiting his home so they could arrest him on a misdemeanor warrant that limited their arrest power to public places.

4.7   PEOPLE v. CASCIO (COLO. 1997)
(*Arrest*)

While on night patrol in Pike National Forest, deputies spotted a van parked illegally. The defendant and his brother were in the van. The deputies parked their patrol car 10 to 20 feet behind the van and trained their spotlight on the van. Both deputies used their flashlights to see into the van. The deputies did not, however, activate the patrol car's overhead light bar. Both deputies approached the passenger side of the van on foot. Deputies warned the men that they were in an area where parking and camping were not permitted. A deputy asked the driver, Cascio, if it was his van; Cascio said it was. The deputy then asked whether the Cascios had any weapons in the car; they answered in the negative. The deputy requested and received permission from Cascio to search the van for weapons. The deputy asked the Cascios to get out of the van but did not pat them down. He spotted a gram of fine white powder on a business card on the van's dashboard and a hot propane torch located between the driver and passenger seats. When asked by the deputy whether they were smoking crack cocaine, the Cascios failed to respond. At that point, the deputy read the Cascios their rights; subsequently, Scott Cascio explained that the powder was a combination of cocaine and methamphetamine.

The trial court ordered suppression of the drugs and other evidence obtained during the warrantless search of the van. The state appealed.

- ■ *Why would the trial court have concluded that evidence of cocaine should be suppressed?*
  - • *Was the trial court correct? Explain.*

People v. Cascio (Colo. 1997): 60 CrL 1533

The court said it was faced here with circumstances that present a close question and accentuate the sometimes subtle distinction between a consensual encounter and an investigatory stop. Not all police–citizen encounters implicate the 4th Amendment. "Only when the officer, by means of physical force or show of authority, has in some way restrained the liberty of a citizen may we conclude that a 'seizure' has occurred" [*]. "The test for determining if the encounter is a consensual one is whether a reasonable person under the circumstances would believe he or she was free to leave and/or to disregard the official's request for information" [*]. "The test [to determine if someone reasonably feels free to leave] is necessarily imprecise, because it is designed to assess the coercive effect of police conduct, taken as a whole, rather than to focus on particular details of that conduct in isolation. Moreover, what constitutes a restraint on liberty prompting a person to conclude that he is not free to 'leave' will vary, not only with the particular police conduct at issue, but also with the setting in which the conduct occurs" [*]. The "free to leave" test is not dependent on the state of mind of the individual approached by the police, but on the objective standard of a reasonable person. Moreover, the "inherent social pressure to cooperate with the police" does not elevate every police–citizen encounter to a seizure [*].

In applying this contextual approach, courts have deemed important the position of the patrol car relative to the motorist's vehicle. Here, the Cascios' egress was only slightly restricted by the deputies' patrol car with approximately 10 to 20 feet between the two vehicles. One deputy testified that the Cascios would have been able to leave by maneuvering their van in a manner akin to parallel parking. The other deputy testified that it would not have been difficult for the van to leave. Therefore, the Cascios were not physically restrained from departing.

The totality of the circumstances surrounding the encounter did not support a finding that the encounter was an investigatory stop rather than a consensual encounter. Although there were two deputies, they did not act in a threatening manner. The deputies did use flashlights and activated their spotlight. Although the use of a spotlight can be a means of intimidation, there were no findings or implications here that indicate that was the case. Instead, the lights were used as a matter of practical necessity as the encounter took place when it was getting dark, and no significance was attributed to their use.

Here the encounter was consensual because the Cascios' liberty was not restrained, and their voluntary cooperation was elicited through noncoercive questioning [*]. Thus, aside from the inherent pressure felt by any citizen to cooperate with law enforcement officers, the circumstances of this encounter were not so intimidating as to communicate to the Cascios that they were not free to leave or to decline to respond.

The district court deemed the Cascios' consent to the search voluntary and court deferred to that finding, reversing the suppression order.

4.8 STATE v. NORRIS (OHIO CT.APP. 1999)
(Arrest/Hot Pursuit)

The defendant was the subject of a domestic violence complaint. The state had a statute authorizing warrantless arrests in public places in such cases. Told by the complainant that the defendant was staying at a motel, officers went there and knocked on the door to the defendant's room. The defendant opened the door inward without crossing the threshold. With the defendant still inside the room, the officers told him he was under arrest. They then entered the room and struggled with the defendant while attempting to handcuff him. During the struggle, cocaine fell out of the defendant's pocket.

At the defendant's trial on a drug possession charge, he argued that the cocaine had to be suppressed as the fruit of an illegal entry into the hotel room. The state argued that by opening the door to the room, the defendant exposed himself to public view and abandoned any reasonable expectation of privacy he had in the room. In the alternative, the state argued, the officers' entry into the room was justified by the "hot pursuit" doctrine.

- *Was it an illegal entry? Justify your answer.*
- *Was the police entry justified by hot pursuit? Explain.*

State v. Norris (Ohio Ct.App. 1999): 66 CrL 133

The issue is whether the arrest occurred in a public place or in the motel room. If the former, the arrest would be upheld as a warrantless arrest in a public place; if the latter, the arrest would be considered unconstitutional as a warrantless arrest inside a home.

The court found the arrest occurred in the motel room. The defendant here was "at all times inside his motel room." Absent a warrant or exigent circumstances, the police could not enter the room to arrest him.

With respect to the state's argument of hot pursuit, the court defined hot pursuit as "an exigent circumstance that relieves the police of the warrant requirement where the delay attendant upon obtaining the warrant would result, inter alia, in the escape of a suspect or the destruction of evidence." The court indicated that hot pursuit must entail immediate and continuous pursuit from the moment that probable cause developed.

The court concluded that the police were not in hot pursuit at the time of the defendant's arrest. The first officer on the scene was sufficiently relaxed to wait for backup before approaching the room. If the police had concerns about waiting for an arrest warrant, they could simply have kept the room under surveillance while waiting. There was no suggestion that destruction of evidence was a concern.

4.9   UNITED STATES v. JEREZ (SEVENTH CIR. 1997) (*Arrest v. Stop*)

Deputy sheriffs, members of a drug interdiction unit, were patrolling in the area of the airport in search of "target vehicles"—vans and two-door cars said to be preferred by drug couriers—from "source states." Noticing such a vehicle in a motel parking lot, they ran a computer check, which revealed the registered owner's name and the fact that the vehicle was not stolen. They also learned that the owner, Carlos Solis, was staying in Room 161 of the motel with another person. Further checks revealed that Solis' driver's license was suspended and he had a recent arrest for smuggling some sort of contraband into a Florida jail; however, he had no extraditable felony warrants. They decided to try to get Solis and his companion to consent to a search.

The suspects' room was quiet. The deputies took turns knocking on the door for about 3 minutes. During that time, one of them said, "Police. Open up the door. We'd like to talk to you." When this proved fruitless, one deputy went to the window of the room and knocked on the window for about a minute and a half, while his partner continued knocking at the door. The deputy also shined his flashlight through a small opening in the drapes and saw a man on the bed. Finally the man, Solis, opened the drapes, which allowed him to see the deputy whose jacket identified him as a member of the drug enforcement unit. The deputy asked Solis to open the door. Solis did so.

Solis was dressed only in his underwear and the room was dark. The officers identified themselves and asked if they could speak with them. Solis agreed. His companion, Jerez, who was still in bed, also agreed to speak with the deputies. The officers requested and received permission to search the room and the suspects' belongings. The search yielded sizable amounts of cocaine.

The defendants moved unsuccessfully to suppress the evidence. The court ruled that the initial encounter between the deputies and the defendants did not constitute a seizure and that the subsequent search followed the defendants' voluntary consent. The defendants then entered conditional guilty pleas. On appeal, they claimed that the officers' knocking on their motel room's door and window and shining a flashlight through the room's window amounted to a "seizure." The state argued that officers had reasonable suspicion to stop the men and investigate criminal activity.

- *Was there reasonable suspicion to stop Solis and his companion? Justify your conclusion.*
- *Was the encounter at the motel a seizure for 4th Amendment purposes? Explain.*

United States v. Jerez (Seventh Cir. 1997): 60 CrL 1532

The U.S. Supreme Court has formulated two approaches for determining whether a person has been "seized" under the 4th Amendment. The first approach is used when the police approach an individual in a place such as an airport, rail terminal, or on the street. As a general matter, law enforcement officers can approach a willing individual in a public place and ask that person questions without violating the 4th Amendment. A "seizure" in such situations occurs only if a reasonable person in similar circumstances would not have felt "free to leave," as in *Michigan v. Chesternut,* 486 U.S. 567 (1988). The second approach applies when the police approach an individual in a confined space such as a bus. Because a person on a bus or in an otherwise confined space "has no desire to leave" and would wish to remain even if police were not present, "the degree to which a reasonable person would feel that he or she could leave is not an accurate measure of the coercive effect of the encounter," as in *Florida v. Bostick,* 501 U.S. 429 (1991). When a person's "freedom of movement [is] restricted by a factor independent of police conduct—i.e., by his being a passenger on a bus ... , the appropriate inquiry is whether a reasonable person would feel free to decline the officers' request or otherwise terminate the encounter."

This second formulation is the appropriate analytical approach in this case. The movements of Jerez and Solis were confined as a natural result of their voluntary decision to stay in the motel. It was the middle of the night and at least one of them was clad only in his underwear. As a practical matter, they could not have expressed their desire to terminate the encounter with the police by leaving the scene. Like the person seated on the bus, a person staying in a motel room has no desire to leave and would remain whether police were present or not. Jerez and Solis, therefore, were "seized" within the meaning of the 4th Amendment if a reasonable person would not have felt free to decline deputies' requests to open the door or to otherwise ignore the deputies' presence. The test, as with the "free to leave" formulation, is an objective one that requires a contextual approach.

In making the assessment of whether a seizure occurred, the circumstances must, of course, be assessed in terms of the values protected by the 4th Amendment. Here the district court failed to consider adequately two significant factors: the place and the time of the encounter. The police confronted the appellants in the middle of the night and sought admission to their dwelling place. Because our law and legal traditions long have recognized the special vulnerability of those awakened in the night by a police intrusion at their dwelling place, our 4th Amendment jurisprudence counsels that, when a knock at the door comes in the dead of night, the nature and effect of the intrusion into the privacy of the dwelling place must be examined with the greatest of caution. "There is no rule of private or public conduct which makes it illegal per se, or a condemned invasion of the person's right of privacy for anyone openly and peaceably at high noon, to walk up the steps and knock on the front door on any man's 'castle' with the honest intent of asking questions of the occupant thereof—whether the questioners be a pollster, a salesman, or an officer of the law" [*]. The same does not hold true, however, when the knocking occurs in the middle of the night and lasts for 3 full minutes. The 3 minutes of silence by Room 161's occupants, when combined with the other circumstances of this case, especially the lateness of the hour, amounted to a refusal by Jerez and Solis to answer the door. Once the officers had been refused admittance, their continued efforts to rouse the occupants out of bed certainly prevented them from ignoring the continued requests and from maintaining the privacy and solitude of their dwelling. The deputies' persistence, in the face of the refusal to admit, transformed what began as an attempt to engage in a consensual encounter into an investigatory stop. In addition to knocking on the room's only door, the deputies then knocked on the room's only window, and then shone a flashlight through the small opening in the window's drapes, illuminating Mr. Jerez as he lay in the bed. This escalation of the encounter renders totally without foundation any characterization that the prolonged confrontation was a consensual encounter rather than an investigative stop. When a person is in a confined area, encircling the area in an intimidating fashion contributes to a reasonable belief that ignoring the law enforcement presence is not an option.

Simply stated, this was a case in which the law enforcement officers refused to take "no" for an answer. Their actions, when objectively assessed, "convey[ed] a message that compliance with their requests [was] required" [*]. The court held that a seizure took place.

The deputies articulated four facts that made them suspect Solis might have been involved in criminal activity: (1) he had a two-door vehicle, a "target" vehicle; (2) it had a license plate from Florida, a source state; (3) it was parked near an airport and an interstate; and (4) a criminal history check revealed that Solis had a suspended driver's license and an arrest or conviction for smuggling some type of contraband into a Florida jail. These facts, when considered together, did not provide reasonable suspicion under *Terry v. Ohio,* 392 U.S. 1 (1968). Furthermore, the subsequent consent to search was not sufficiently attenuated from the illegal seizure.

4.10   WASHINGTON v. LAMBERT (NINTH CIR. 1996) (*Stop*)

Police thought the two Black men they saw at a restaurant resembled very general descriptions of two suspects being sought for a string of armed robberies.

Police officers shined searchlights on the suspects' car, ordered them out of the vehicle at gunpoint, handcuffed their hands behind their backs, and placed them in separate police cars for at least 5 minutes.

- *Was this an arrest? Or a stop?*
- *Was there probable cause for an arrest?*

Washington v. Lambert (Ninth Cir. 1996): 60 CrL 1155

Under the circumstances facing the police, this was an arrest, rather than a mere investigative detention. The majority observed that there is no bright line separating arrests and stops; instead, proper categorization depends on the totality of the circumstances, including the need in this particular case for aggressive police conduct. Prior cases [*] allow the use of "especially intrusive" means of effecting a stop only "in special circumstances such as (1) where the suspect is uncooperative or takes action at the scene that raises a reasonable possibility of danger or flight; (2) where the police have information that the suspect is currently armed; (3) where the stop closely follows a violent crime; and (4) where the police have information that a crime that may involve violence is about to occur." Other relevant factors are the specificity of the information that the persons being stopped are the persons being sought, that they are likely to use force themselves, and the number of police involved.

In this case, neither of the men did anything prior to or during the confrontation to justify use of the "intrusive and threatening procedures" employed by the police, the majority said. Furthermore, the officers outnumbered the men and the men did not fit the specifics of the descriptions very well. The majority commented that "if the general descriptions relied on there can be stretched to cover [these men] then a significant percentage of African-American males walking, eating, going to work or to a movie, ball game or concert, with a friend or relative, might well find themselves subjected to similar treatment, at least if they are in a predominantly white neighborhood."

4.11   MCGEE v. COMMONWEALTH (VA.CT.APP. 1996) (*Arrest/Consent*)

At about 5:00 p.m. on a July afternoon, Officer Loperl received a radio dispatch, based on a report from an anonymous informer, that "a Black male wearing a white t-shirt, black shorts, and white tennis shoes" was selling drugs on a particular street corner. Approximately 2 minutes after receiving the dispatch, Loperl and two other officers, all of whom were in uniform, arrived at the location in two marked police cruisers. The only persons observed at the location were the defendant and a female companion.

After parking their cars, the officers approached the defendant, who was sitting on a small porch in front of a store. Officer Loperl testified that they did not block the defendant's path in any direction or draw their weapons. Loperl testified that he stated to the defendant, while speaking in the same tone of voice he was using in court, "I had received a call that you were on this corner selling drugs and said you matched the description." According to Loperl, the defendant was free to leave, although the officer did not expressly so inform the defendant.

Loperl then "asked [the defendant] could I pat him down to make sure he didn't have any weapons on him." The defendant responded by standing up and extending his arms in front of him with both fists clenched. The fists were clenched so tightly the officer could not see what was in them. Loperl testified that the defendant could have been holding a "small pocket knife" or "a razor" in his closed fists. Therefore, after patting down the defendant and finding no weapons, Loperl asked the defendant to open his hands. Although Loperl could not remember the exact words used, he testified that, "I know I asked him. I know I didn't tell him. I asked him." The defendant opened his hands, which contained money, a torn plastic bag, and "a little piece of white substance." Loperl placed the defendant under arrest. In the search of the defendant incident to that arrest, Loperl found twenty-five bags containing crack cocaine.

- *Was this defendant "seized" before the officer found the items in his fists? Explain.*
- *Was the defendant's consent to search voluntary? Explain.*

McGee v. Commonwealth (Va.Ct.App. 1996): 60 CrL 1150

"The uncontroverted evidence in this case establishes that the initial encounter between the defendant and the police was consensual and that the officers did not seize him for 4th Amendment purposes. The officers approached the defendant in a public place and initiated a conversation in the course of investigating the anonymous report of drug dealing. The police officers had a duty to investigate the complaint of criminal activity, and it was reasonable for them to question the defendant, who was the only male at the reported location. Although the three officers who confronted the defendant were in uniform, they made no show of force. They did not 'run up to' the defendant and did not draw their weapons. According to Loperl, the officers were standing in front of the defendant but did not block him from leaving in any direction. Loperl testified that he spoke to the defendant in the same tone of voice he was using while testifying and that none of the officers touched the defendant before he consented to the pat-down search. Loperl approached the defendant, explaining that the police had received a report of someone selling drugs on that street corner, and said that the defendant matched the description. Loperl, however, did not accuse the defendant of selling drugs. Rather, Loperl simply told the defendant the reasons for approaching and asking him questions. Under these circumstances, we hold that no 4th Amendment seizure occurred."

The majority took issue with the dissenting position, finding that a reasonable person would not feel free to leave after being approached by a police officer and informed that he was suspected of drug dealing. The effect of the dissenting opinion, according to the majority, "is to hold that a 4th Amendment 'seizure' occurs per se any time a police officer advises a suspect the police had received information that the suspect had been selling illegal drugs at a particular location. In accordance with this view, without implicating the 4th Amendment, the police could not investigate a citizen complaint and respond truthfully to a suspect's questions about why the police were present and had approached that individual. In *Florida v. Bostick,* 501 U.S. 429 (1991), the Supreme Court stated, 'We adhere to the rule that, in order to determine whether a particular encounter constitutes a seizure, a court must consider all the circumstances surrounding the encounter to determine whether the police conduct would have communicated to a reasonable person that the person was not free to decline the officers' requests or otherwise terminate the encounter.'"

The majority went on to say that the dissent "focuses upon the possible effect upon the suspect of such a statement when made by a police officer. The Supreme Court has emphasized, however, the objective nature of the test to be applied in determining if a person has been seized within the meaning of the 4th Amendment."

The court then concluded that "based on the officer's testimony about the language he used in requesting that the defendant open his fists, that the defendant's consent to do so was voluntary."

Search and Search Warrants

Constitutional issues arise at two points with respect to search warrants: The warrant must be *issued* constitutionally and it must be *executed* constitutionally.

Constitutional issuance of a search warrant requires the police to demonstrate and the judge to find probable cause to believe that a crime has been committed and that evidence of that crime will be found in the place where the police want to look for it. Beyond that, the constitution requires the government to specifically describe the place to be searched and the things to be seized.

The police demonstrate facts to support a finding of probable cause by filing an affidavit or testifying under oath about the facts they have. This is a critical point in the procedure because if the police make a mistake (if, for example, they omit reference to a fact that they actually know and that is necessary to find probable cause), they are not allowed to rehabilitate the affidavit and correct that mistake after the fact. If the police make a mistake in their affidavit and they fail to show facts sufficient to establish probable cause, the warrant will be declared constitutionally insufficient. In that case, the exclusionary rule operates and any evidence found will be suppressed. If, however, the magistrate makes an error in declaring probable cause when the facts did not support that conclusion, the good faith exception to the exclusionary rule may apply and the evidence found could still be used.

In setting out the facts to support a finding of probable cause for a search warrant, the police must show that their facts are current. That is, their information must not be stale. If they want to search a particular place for evidence, they must have probable cause to believe that evidence will be found at that place at the time they want to search for it. It is not enough

---

When the appellate court has cited and relied upon a U.S. Supreme Court opinion in reaching its decision, those citations are set out in full so you will know what Supreme Court authority the court relied upon. When you see an asterisk [*] in the court's opinion, that means the appellate court has referenced and relied upon a lower court case in reaching its decision. Those case citations are not included here.

for the government to show that evidence of the crime was at the place to be searched at some time in the past or might likely be there at some time in the future; the government must establish probable cause to believe that evidence is presently at the place to be searched.

Constitutional execution of a search warrant requires that the facts establishing probable cause are not stale at the time the warrant is executed. It is not enough to show that at the time the warrant was issued, there was probable cause to believe evidence would be found in a particular place. A constitutional search requires probable cause to believe evidence might be found in a particular place at the time the police enter and search that place.

This issue of staleness is important in the issuance and execution of search warrants because evidence can be moved; just because evidence was once at a spot does not mean there is probable cause to believe it is still there. The policy underlying the rule is that it would be unreasonable to allow the police to search a place if they did not have probable cause to believe evidence would be found there, hence the requirement that the probable cause not be stale at the time of the search.

Staleness does not come into play with respect to arrest warrants, because probable cause to believe a crime has been committed and that a particular person committed the crime cannot get stale. If the facts do not change, once there is probable cause to believe a crime has been committed, there is always probable cause to believe a crime has been committed. That likelihood does not diminish with time. If the facts do not change, once there is probable cause to believe a particular person has committed a crime, that likelihood is not diminished simply by the passage of time. However, probable cause to believe a particular thing is in a particular place at Time A does not necessarily suggest it is there at Time B because things can be moved. As a consequence, search probable cause has a temporal quality not present in crime or arrest probable cause.

Constitutional execution of a search warrant also requires consideration of the knock-and-announce principle and consideration of the time of day or night the warrant is executed. The U.S. Supreme Court has declared that an element of a reasonable search is having the police knock and announce their presence before entering. Presumably that will help to preserve safety for the occupant and the police, who might otherwise be hurt if police break in and startle occupants who do not recognize them as police. Additionally, and less important of course, is that fact that knocking and announcing allows the occupant to open the door and may preserve property by making it unnecessary for the police to break in.

The knock-and-announce principle is an element of reasonableness. It can be dispensed with in the face of exigent circumstances or if the magistrate has authorized a no-knock warrant based on facts presented in the affidavit in support of the search.

Most states require that search warrants be executed during the daytime. Like a no-knock entry, a nighttime search might be constitutional in the face of exigent circumstances or if the magistrate authorized it based on facts presented in the affidavit in support of the search.

5.1   UNITED STATES v. HUSBAND (SEVENTH CIR. 2002) (*Search*)

Police officers saw the defendant place an object in his mouth as they were arresting him for drug distribution. While the officers were obtaining a warrant to search his mouth, the defendant began to sweat and twitch as though he were about to have a seizure. The officers took the defendant to a hospital, but the defendant still refused to open his mouth.

Eventually, a doctor told the defendant that if he did not open his mouth, the doctor would introduce a general anesthetic into the defendant's IV that would render him unconscious. The defendant continued to withhold cooperation. When the drug made the defendant unconscious, the officers retrieved from his mouth plastic packets containing more than 20 grams of cocaine. The drug made the defendant stop breathing, but the doctor was able to revive him.

- *What would the defendant argue in support of his position that this search was unconstitutional?*
- *What would the state argue in support of its position that this search was constitutional?*
- *What result? Why?*

United States v. Husband (Seventh Cir. 2002): 72 CrL 136. Earlier proceedings at 226 F.3d 626, 67 CrL 739

Police officers who obtained a warrant authorizing them to search a defendant's mouth for packets of drugs did not violate the 4th Amendment by using anesthesia to execute the warrant after the defendant refused to open his mouth. The court decided that the execution of the search was reasonable under the balancing test set out in *Schmerber v. California,* 384 U.S. 757 (1966).

In *Schmerber,* the Supreme Court applied a balancing test to hold that the 4th Amendment did not prohibit the police from forcibly taking a blood sample from a drunk driving suspect. Under the *Schmerber* balancing test, a court must weigh the following:

- The extent to which the procedure could threaten the safety or health of the individual.

- The extent of intrusion on the individual's dignitary interests in personal privacy and bodily integrity.

- The community's interest in fairly and accurately determining guilt or innocence.

In *Winston v. Lee,* 470 U.S. 753 (1985), the Court again applied the *Schmerber* balancing test to hold that, in the circumstances of that case, the 4th Amendment precluded the use of a compelled surgical procedure to remove a bullet from beneath the defendant's skin.

The first time the Seventh Circuit looked at this case, it held that the 4th Amendment did not require the officers to obtain prior judicial approval for the use of anesthesia in executing the warrant. It also decided that the use of anesthesia was more intrusive on the defendant's dignity and privacy interests than the blood test in *Schmerber,* but that the search of his mouth was less invasive than the surgery in *Winston.* However, the court ultimately remanded the case and ordered further development of the record regarding (1) the risk posed by the particular anesthetic, (2) the medical emergency facing the defendant from the object in his mouth, and (3) the potential for the loss of evidence.

Aided by the additional fact finding, the court decided that the officers' use of anesthesia in executing the warrant was reasonable.

The anesthetic is one routinely used in hospital emergency rooms, and the doctors who authorized the use of the drug testified that it was the safest way to extract the object from the defendant's mouth. Although the drug carries the risk that the patient will stop breathing, the court decided that "the dangers associated with the risk were low given the ability to use forced breathing methods," including the one used to revive the defendant.

The doctors' concern that the object in the defendant's mouth was cocaine was reasonable in light of the defendant's medical condition, and the district court's finding that the defendant's ingestion of such a large amount of cocaine would have posed an extremely serious medical emergency was supported by the doctors' testimony as well. It added that the district court did not clearly err by discounting the credibility of testimony by the defendant's medical expert that the prosecution's doctors exaggerated the risk posed by the cocaine in the defendant's mouth.

The doctor who administered the anesthesia in this case insisted on waiting for the search warrant before proceeding, and the court acknowledged that this decision to delay cuts against the immediacy of the medical emergency. The court, nevertheless, upheld the district court's decision to give little weight to this fact. The time between the defendant's arrival at the hospital and the doctor's decision to wait a short time for the warrant could have been based on considerations other than the seriousness of the defendant's condition, the court said. It suggested that the doctor might have believed that the warrant would protect him legally, or that the defendant would comply with the warrant and open his mouth.

"Considering the low risk of danger associated with [the anesthetic drug] and the immediate and severe medical emergency caused by the [defendant's] refusal to open his mouth, we conclude that the method by which the warrant was executed was reasonable," the court decided. It added that it was not addressing whether the result would be different if a safer way of obtaining the evidence had been available, if the situation had not presented a threat to the defendant's life, or if the police had not obtained a warrant.

5.2   UNITED STATES v. OWENS (D.C. 2002)
(*Search: Knock-and-Announce*)

Police officers obtained a warrant to search for firearms in an apartment that was thought to be the site of drug trafficking. One of the officers on the warrant team worked as a security guard at the apartment complex, knew the apartment's occupants, and, in the course of his private employment, had knocked on the door on previous occasions to warn the occupants that marijuana smoke was emanating from the premises.

Three times during a half-minute span, the officer knocked on the door and said in a loud voice, "Andre, it's me, Officer Hicks." Receiving no response during the initial 30 seconds, the officer said "Police. We have a search warrant." After another 15 seconds or so, during which there was nothing to suggest someone was coming to the door, the team forcibly entered the apartment. The entry led to the discovery of an illegal firearm in a coat belonging to the defendant.

The trial court held that the police violated the local knock-and-announce statute, which incorporates the corresponding federal provision, by not waiting long enough before making their forcible entry. In reaching its conclusion, the trial court ruled that only the 15 seconds that elapsed after the officer announced his authority and purpose counted in the determination of whether there was a sufficient time lapse for the search team to reasonably conclude that they were being refused entrance into the apartment.

- *What is the purpose behind the knock-and-announce requirement?*
- *With the policy behind the requirement in mind, consider these questions: Should the initial 30 seconds have counted in the knock-and-announce analysis? Or was the trial court correct in saying that the time does not begin to run until the police announce that they have a warrant? Explain your reasoning.*

United States v. Owens (D.C. 2002): 70 CrL 328

The time between the police officer's knock at the door and announcement of identity and the slightly later point at which he announced the purpose and authority behind his demand for entry should have been counted in determining whether the officer waited long enough before breaking down the door, according to a majority of the District of Columbia Court of Appeals. Merely by identifying himself, the officer alleviated any concern by those inside that they were in danger from an unknown intruder, thereby satisfying a major purpose of the constitutional and statutory knock-and-announce requirements.

The majority concluded that the entire time period following the initial knock should be counted. Even though the officer's declaration that he had a warrant came 30 seconds into the overall waiting period, he had already made clear to the presumed occupant of the apartment who he was. The majority therefore agreed with the government that the initial 30 seconds "furnished decisive context for the reasonableness of the succeeding 15-second wait."

One of the major concerns of the knock-and-announce rule is to alleviate "the shock and fear" associated with not knowing who is seeking entry and whether it is safe to admit the person. Under the circumstances of this case, it was reasonable for the officer to believe that he had conveyed to the occupants the fact he was not an unknown person but a police officer, the majority said. Any concern of the occupants of the apartment as to who was at the door was dispelled with the first knock. The occupants' initial lack of knowledge as to why the officer was seeking to enter and whether they were obliged by law to admit him was not determinative, the majority indicated.

Noting that determining the adequacy of a knock-and-announcement demands a "highly contextual analysis," the majority concluded that the 15-second wait, when viewed in context with the prior 30-second period, was long enough.

Although 15 seconds could be too short a time in other contexts, particularly in cases in which entry is attempted at hours when occupants are likely to be asleep and disoriented when awakened, it was adequate for an entry that took place in the afternoon, the majority said. Another relevant factor, it said, was the relatively small size of the premises—a one- or two-bedroom apartment in which residents would certainly hear a knock at the door wherever they were inside and would need little time to respond. Finally, the majority emphasized that the warrant was based on allegations of drug activity and firearms in the apartment. When officer safety is at issue, searchers can reasonably infer refusal to open up more readily than under other circumstances.

One judge concurred but did not agree that the suspicions regarding weapons had anything to do with the issue on appeal. "Inclusion of a generalized safety concern in evaluating whether there has been a constructive refusal to admit dilutes the evidentiary standard we have established to ensure that there is a reasonably-based government interest countervailing full compliance with the statute."

Note: In December 2003, the U.S. Supreme Court decided *United States v. Banks*, 540 U.S. 31 (2003) [74 CrL 160], a case in which the Court had to decide whether officers, executing a search warrant, acted properly when they forcibly entered a home only 15 to 20 seconds after announcing their presence and purpose. The Court approved the entry.

That case does *not* stand for the proposition that police may enter forcibly after 15 to 20 seconds. The question will always be one of reasonableness. In *Banks,* the Court concluded the entry was reasonable because the warrant authorized a search for cocaine, a substance subject to quick, easy destruction. Had the warrant authorized a search for illegal aliens or cannons, the result might well have been different.

5.3   COMMONWEALTH v. JIMENEZ (MASS. 2002)
(*Search: No-Knock*)

After several months of police work that included extensive surveillance, law enforcement officers applied for a warrant to search the defendant's apartment for evidence of drug trafficking. In seeking authority to avoid compliance with the knock-and-announce rule, the police included the following allegations in the warrant affidavit:

- The defendant and his accomplice kept secret the location of the apartment where drugs were stored and moved it at least once during the period of police surveillance.

- The apartment was located on the third floor of a building with a street-level door that was kept locked.

- Drugs could easily be flushed down the toilet.

- It is common for drug dealers to have firearms, and members of the police department's vice squad "commonly confiscated firearms in the service of search warrants of this type."

The magistrate approved the no-knock provision. He did not state whether he did so on the basis of officer safety, likely destruction of evidence, or both.

Officers executed the warrant after dark. Suspects were not seen at the windows keeping an eye on the approach to the building. The door on the first floor opened easily when pushed. Police broke down the apartment door with a battering ram and entered.

The trial court concluded that the affidavit demonstrated both safety and evidence destruction concerns, and the judge denied the defendant's motion to suppress the drugs, drug paraphernalia, cash, and handgun seized in the search. The defendant appealed.

- *What should the police have to demonstrate to secure a no-knock warrant?*
  - *Should they have to have probable cause to believe their factual allegations in support of the no-knock entry?*
  - *Or should reasonable suspicion be enough? Why?*
- *Once you have decided what you think the standard should be, decide whether the police met that burden here.*
- *Was this no-knock warrant justified? Explain.*
- *Was this no-knock entry justified? Explain.*

Commonwealth v. Jimenez (Mass. 2002): 72 CrL 277

Massachusetts adheres to a probable cause standard for approval of a no-knock warrant. The magistrate issuing the no-knock warrant erred here by giving no-knock authority on the basis of allegations that drug dealers commonly have firearms and that local police commonly confiscated weapons when serving such warrants. Other averments in the warrant, concerning features of the building in which the target premises was located, raised sufficient concerns about possible destruction of evidence to justify no-knock authority. However, the situation the officers encountered at the scene should have led them to reappraise the necessity of a no-knock entry, and their failure to do so required suppression of the evidence seized under the warrant.

Officer Safety

Beginning with the officer safety justification, the majority said the affidavit described only general concerns present in the execution of any search warrant for drugs. The absence of particular facts or circumstances suggesting that there might be weapons on the premises or that the defendant had a history of weapons possession or violence made the affidavit inadequate to establish either probable cause or reasonable suspicion of a threat to the officers' safety.

To find sufficient averments about what drug dealers "commonly" do or what police "commonly" find when searching for drugs would be tantamount to holding that any search warrant for drugs justifies a safety-based exception to the knock-and-announce rule. Such a per se rule was rejected by the U.S. Supreme Court in *Richards v. Wisconsin*, 520 U.S. 395 (1997).

Destruction of Evidence

The features of the apartment building that could have delayed the officers' entry and allowed a watcher in the apartment to spot them were sufficient, when combined with the secrecy of the drug operation and the movement of its headquarters during the surveillance, to support a grant of no-knock authority on the basis of likely destruction of evidence. However, the majority added, this concern was absent at the time the warrant was executed.

The officers came to the apartment after dark when they could not be easily identified. Furthermore, the majority pointed out, the suspects were not seen at the windows keeping an eye on the approach to the building, and the door on the first floor opened easily when pushed. Thus, the majority said, by the time the police reached the threshold of the defendant's apartment, they no longer had a basis to believe the defendant was aware of their presence and might be destroying evidence.

The police were required to make a "threshold reappraisal" of the actual circumstances before disregarding the knock-and-announce rule. On the facts here, the majority concluded a no-knock entry was not justified. Accordingly, the police acted unlawfully in breaking down the apartment door with a battering ram, and the evidence had to be suppressed.

One judge dissented, arguing that she would have upheld the no-knock entry on an officer safety rationale. This judge also questioned the majority's insistence that the justification for a no-knock warrant be found by probable cause rather than mere reasonable suspicion. Use of the higher standard is at odds with [*] and with "virtually every other jurisdiction that has considered the issue." The majority responded to that observation in a footnote, and said that use of the more demanding probable cause standard is consistent with the state constitution.

5.4   COMMONWEALTH v. SENG (MASS. 2002)
(*Inventory Search*)

Police arrested the defendant for murder. They inventoried his wallet after his arrest and found a card with checking and savings account numbers handwritten on the back. As a result of that search, prosecutors issued a summons for the defendant's bank records prior to trial. The defense filed a motion to suppress "all evidence obtained pursuant to a warrantless search of defendant's wallet, as well as the fruits of that search [because] it went beyond a mere search incident to arrest, and instead amounted to a full investigation of the contents of the wallet." The prosecution answered that the search was a lawful custodial inventory search. The trial court found that the account numbers on the back of the card were "clear and obvious."

- *What is the purpose of an inventory search?*
- *Was this a proper inventory search? Explain.*

Commonwealth v. Seng (Mass. 2002): 71 CrL 147

There is a difference between observing and recording the bank's name and logo on the front of the card for inventory purposes and examining the card closely enough to recognize and record the account numbers written on the back. The bank records derived from account numbers found in the defendant's wallet were suppressed, because the reading and recording of those numbers went beyond an inventory search and amounted to a warrant-less investigatory search.

"It may be … that in some situations, recording the numbers on a card in a wallet may serve a valid inventory purpose," such as protecting the police against claims of theft or misuse of a credit card or check card. However, the card in this case was not such a card.

Other courts have held or suggested that reading papers falls outside the bounds of a lawful inventory, the court noted. Additionally, the U.S. Supreme Court observed in *South Dakota v. Opperman,* 428 U.S. 364 (1976), that police conducting an inventory search could find items such as letters or checkbooks, which might "touch upon intimate areas of an individual's personal affairs" and "reveal much about a person's activities, associations, and beliefs." In an inventory search, police are required to limit themselves to removing that property for storage without examining its contents.

Police need not blind themselves to information or evidence visible during an inventory search, but they cannot read materials that do not declare their nature on sight. As applied to this case, this means that the officers were not allowed to investigate the information in the wallet without obtaining a search warrant. The information on the back of the card was not overtly incriminating.

The police might have been able to get the account numbers just by knowing the bank's name. In this case, however, it appears that the access to the bank account data resulted from an impermissible investigatory search of the handwritten numbers on the back of the card. The evidence should not have been admitted.

5.5   STATE v. HENDRICKS (KAN.CT.APP. 2003)
(*Search Warrant/ Exclusionary Rule: Good Faith Exception*)

The defendant's roommate told police where they could find the defendant's brother, who was being sought on an arrest warrant. The defendant himself had denied knowledge of his brother's whereabouts.

On being approached by police, the defendant's brother at first denied being the wanted man. After admitting his identity and being taken to jail, he turned informer. He claimed that the roommate ran a prostitution ring and was a drug dealer. He also said that methamphetamine could be found at the residence and described a concealed compartment there in which marijuana was allegedly stored.

An officer prepared a search warrant affidavit using this information but omitting the fact that the informer had attempted to deceive the police about his identity. The affidavit also did not relate the fact, known to the affiant, that an officer who questioned the informer suspected him of involvement in a check-kiting scheme and doubted his credibility. When the warrant was executed, police found some drugs and drug paraphernalia, although not the locked compartment, marijuana, or methamphetamine described by the informer. The trial court granted the defendant's motion to suppress.

- *The officer chose to omit facts in his affidavit that detracted from the informant's veracity. What effect, if any, does that have on the affidavit and the warrant issued pursuant to it?*

- *Is the warrant good?*
- *If not, can the police use the good faith exception to save the search? Explain.*

State v. Hendricks (Kan.Ct.App. 2003): 72 CrL 353

Information casting doubt on the veracity of an informer was material to a finding of probable cause and should have been included in a search warrant affidavit based on a tip from an informer. The informer, an arrestee accusing the person who had turned him in to police, did not qualify as a good citizen informer whose information could be presumed reliable, the court said. Noting that the omission was deliberate, the court declined to declare the fruits of the warrant admissible under the good faith exception to the exclusionary rule.

The suppression order was appropriate. The deliberate or reckless inclusion of false material statements in, or the omission of material information from, a warrant affidavit requires suppression of the fruits of the warrant. An omission is material for this purpose if the affidavit, when supplemented with the omitted information, would not establish probable cause.

The trial court determined that the omissions were material because the informer had a motive for lying. The state argued that the informer should be classified as an identified citizen informer, a class of informer whose tip is considered highly reliable in part because his false report might expose him to prosecution. Under that view, information about the informer's credibility would not be material.

Rejecting the state's contention, the court pointed out that not all identified informers are disinterested citizen witnesses. Here, the affidavit established that the informer was an arrestee who believed that the defendant's roommate was responsible for turning him in to the authorities. Therefore, the trial court correctly determined that the informer had to be treated as "an informer from the criminal milieu." A warrant based on information from such an individual does not establish probable cause unless the police provide information about his veracity and credibility along with corroboration of his allegations.

No such information was provided here, and nothing in the affidavit supported a finding of probable cause except an officer's earlier visit to the residence confirming that it was occupied by the defendant and his roommate. Had the issuing magistrate been apprised of the omitted information, the court concluded, the "combined bits and pieces of information" would have failed to establish that probable cause existed for the issuance of a search warrant.

5.6   STATE v. GARCIA (N.M.CT.APP. 2002)
(*Search Warrant: Nighttime*)

Police officers observed people taking a truckload of trees and shrubbery into an apartment at night, but the people had left by the time the officers reached the truck. A local hardware store confirmed that trees and shrubbery had been stolen. A magistrate issued search warrants authorizing nighttime searches of the truck and apartment.

The defendant argued that the nighttime searches were unconstitutional. Police had already secured the premises. They could have kept evidence from being destroyed or hidden simply by maintaining surveillance until daylight. Absent exigent circumstances, the defendant argued, a nighttime warrant should not have been issued.

- *Discuss the propriety of the nighttime warrant in this case.*
- *Should it have been issued and executed?*

State v. Garcia (N.M.Ct.App. 2002): 71 CrL 172

The court rejected the defendant's contention that police need exigent circumstances to justify a nighttime warrant. So long as police have the "reasonable cause" to conduct a nighttime search, a nighttime search is constitutional.

The court was not persuaded by the defendant's surveillance argument. The police might have been required to abandon the surveillance of the property before daylight by circumstances unforeseen. Police were not required to allege in the affidavits that they could not continue the surveillance until daylight.

Finally, the court noted that the police had observed the suspects moving the evidence at night, and that the officers had not delayed or sought permission to search on the basis of probable cause developed during business hours. "The intrusiveness of the nighttime search in this case is considerably lessened because of these circumstances, making the showing of necessity sufficient under constitutional scrutiny."

5.7 ILO v. STATE (ARK. 2002)
(*Search Warrant: Staleness*)
(*Search: Knock-and-Announce*)

A police officer amassed probable cause to believe the defendant and her husband were selling drugs out of their home. The officer had stopped one of the many short-term visitors to the home and recovered a quarter-pound of marijuana. The detained buyer said he had been purchasing marijuana from the defendant for 1 year, and that a handgun had been present at drug sales on at least two occasions in the past year. The buyer also responded to a question about firearms by stating that he had seen a handgun in the defendant's home a couple of times—the most recent time being 2 weeks earlier.

The trial court held "that merely seeing a handgun at a residence 2 weeks earlier is too remote in time to predicate a fear that such handgun will continue to be present and endanger officers, absent any other compelling facts to suggest otherwise."

- *What does it mean for information to be "stale"?*
- *Is this information about the handgun too stale to serve as a basis for allowing police to execute a search warrant without complying with the knock-and-announce requirement of the 4th Amendment? Why?*

■ *Is this information about the presence of a handgun on the premises sufficient to serve as a basis for authorizing a no-knock entry? Why?*

Ilo v. State (Ark. 2002): 72 CrL 24

Information that a handgun was seen 2 weeks earlier inside the home of suspects believed to be selling marijuana was not too old to give rise to a reasonable suspicion that compliance with the 4th Amendment's knock-and-announce rule would endanger officers executing a search warrant at the residence.

The decision as to whether information is too old is necessarily a fact-specific inquiry, dependent on the circumstances present in a particular case. The court noted here that there are only a couple of published decisions on the issue of staleness with regard to the justification for a no-knock entry.

The court emphasized that the narcotics dealing of which the defendant was suspected was continuous in nature. The information from the buyer also established there was a handgun present during drug sales on at least two occasions over the previous year. The fact that the more recent sighting of the handgun was 2 weeks old did not make the officer's suspicion that the handgun would be present when he executed the warrant unreasonable.

The court said it felt compelled to note that the vast majority of cases considering the issue have held that the mere presence of firearms on the premises, standing alone, is not sufficient to justify dispensing with the knock-and-announce requirement of the 4th Amendment. However, the court decided that it did not need to answer this question in the instant case because the defendant argued that the sighting of the handgun was stale, not that it was insufficient by itself to establish the exigency justifying the no-knock entry.

chapter 6

Exclusionary Rule:
Operation and Extenstion
to Secondary Evidence

The 4th Amendment prohibits the government from searching or seizing us, or our homes, property, or effects, unless it has probable cause and (preferably) a warrant. However, the 4th Amendment does not specify what the penalty should be if the government disobeys.

For decades, cases went up to the U.S. Supreme Court in which the police had searched for and seized evidence without probable cause or a warrant, and the Court would find a 4th Amendment violation and tell them not to do it again. Another violation would make its way to the Supreme Court and the Court would tell them again. Finally, the Court created a remedy, a penalty to punish the police for violating our constitutional rights.

That remedy is the Exclusionary Rule. In essence, it says this to the police: If you seize evidence illegally, it will be excluded from the trial. If you seize evidence unconstitutionally, you cannot use it.

The Exclusionary Rule applies to primary evidence (the evidence actually seized illegally) and to secondary or derivative evidence (evidence developed from illegally seized evidence). Application of the Exclusionary Rule to secondary evidence was established in the Court's discussion of the fruit-of-the-poisonous tree doctrine. The theory is simple: If the tree is poisonous, the fruit of that tree is also poisonous. If the evidence seized was unconstitutionally seized, the evidence derived from that evidence is also unconstitutional and it must be excluded.

The Court made it clear that the main thing it was trying to do was to deter the police from acting unconstitutionally. This is an effective deterrence because if the police act

---

When the appellate court has cited and relied upon a U.S. Supreme Court opinion in reaching its decision, those citations are set out in full so you will know what Supreme Court authority the court relied upon. When you see an asterisk [*] in the court's opinion, that means the appellate court has referenced and relied upon a lower court case in reaching its decision. Those case citations are not included here.

unconstitutionally, their efforts are wasted—because the evidence seized illegally cannot be used in criminal prosecution of the defendant whose rights were violated.

Exceptions to the Exclusionary Rule

Good Faith: Because the main objective of the Exclusionary Rule is to deter the police from violating constitutional protections, it is important to distinguish those cases in which the police have made a constitutional error (in which case evidence will be suppressed) from those cases in which the judge has made a constitutional error, most typically in issuing a warrant without sufficient probable cause. When the judge has made a constitutional error, the good faith exception comes into play and the evidence is not suppressed if a reasonably competent officer would have thought the warrant was good.

Inevitable Discovery: If the police have gathered evidence illegally, but if they can show that they would have inevitably found the evidence constitutionally, the Exclusionary Rule does not apply. This exception is based on the premise that if the police can establish by a preponderance of the evidence that the information ultimately or inevitably would have been discovered by lawful means, they should not be precluded from using it, even though it was actually found unlawfully. This exception will most likely only be used when the illegal police conduct occurred during the course of an ongoing investigation in which the evidence would have been discovered by investigatory procedures in progress (LaFave & Isreal, 1985).

Independent Source: If the police seized evidence illegally, but can show that they also had a constitutional source of information that would have led to constitutional seizure of the evidence, the Exclusionary Rule does not apply, because there would be no deterrent value in excluding that evidence from trial.

Attenuation: If the police acted unconstitutionally, but can show that there was a causal break in the chain of events from their unconstitutional conduct to the seizure of the evidence (i.e., their unconstitutional conduct did not cause the production of the evidence), then the Exclusionary Rule does not apply.

Of these exceptions to the application of the Exclusionary Rule, the good faith exception and inevitable discovery are the most commonly encountered.

6.1   STATE v. FORD (OHIO CT.APP. 2002)
(*Exclusionary Rule*)

Police officers unconstitutionally stopped the defendant in the absence of reasonable suspicion. During the stop, they asked for the defendant's identification, which led to the defendant's arrest on outstanding warrants. The officers later found drugs in the defendant's possession.

The state argued (and the court agreed) that "where there is an outstanding warrant, the authority for the arrest does not derive from unlawful conduct, but from the warrant." The defendant argued that, unless evidence discovered during unconstitutional stops is suppressed, the police would have free rein to conduct sweeps of large numbers of people without any particularized suspicion in the hopes of catching a few people with outstanding warrants.

> ■ *Should the fruits of the unconstitutional stop be excluded from trial? Explain.*

State v. Ford (Ohio Ct.App. 2002): 72 CrL 90

Physical evidence obtained as a result of an arrest on an outstanding warrant discovered during an unconstitutional stop must be suppressed.

    When a police officer learns of a suspect's identity unlawfully, the subsequent search of the suspect's vehicle under an outstanding warrant violates the 4th Amendment. The court, therefore, affirmed an order suppressing the drugs.

6.2   UNITED STATES v. KESZTHELYI (SIXTH CIR. 2002) (*Exclusionary Rule/Inevitable Discovery*)

Federal agents executed a search warrant and searched the defendant's home for drugs and other evidence of drug dealing. They arrested the defendant in the afternoon and searched until 5:00 p.m. They found numerous items associated with drug trafficking, but they only found 4 grams of cocaine and $1,000 in cash. The agents who conducted this first search testified that they believed they had done a thorough job and that drug-detecting dogs had not alerted to the presence of more drug evidence.

    An agent who did not participate in the search "felt very strongly" that the other agents had missed something, and he and the other agents searched the house again the following day. This time, the officers found an ounce of cocaine hidden behind the oven. The government argued that the search the following day was a continuation of the original search and was not a new, independent search.

    In the meantime, after the defendant was in custody, agents contacted a number of his buyers. The buyers informed the agents that the defendant had buried money on his property. On the basis of that information, the agents obtained a second warrant and searched the home for drugs and cash a third time, but found no more drugs or money.

> ■ *Should evidence from the second search be excluded as the result of an unconstitutional search and seizure, or should it be allowed as a continuation of the first search? Explain.*
>
> ■ *Was the third search (based on a new warrant) constitutional? Explain.*

United States v. Keszthelyi (Sixth Cir. 2002): 72 CrL 101

Most circuit courts have held that a single search warrant can authorize more than one entry into the premises identified in the warrant "as long as the second entry is a reasonable continuation of the original search." Even so, this line of cases does not reject "the general rule that a warrant authorizes only one search" and does not approve unlimited access to the premises identified through the entire period set out in the warrant. If that were the rule, it would allow for too much disruption of suspects' quiet enjoyment of their homes and too great a risk of police abuse.

Cases in which police were allowed to discontinue the search and continue again without a new warrant include these: In [*], officers had a warrant to search for stolen business equipment; they wrote down serial numbers of equipment found, left the premises to check the numbers against a list of stolen equipment, and then returned the next day to seize items on the list. That decision to suspend the search was found reasonable because the alternative was more intrusive (seizure of all of the equipment for a check of serial numbers at the officers' leisure). In [*], on Friday, officers found a vehicle pursuant to their warrant, but they could not operate the release lever for the hood; they returned the following Monday with a mechanic to open the hood. The court found that to be a reasonable continuation of the first search: Officers had probable cause to believe there was evidence under the hood and their delay to get a mechanic to open it avoided the more intrusive alternative of damaging the hood to open it.

The court explained that officers executing a search warrant can take as long as "reasonably necessary to execute the warrant" and "generally may continue to search the premises described in the warrant until they are satisfied that all available evidence has been located." When the execution of the warrant is complete, its authority terminates.

In this case, the first search of the defendant's home continued "until [the agents] were content that all available evidence had been located." There was no evidence at the suppression hearing indicating that, at the time the first search ended, there was any aspect of the search that was left incomplete or that agents were unable to search any area specified in the warrant. The thoroughness of that first search was established by the agents' testimony, the use of drug-detecting dogs, and the broad range of items found. Thus, the court concluded that the search was completed when the agents ended their search on that first day. "If the agents desired to conduct an additional search after that time, we think they were required to apply for a new warrant or identify a valid exception to the warrant requirement authorizing re-entry."

Noting the risk that would accompany a decision to the contrary, the court explained, "If law enforcement agents could resume an already-completed search based only on a 'feeling' that evidence remained on the property, there would be no limit to the number of official intrusions that could be carried out pursuant to a warrant."

Beyond that, the agents here took no steps to minimize the intrusiveness of the second search, which appeared to have been as thorough as the first one.

The defendant's conviction, however, was upheld. The court relied on the inevitable discovery exception to the Exclusionary Rule. The buyers' statements to police, "combined with the fact that the amount of cash found during the initial search of defendant's residence was less than expected, strongly suggested that additional evidence remained on the defendant's property, notwithstanding the fact that a search had already been conducted of the defendant's house." The agents had always planned to interview the buyers after the defendant was arrested, and their statements gave the agents new information that gave rise to probable cause for a new search warrant.

6.3 PEOPLE v. HAMILTON (CAL.CT.APP. 2002)
(*Exclusionary Rule/Good Faith Exception*)

Police officers ran a computer check on the defendant's vehicle license tags, and the Department of Motor Vehicles (DMV) reported that the vehicle's registration had expired. In fact, the defendant had renewed his registration. The defendant, however, was unable to produce his registration card when stopped by the police. The encounter led to the officers' discovery of evidence used to convict the defendant of narcotics and firearms offenses.

- *Should the evidence be suppressed, or does the good faith exception apply here? This is not a judicial error; this is an error made by the DMV. What should the result be? Why?*

People v. Hamilton (Cal.Ct.App. 2002): 72 CrL 90

The good faith exception to the 4th Amendment's Exclusionary Rule applies to evidence obtained during an unconstitutional vehicle stop that was premised on inaccurate information supplied to police by the state's DMV.

In *Arizona v. Evans,* 514 U.S. 1 (1995), the U.S. Supreme Court held that errors by court clerks relating to warrant records do not preclude application of the good faith exception to evidence found by officers who rely on the warrants. The Court emphasized that the Exclusionary Rule is aimed at deterring misconduct by law enforcement officers, and reasoned that court clerks, who have no stake in criminal prosecutions, are not "adjuncts to the law enforcement team."

The same is true of DMV data entry clerks. Although some upper level employees of the DMV are designated by the legislature to be peace officers, the court said, "the data entry clerk who—we infer—made the error leading to the detention and search of [the defendant] and his vehicle does not appear to be among these enumerated employees." The court found the DMV data entry clerk to be analogous to the court clerk in *Evans,* and it affirmed the defendant's conviction.

Note that the Florida Supreme Court reached a contrary conclusion in *Shadler v. State,* 761 So.2d 279 (2000), 66 CrL 287.

6.4 STATE v. TYE (WIS. 2001)
(*Good Faith Exception*)

An experienced investigator prepared an affidavit to search the defendant's home and presented it to a magistrate. The investigator did not sign and swear to the truth of the affidavit, and neither the prosecutor who reviewed the affidavit nor the magistrate to whom it was presented caught the mistake. The investigator did not give sworn testimony attesting to the truth of the affidavit.

The investigator discovered his mistake after executing the warrant. He notified the prosecutor's office and prepared a second affidavit in which he described the warrant application process, his failure to sign and swear to the original affidavit, and his subsequent discovery of his mistake. He also stated that the contents of the initial affidavit were true. The second affidavit was sworn.

The state conceded that the warrant violated the state and federal constitutional provisions on searches and seizures. The state offered several grounds, however, for holding that the evidence was admissible: Although the oath is not a mere technicality, it is a formality, rather than substance. The correct second affidavit made up for the faulty first affidavit. The good faith exception should operate here to save this search.

- *What about it? Is this a good faith case? Explain.*

State v. Tye (Wis. 2001): 70 CrL 189

Evidence seized under a search warrant issued without the support of any statement made under oath or affirmation must be suppressed. Neither the good faith exception to the Exclusionary Rule nor the submission, after the search, of a sworn affidavit saves the evidence in such a case.

The majority opinion began with a historical overview of the oath requirement in the 4th Amendment and its state constitutional counterpart. The court noted that the lack of such a requirement was one feature of the much-loathed colonial era writs of assistance, and that most states, including Wisconsin, have followed the example set in the 4th Amendment by making oath or affirmation a constitutional requirement for search warrants. This history, the majority said, "demonstrates the critical importance that the drafters of the federal and state constitutions have placed on the oath to support a search warrant."

The state acknowledged that the absence of the oath could not be deemed a mere failure to comply with a technicality. Nevertheless, one of its arguments against suppression in this case was that, although the oath is not a technicality, it is a matter of formality that did not affect the substantial rights of the defendant.

The majority disagreed and said that the oath "is a matter of substance, not form" and is "an essential component of the 4th Amendment and legal proceedings." The majority noted the oath's purpose of impressing on the affiant "an appropriate sense of obligation to tell the truth" and its role in protecting search targets by creating criminal liability for those who abuse the warrant process by giving false or fraudulent information.

The second affidavit did not make up for the absence of a sworn statement when the warrant was issued. "An after-the-fact oath or affirmation disregards the historical importance of the oath or affirmation as the basis upon which a neutral magistrate issues a warrant." Treating the two affidavits as interchangeable would eviscerate the oath or affirmation requirement, the majority concluded, adding that there was no authority from other states approving of such a remedy.

The state also relied on the good faith exception to the Exclusionary Rule, which the court recognized as a matter of state constitutional law [*]. Responding briefly to this argument, the majority said it would "not extend the good faith exception to a warrant issued on the basis of a statement that totally lacks an oath or affirmation, as in the present case."

Three judges concurred but wrote separately to expand on why the good faith exception should not apply. A warrant issued without oath or affirmation falls into the category of warrants so facially deficient that reliance on them is unreasonable. Wisconsin cases and *United States v. Leon,* 468 U.S. 897 (1984), recognize that category as one to which the rule of exclusion, rather than the good faith exception, should apply.

6.5   PEOPLE v. GONZALES (ILL.APP.CT. 1994) (*Fruit-of-the-Poisonous Tree*)

About an hour after a shooting that left one person dead, the defendant and others were arrested in an apartment building. There was not sufficient probable cause to justify their arrests. Events following that arrest led the defendant to name Enrique Hernandez as his accomplice. Hernandez later testified at trial against the defendant. The defendant appealed, claiming that the identification of Hernandez should have been suppressed because it was the product of an illegal arrest, hence fruit of the poisonous tree.

- *What do you think? Analyze it.*
- *If you "need more facts," which facts do you need?*
    - *How would your answer and analysis be different depending on how those facts develop?*

People v. Gonzales (Ill.App.Ct. 1994): 56 CrL 1231

The trial court admitted the testimony, but the court of appeals reversed. The U.S. Supreme Court listed a number of factors for courts to consider when deciding whether testimonial evidence should be suppressed as fruit of a 4th Amendment violation in *United States v. Ceccolini,* 435 U.S. 268 (1978). Here, the 4th Amendment violation was clear, and the witness's identity came to official attention as a direct result of the unlawful arrest. Moreover, the statement of the witness (Hernandez), who was also unlawfully arrested on the day of the shooting, could not be deemed what *Ceccolini* called the "product of detached reflection and a desire to be cooperative." The witness was facing charges for an unrelated killing and stated that he expected "some consideration" in exchange for his testimony against the defendant. Under the circumstances, the witness's statement was "inextricably tainted" by the defendant's illegal arrest.

6.6   UNITED STATES v. AKRIDGE (SIXTH CIR. 2003) (*Exclusionary Rule: Attenuation*)

A police officer responding to an anonymous tip about drug dealing went to the defendant's residence to conduct a "knock and talk." When the officer requested permission to search, the defendant stated that he would have to ask his roommate and his girlfriend, who were also on the lease. After the defendant had identified the other residents of the apartment, the officer induced the residents' consent to a search of the apartment by falsely representing that he had specific information about drugs in the apartment and that federal officers possessing a search warrant were nearby. The search turned up drugs and firearms.

At the time of the search, the roommate was under investigation for possession of firearms as a convicted felon. The officer suggested that the three residents decide who should accept the blame for the contraband. As a result, the girlfriend was taken to jail and later released, while the other two remained at the apartment.

Later, all three residents of the apartment were arrested for drug trafficking and firearms possession. The girlfriend entered into a plea agreement 1 week after her arrest, and the roommate did so approximately 3.5 months after his arrest. Prior to the date that the girlfriend's guilty plea was entered into the record, a magistrate judge recommended that the defendant's motion to suppress the physical evidence be granted. The district court granted that motion but denied the defendant's later motion to enlarge the scope of the suppression order to encompass statements and trial testimony by the roommate and the girlfriend.

- ■ *Does the attenuation exception to the Exclusionary Rule operate here? Explain.*
  - • *Be specific in identifying the facts on which you rely in reaching your conclusion.*

United States v. Akridge (Sixth Cir. 2003): 74 CrL 36

The attenuation doctrine operates here and the evidence is not excluded. Testimony of co-conspirators complying with plea agreements entered into after police seized physical evidence incriminating them and a defendant in an illegal search is admissible. The Sixth Circuit concluded that the degree of free will exercised by the co-conspirators in cooperating with the state, and the passage of time between the illegal search and the subsequent plea agreements and trial testimony, sufficiently attenuated the testimony's link with the search to render the testimony admissible.

The court applied the standards set out in *United States v. Ceccolini,* 435 U.S. 268 (1977), a case in which the Supreme Court addressed the issue of attenuation in the context of verbal evidence. In *Ceccolini,* the Court rejected a statement it had made in *Wong Sun v. United States,* 371 U.S. 471 (1963), that physical and verbal evidence should be treated identically for purposes of the Exclusionary Rule. The Exclusionary Rule will not invariably bar testimony, the *Ceccolini* court said. "[S]ince the cost of excluding live-witness testimony often will be greater, a closer, more direct link between the illegality and that kind of testimony is required" for suppression.

In *Ceccolini,* a local police officer, chatting with an employee of a flower shop, picked up an envelope from the counter and saw it contained money and gambling slips. The officer knew the flower shop had earlier been under surveillance by the FBI as a suspected gambling operation. Without mentioning what he had seen, the officer asked the shop employee whose envelope it was; the employee provided the defendant's name. The officer relayed that information to the FBI, and 4 months later federal agents interviewed the flower shop employee. The employee willingly assisted the FBI and subsequently testified against the defendant. In ruling that the witness's testimony was admissible despite having been derived from an admittedly illegal search, the *Ceccolini* court emphasized that the witness's testimony was voluntarily given; the police already knew of the witness's relationship to the defendant before the illegal search occurred; and substantial amounts of time separated the illegal search, the initial contact by the FBI, and the witness's trial testimony.

Drawing on *Ceccolini* and other circuit cases [*] applying it, the Sixth Circuit drew up a list of four factors to be considered in ruling on the admissibility of testimony after an illegal search:

1. The degree of free will exercised by the witnesses.
2. The role of the illegality in obtaining the testimony.
3. The time elapsed between the illegal behavior, the decision to cooperate, and the actual testimony at trial.
4. The purpose and flagrancy of the officers' misconduct.

The most important factors in this case were the degree of free will exercised by the witnesses and the temporal attenuation between events.

1. *The degree of free will:* The court noted that the girlfriend and the roommate voluntarily agreed to accompany police to the station for questioning prior to their arrests. When the roommate made his decision to cooperate with the prosecution, he gave as his reasons his knowledge that he faced an enhanced sentence as a career offender, his feeling that he had been a poor role model for his son by getting involved in drug trafficking, and his desire to "turn his life around."

    The court acknowledged that this fact pattern was not as clearly voluntary as in *Ceccolini,* where the witness had not been a putative defendant; nevertheless, it concluded that the roommate's testimony was freely given.

2. *The time elapsed:* The lapse of time between events also worked in favor of admissibility. Six weeks elapsed between the illegal search and the stationhouse questioning, and nearly 4 months passed from the roommate's arrest to his decision to cooperate. Taken together, these factors support a conclusion that the connection between the roommate's arrest and his statement had become so attenuated as to dissipate the taint of the illegal search.

    As for the girlfriend's testimony, the court noted that, although she executed a plea agreement only 1 week after her arrest, her guilty plea was not entered into the record until much later, at a time when the magistrate judge's recommendation that the physical evidence be suppressed was before the district court. The girlfriend also stated that she knew she could attempt to challenge the evidence against her but preferred to cooperate with the prosecution and tell the truth. Had her motivation been solely to avoid prosecution, she could have waited for a suppression ruling, the court observed. That she entered her guilty plea without challenging the admissibility of the evidence against her demonstrated the voluntariness of her testimony.

3. *The role of police illegality and misconduct:* The officers' misconduct could not be considered flagrant insofar as they were not in search of the evidence sought to be suppressed here—that is, the testimony—when they responded to a complaint about drug trafficking in the apartment, the court said. More difficult to reconcile

was the fact that the illegal seizure and accompanying threat of prosecution played some role in obtaining the testimony of the two roommates. Nonetheless, the court concluded that their testimony was, for the most part, voluntarily given.

One judge dissented, arguing that the police's action in flatly and repeatedly lying to the defendant to get in the door was flagrant misconduct, and that the witnesses' testimony could be viewed as voluntarily given only in the sense that any defendant who entered into a plea agreement does so "voluntarily."

6.7 HAYNES v. STATE (ARK. 2003)
(*Exclusionary Rule: Inevitable Discovery*)

Arkansas state law requires that a DNA sample be taken from offenders convicted of specified crimes before they are released from incarceration.

The defendant ran afoul of the law on three occasions. First, he was incarcerated for nonpayment of child support. At that time, prison officials illegally took a blood sample on the mistaken belief that, under the DNA database statute, the defendant's offense was a qualifying offense for which a DNA sample had to be taken.

Second, the defendant was incarcerated on a conviction of residential burglary. That offense was a qualifying offense under the statute; however, there was no evidence that a sample was taken from the defendant.

Third, he was convicted in the instant case of rape and burglary. A key piece of evidence in the state's circumstantial case was a match between DNA found on a ski mask worn by the assailant and the illegal DNA sample taken in connection with the defendant's "deadbeat dad" conviction. The match served as the basis for obtaining a new DNA sample that confirmed the earlier match between the illegal sample and the DNA found on the ski mask. The defendant argued that both the original, illegal sample and the recent, confirming sample should have been suppressed.

The inevitable discovery exception to the Exclusionary Rule, recognized in *Nix v. Williams,* 467 U.S. 431 (1984), allows the admission of illegally obtained evidence, otherwise subject to suppression, if the state proves that police would inevitably have discovered the evidence by lawful means.

The defendant argued that no DNA sample was actually taken in connection with his release from his residential burglary conviction, an offense for which DNA was required to be drawn. Therefore, he argued, the state failed to meet its burden of proof that discovery of his DNA was inevitable.

The state countered that argument with testimony from a supervisor of the forensic biology section of the state crime lab, who stated that blood samples were obtained from all prisoners as required by the act.

- *Does the defendant's DNA qualify as evidence that would have been inevitably discovered for purposes of operation of the rule? Why? Explain your reasoning.*

Haynes v. State (Ark. 2003): 74 CrL 101

A state statute required that a DNA sample be obtained from prisoners before their release. That requirement satisfied requirements for inevitable discovery with respect to DNA evidence incriminating the defendant that was actually obtained using an earlier, illegally obtained sample. The court said it presumed that law enforcement officers complied with the law requiring the taking of a DNA sample from prisoners even though no evidence established that the later sample was actually taken from this defendant.

In this case, the fact that the state DNA database act identified the defendant's residential burglary conviction as a target offense requiring that a sample be obtained before the prisoner is released meant that the state would inevitably have discovered the defendant's DNA profile by lawful means.

The court rejected the defendant's argument that the state had not proved that discovery of his DNA was inevitable. "A presumption exists that public officials will follow the law in performance of their duties," the court said. The defendant failed to rebut that presumption.

The court also credited the testimony of a supervisor of the forensic biology section of the state crime lab, who stated that blood samples were obtained from all prisoners as required by the act. Taken together, the statutory requirement that DNA samples be obtained from prisoners convicted of target offenses, and the testimony of the crime lab supervisor that samples were taken of all such prisoners, fulfilled the state's burden of showing that the defendant's DNA profile inevitably would have been discovered.

Two judges dissented. They objected to the majority's reliance on a presumption and were unimpressed with the crime lab supervisor's testimony. No evidence showed that blood was actually drawn from the defendant in connection with his release from his residential burglary incarceration. Accordingly, the court should not have found that the state met its burden of proof, and then shifted the burden to the defendant to rebut.

6.8 STATE v. FLIPPO (W.VA. 2002)
(*Exclusionary Rule: Inevitable Discovery*)

The defendant in this case was convicted of murdering his wife in a cabin they had rented. The trial judge denied a motion to suppress certain photographs police found in the cabin, citing a general murder-scene exception to the warrant and probable cause requirements. The U.S. Supreme Court confirmed that no such exception exists and remanded the case.

On remand, the state court held that the warrantless seizure of the photographs was unconstitutional, but the state argued that their admission was justifiable under the inevitable discovery exception.

- *Is that analysis correct? Explain.*

State v. Flippo (W.Va. 2002): 72 CrL 202

The West Virginia Supreme Court held that to take advantage of the inevitable discovery exception to the Exclusionary Rule, the alternative line of police investigation must already have been underway at the time of the constitutional violation.

The court observed that state and federal courts are divided on this point and that the position adopted here is the minority view. The court explained that it adopted this view because this narrower construction is more consistent with the privacy protections of the state constitution. The court agreed with the Minnesota Supreme Court [*] that "[i]f police are allowed to search when they possess no lawful means and are only required to show that lawful means could have been available even though not pursued, the narrow 'inevitable discovery' exception would 'swallow' the [constitutional warrant] protection."

6.9   UNITED STATES v. RHIGER (TENTH CIR. 2003) (*Exclusionary Rule: Exigent Circumstances*)

Federal drug agents observed the defendant driving two people to several locations where the passengers bought materials used to manufacture methamphetamine. The agents also learned that less than a week earlier, the defendant had purchased ingredients used to make methamphetamine. They observed the defendant enter a residence with the purchased materials. After watching the home for an hour, the agents detected the smell of cooking methamphetamine.

Half an hour later, they entered the home without a warrant and, as expected, found a methamphetamine lab. During that half-hour, one of the agents made sure that the odor was not coming from somewhere other than the home under surveillance: He questioned the owner of a nearby mobile home, searched the interior of that mobile home with the consent of the owner, and determined that no illegal drug activity was occurring.

The defendant argued that the entry of the home violated the 4th Amendment in the absence of exigent circumstances.

The government argued that exigent circumstances existed due to the volatility of chemicals used in a methamphetamine lab and the potential for an explosion.

- *Was entry justified on the grounds of exigent circumstances? Explain.*

United States v. Rhiger (Tenth Cir. 2003): 72 CrL 316

The presence of explosive methamphetamine precursors and a smell of methamphetamine cooking constituted exigent circumstances justifying a warrantless entry of a home.

Tenth Circuit precedents set forth a three-pronged standard for finding exigent circumstances to justify a warrantless entry. Law enforcement officers must have reasonable grounds to believe that there is an immediate need to protect life or property; the search must not be motivated by an intent to arrest and seize evidence; and there must be some reasonable basis, approaching probable cause, to associate an emergency with the place to be searched.

The majority held that exigent circumstances existed in this case. The agents' knowledge of the defendant's purchase and possession of materials used to manufacture methamphetamine, the strong odor of cooking methamphetamine emitting from the home, and their knowledge of the inherent dangerousness of an active methamphetamine lab established a reasonable basis, if not probable cause, to believe there was an immediate need to protect the public by entering the home and discontinuing the lab's production. Testimony by the agents revealed that they acted out of a concern for public safety, not for the purposes of making arrests and seizing evidence, the majority concluded.

The fact that the agents did not enter the home as soon as they smelled the methamphetamine did not detract from the conclusion that a reasonable officer would have perceived a threat to public safety, according to the majority. One of the agents spent the half-hour period between the detection of the odor and the entry making sure the odor was not coming from somewhere other than the home under surveillance. To do so, the agent questioned the owner of a nearby mobile home, performed a consensual search of the interior, and determined that no illegal drug activity was occurring. It was at that point that the agent concluded that there were exigent circumstances justifying an entry of the target premises. That the agent waited half an hour before entering "does not undermine the objective evidence that cooking methamphetamine is an exceptionally dangerous process."

6.10   UNITED STATES v. HOLLOWAY (ELEVENTH CIR. 2002)
(*Exclusionary Rule: Exigent Circumstances/Probable Cause*)

Police officers responded within minutes to the address given in a 911 call about gunshots and arguing and found the defendant and a neighbor in the front yard and the defendant's wife on the front porch. After securing them at gunpoint, an officer stepped onto the porch to begin a warrantless search of the home for victims and weapons. From the porch, the officer saw, on a table, a shotgun that was used to convict the defendant in federal court of being a felon in possession of a firearm. The people present at the scene later told police that the defendant had fired into the air to frighten away some strangers who had been throwing rocks at his house and horses.

- *Were the police constitutionally entitled to engage in a warrantless search of the home in this case? Justify your conclusion.*
  - *If so, how do you deal with the Gates test for using hearsay to establish probable cause?*

United States v. Holloway (Eleventh Cir. 2002): 71 CrL 212

An anonymous 911 caller's report of gunshots and arguing at an address, combined with police officers' confirmation that there were people present at that address, support a reasonable belief in the existence of an emergency situation requiring an immediate, warrantless entry. "[W]hen an *emergency* is reported by an anonymous caller, the need for immediate action may outweigh the need to verify the reliability of the caller" (emphasis in original).

The court characterized the warrant exception it was using as a form of exigent circumstance and it cited passages from a long line of U.S. Supreme Court cases approving of warrantless entries in emergency situations.

The court acknowledged that, in the "typical" exigent circumstances case, there is probable cause to believe a search will disclose evidence of a crime. "In emergencies, however, law enforcement officers are not motivated by an expectation of seizing evidence of a crime. Rather, the officers are compelled to search by a desire to locate victims and the need to ensure their own safety and that of the public .... Thus, in an emergency, the probable cause element may be satisfied where officers reasonably believe a person is in danger."

Here, police had received two dispatches from a 911 operator indicating continued arguing at the defendant's home; they arrived within minutes. On their arrival, nothing at the scene "dissuaded the officers from believing the veracity of the 911 calls." On the contrary, "the presence of [the defendant] and his wife on the front porch supported the information conveyed by the 911 caller."

The court made it clear that its conclusion was consistent with the Supreme Court's decision in *Florida v. J.L,* 529 U.S. 266 (2000), in which the Court held that an anonymous report that a youth had a gun and police officers' observations of a youth matching the description provided by the report did not provide the reasonable suspicion the 4th Amendment requires for an investigative stop. The Supreme Court rejected the idea that the danger posed by someone's possibly illegal possession of a firearm justifies applying a lower standard of reliability than the court has previously required of informers.

The Eleventh Circuit distinguished that case from the present one, noting that in *J.L.* the investigatory stop was not based on an emergency situation. This case, on the other hand, "involved a serious threat to human life" and "concerned an on-going emergency requiring immediate action." Given the nature of the 911 call, "a lesser showing of reliability than demanded in *J.L.* was appropriate in order to justify the search of [the defendant's] home .... Because the police had no reason to doubt the veracity of the 911 call, particularly in light of the personal observations of the officers once they arrived on the scene, their warrantless search for victims was constitutional."

In further support of its conclusion, the court pointed out that 911 calls are "the predominant means of communicating emergency situations," that they "are distinctive in that they concern contemporaneous emergency events, not general criminal behavior," and that "the exigencies of emergency situations often limit the ability of a caller to convey extraneous details, such as the identifying information .... If law enforcement could not rely on information conveyed by anonymous 911 callers, their ability to respond effectively to emergency situations would be significantly curtailed." The court also observed that a 911 caller's decision to remain anonymous out of fear of retaliation or danger "may very well have little bearing" on his or her veracity.

Offering some guidance for the resolution of future cases, the court added that "[t]he fact that no victims are found, or that the information ultimately proves to be false or inaccurate, does not render the police action any less lawful .... As long as the officers reasonably believe an emergency situation necessitates their warrantless search, whether through information provided by a 911 call or otherwise, such actions must be upheld as constitutional."

The court also made clear that the 4th Amendment allows evidence observed in plain view during such warrantless searches to be seized and used as evidence.

6.11   STATE v. DAVIS (CONN.APP.CT. 2002)
(Exclusionary Rule: Exigent Circumstances/Pretrial Identification)

Police had two witnesses who had seen the survivor of a shootout lying injured on a driveway. After learning that the defendant had showed up at a hospital with gunshot wounds, police took the witnesses to the hospital. In separate procedures, each identified the defendant as he lay in bed with a sheet covering his wounds.

- *If the defendant argued that this pretrial identification procedure violated due process guaranteed for pretrial identification, how should the court rule? Make sure you explain what the test is for due process in pretrial identification.*
- *Does that procedure violate due process required for pretrial identifications? Explain.*
- *If the government argued that this pretrial identification procedure was constitutional because these were exigent circumstances, how should the court rule? Explain.*

State v. Davis (Conn.App.Ct. 2002): 71 CrL 281

A "hospital show-up" identification of a murder suspect was not unnecessarily suggestive in light of the exigent circumstances faced by police.

In [*] the Connecticut Supreme Court listed "the need of police to determine quickly if they are on the wrong trail" among exigent circumstances that can justify use of a suggestive identification procedure. In the instant case, the court said, "the police were looking for a murder suspect and it was crucial to ascertain quickly whether the defendant was the man responsible so that, if he were not, the search to find and apprehend the responsible person could resume with a minimum of delay. Under the circumstances, we conclude that although the hospital identifications were suggestive, they were not unnecessarily so because of the exigent circumstances."

The court added that even if the identification procedures were necessarily suggestive, the identifications were sufficiently reliable, under the totality of the circumstances, to justify their admission.

6.12   UNITED STATES v. DAVIS (TENTH CIR. 2002)
(Exclusionary Rule: Exigent Circumstances)

Shortly after 5:30 a.m., officers responding to a report of a possible domestic disturbance were greeted at the door by the defendant who had alcohol on his breath and bloodshot eyes. He told the officers he had been disciplining his child and that was the reason for the noise that prompted the report. He denied that the female resident of the house was present, but she immediately appeared in the doorway and stated that the couple had been arguing. The defendant tried to prevent the woman from talking with the officers. He refused the officers' request to enter the home and, when they said they would enter anyway, ordered the woman outside, retreated into the house, and headed for a back room.

The woman, too, refused to consent to the officers' entry, but the officers went inside anyway. They later testified that they believed the defendant was either going for a weapon or trying to evade them. The entry led to the discovery of drugs and several stolen firearms.

One of the officers knew that the defendant had no history of violence.

The defendant sought to have the drugs and firearms suppressed as evidence, arguing they were discovered in an unconstitutional warrantless search.

The State argued the warrantless entry and subsequent discovery were justified by exigent circumstances.

■ *Evaluate the merits of these arguments.*

United States v. Davis (Tenth Cir. 2002): 71 CrL 244

These facts did not provide exigency and the Tenth Circuit was unwilling to create a special exigency rule for domestic violence calls. The facts that an apparently intoxicated man answered the door for police responding to a domestic disturbance call, falsely asserted that his female cohabitant was not at home, and then retreated to a back room did not add up to exigent circumstances justifying a warrantless, nonconsensual entry of the home. Therefore, evidence obtained when the police followed the man into the home was properly suppressed.

The requirements of the exigent circumstances exception to the warrant requirement are reasonable grounds to believe that there is an immediate need to protect life or property; a purpose other than making an arrest or seizing evidence; and a reasonable basis, approaching probable cause, to associate an emergency with the area or place to be searched. Those requirements were not met here.

The government argued that the defendant's rapid retreat posed a significant and immediate risk to the officers' safety, and that their entry was intended to control the defendant rather than to look for evidence. The government stressed the defendant's obvious untruthfulness and the perspective the officers had on the situation from their training and experience.

The court concluded, however, that the facts known to the officers provided no more than equivocal support for a belief that the defendant's retreat posed a risk to the officers' safety. There was no evidence that the officers believed the defendant had a reputation for violence; on the contrary, one of the officers knew that the defendant had no history of violence. Nor did the defendant display a threatening or aggressive manner when he initially contacted the officers. Any concern generated by his lie as to the woman's whereabouts should have been allayed when she appeared without any signs of harm.

Moreover, the defendant's only manifestation of resistance was his insistence on keeping the officers outside of his home. Even the woman, the suspected victim, tried to keep the officers out. The court also said that the officers' knowledge that the defendant had a child should have indicated that his withdrawal from police presence was nonthreatening. The early hour and the defendant's apparent intoxication did not require the district court to ignore the officers' knowledge of facts cutting against a finding of exigency—the defendant's "historically peaceable manner" and the fact that he was a father.

The trial court was not required to defer to the officers' judgment that the situation could quickly spin out of control. The government was essentially asked for "a special rule for domestic calls because they are inherently violent, and the police, responding to these calls, are automatically at greater risk." Rejecting this argument, the court said that granting unfettered permission to officers to enter homes, based only on a general assumption that domestic calls are always dangerous, would violate the 4th Amendment.

The U.S. Supreme Court refused to create an analogous rule for drug cases in *Richards v. Wisconsin,* 520 U.S. 385 (1997).

6.13   UNITED STATES v. HOWARD (FIFTH CIR. 1997)
(*Exclusionary Rule: Exigent Circumstances*)

As a result of information received from a cooperating suspect, Drug Enforcement Agency (DEA) agents performed spot surveillance of the defendant's home for several months. They observed narcotics-related pedestrian and vehicular activity there. With the help of another cooperating suspect, agents targeted Hillis, who allegedly worked with the defendant, for a "reverse sting." Hillis was arrested when he tried to buy 5 kilograms of cocaine from the cooperating suspect, and he immediately agreed to cooperate as well. He told the DEA that the defendant was storing a large quantity of marijuana in a freezer at the defendant's house, the defendant was the source of the $10,000 Hillis brought for the cocaine buy, and the defendant expected him to return to the defendant's house with 1 kilogram of the cocaine.

The DEA ordered the defendant's residence placed under surveillance. Prior to Agent Hildreth's arrival at the house, officers stopped a vehicle, apparently some distance from the house. When Hildreth arrived, he was informed that a second vehicle, "directly beside the residence in view of the residence," was stopped while leaving the defendant's house and that cocaine had been found. Hildreth did not know why the officers stopped the second vehicle in front of the defendant's house. In addition, Hildreth testified that when he arrived at the house, a small crowd had gathered at the scene of the stop. The defendant's neighbor testified that the small crowd consisted of police officers. Agent Hildreth testified that he was concerned that the defendant would notice the commotion and attempt to destroy evidence. Hildreth also stated that although he knew that the defendant had a vision problem, he did not know how many people were inside the defendant's house and he feared for the safety of the officers.

Accordingly, Agent Hildreth and other officers made a warrantless entry to secure the premises and then conducted a protective sweep of the house. The defendant consented to a search of his residence and agents found marijuana in a freezer in the garage.

The defendant said the warrantless search was illegal. The government asserted five exigent circumstances:

- *Probable cause to believe there were illegal drugs and paraphernalia in the house.*
- *Concern about the safety of the officers.*
- *Fast-moving character of the investigation.*

- *Because a crowd gathered, someone inside might have become alerted to the presence of officers.*
- *Evidence might have been removed from or destroyed in the house.*
  - *Was the warrantless search justified by exigent circumstances? Explain, addressing each of the claims made by the government.*

United States v. Howard (Fifth Cir. 1997): 60 CrL 1491

The court began by examining the exigent circumstances the government claimed were present, and analyzed each as follows: "First, the government asserts that Agent Hildreth had probable cause to believe that there were illegal drugs and paraphernalia in the house. Presence of drugs alone does not give rise to exigent circumstances justifying a warrantless entry and search.

"Second, Hildreth claimed to be concerned about the safety of himself, his fellow officers, and the community. There was no direct or circumstantial evidence supporting the belief that the defendant or anyone with him posed a specific danger to anyone. However, given the fact that it is common for drug traffickers to carry weapons, we must conclude that Hildreth's fear for safety qualifies as a factor favorable to the government.

"Third, the government relies upon the allegedly fast-moving character of the investigation. According to the record, there was an approximately 20-35 minute window during which Hildreth could have obtained a telephonic warrant. Whether Hildreth had a sufficient factual basis for believing an exigency existed is a close call. According to Hildreth he harbored a reasonable belief that the defendant would become suspicious upon Hillis' failure to return with the cocaine. This suspicion, the government argues, could have prompted the defendant to destroy evidence. There is no direct evidence in the record suggesting that Hillis was supposed to return to the defendant's residence at any particular time; nevertheless, at some point the defendant would have become apprehensive about Hillis' failure to return. We will not second-guess the judgment of law enforcement officers when reasonable minds may differ on the exigency of any particular situation. We conclude that Hildreth did not have enough time to obtain a warrant.

"The fourth alleged exigency is that because a crowd gathered outside the defendant's house, he or someone inside might have become alerted to presence of the police and would have begun destroying evidence. There is no direct evidence that the defendant had such awareness. However, we refuse to require direct evidence. The residence was not under surveillance for long before the crowd gathered, Agent Hildreth did not know whether there was anyone else inside, and the defendant's home was a busy one. The court's factual finding that the crowd outside of the defendant's residence gave rise to exigent circumstances was not clearly erroneous.

"Finally, the government contends that Hildreth had reason to believe evidence might be removed from or destroyed in the house. This contention rests on three inferences: the defendant had cocaine in his house, the defendant was aware that the officers were outside of his house and, thus, might have been prompted to destroy the cocaine, and the defendant would become concerned that something had gone wrong and that the police were en route. We have already concluded that each of these inferences is supported in the record.

Thus, the district court did not err by concluding that Hildreth was reasonable in believing that the defendant could have been in the process of destroying evidence. We hold that the warrantless entry was justified by exigent circumstances."

6.14   PEOPLE v. LEWIS (COLO. 1999)
(Exclusionary Rule: Fruit-of-the-Poisonous Tree/Exigent Circumstances/ Pretrial Identification)

Clerks at a convenience store reported that a Black male, 6'1" to 6'3" tall, with an athletic build, wearing a Colorado Rockies hat and a black coat, had robbed the store at gunpoint with a silver handgun. Approximately 5 minutes after receiving the dispatch, an officer arrived near the location of the robbery, but did not observe anyone on the street in the direction in which the robber reportedly ran.

The officer proceeded to a motel located about a half-block from the convenience store. In the courtyard of the motel, the officer saw a woman talking to a tall Black man in dark clothing who was standing inside the open door of the room. On seeing the officer, the woman shut the door from the outside.

The officer directed the woman to open the door, and he observed inside the room four Black males who met the description of the robbery suspect. At this point, nearly 10 minutes had passed since the original dispatch. When backup officers arrived, they entered the room and recovered a Colorado Rockies hat, a silver handgun, and items taken in the robbery. The convenience clerks were brought to the scene, and one of them identified one of the men, the defendant, as the robber.

- ▪ *Analyze the case. Be specific in your analysis about:*
  - *The entry to the motel room.*
  - *The evidence found and seized there.*
  - *The identification of the defendant.*

People v. Lewis (Colo. 1999): 65 CrL 47

Should evidence from the motel room be suppressed? If so, why?

For the warrantless entry to be lawful, the 4th Amendment required the state to show that the entry was justified by probable cause and exigent circumstances. However, the officer's observation of a man inside the motel room whose general appearance was consistent with the description of the robber was insufficient to establish probable cause.

The court pointed out that the state even conceded that the description on which the officer relied was vague. Further, the most distinctive feature in the description, the Rockies hat, was missing. Indeed, the description was so general that it matched three other persons in the motel room. Moreover, probable cause was lacking, the court reasoned, even taking into account the lateness of the night, the absence of other persons on the street, proximity of the motel to the crime scene, and the woman's closing of the door on seeing the officer. None of these facts "gave the officer any additional reason to think that the particular individual in the motel room doorway had committed any crime."

In the absence of probable cause, the state's argument that exigent circumstances, namely "hot pursuit," justified the warrantless entry also failed. In reaching this decision, the court emphasized that probable cause is a threshold requirement for the consideration of exigent circumstances. Even if probable cause existed, the facts here do not rise to the level of hot pursuit. A warrantless entry is only justified as hot pursuit if the police had some direction leading them to a particular location. In the instant case, the officer's presence at the motel was the result of happenstance.

Should the out-of-court identification be suppressed as "fruit-of-the-poisonous tree"?

The independent source doctrine allows illegally obtained evidence to be admitted if the state can demonstrate that the evidence was also discovered "by means wholly independent of any constitutional violation." In [*] the Colorado Supreme Court established a two-part standard to govern the application of the independent source doctrine to an out-of-court "show-up" identification, which requires that (1) the police were aware of the defendant's identity and location before the 4th Amendment violation, and (2) the witness's identification is based on contemporaneous observation of the criminal activity.

The court here said the state was incorrectly seeking a standard closer to that for in-court identification, which permits application of the independent source doctrine solely on the basis of the witness's recollection. However, under such an interpretation, all out-of-court identifications would be admissible, regardless of any police misconduct, and thus the exception would "swallow the rule." Therefore, the court explained, the witness's recollections cannot constitute an independent source in the context of an out-of-court identification absent satisfaction of this first prong of the test. The proper inquiry for the out-of-court identification in this case was whether an independent basis existed for the defendant's presence at the show-up identification.

Here, it was the officer's unlawful entry that led to the observation of four Black males who fit a vague description of the robber, an observation that resulted in the detention of the men, as well as the clerk's identification of the defendant. "The record does not include evidence of any alternate independent basis which would have allowed the police to secure the defendant's presence at the show-up identification, absent his illegal seizure at the motel."

6.15   UNITED STATES v. BLOUNT (FIFTH CIR. 1996)
(Exclusionary Rule: Exigent Circumstances/Protective Sweep/ Open Fields/Probable Cause/Hot Pursuit)

Plainclothes officers and Bureau of Alcohol, Tobacco, and Firearms (ATF) agents executed a search warrant on 3717 Campbell Street, a suspected crack house. As the police entered the house, a person matching the description of Richard J. Thomas, whom the police suspected might be present and armed, exited the rear of the house and fled on foot. (This suspicion was based on a police computer entry reporting a sexual assault involving a firearm at the Campbell address. This report, entered 2 months prior to the execution of the search warrant, listed persons named "Ricky" and "Lamont" as suspects. At the time the Campbell Street warrant was executed, there was no extant arrest warrant for Thomas.) Drugs, money, and a handgun were retrieved from the home.

After the Campbell Street residence had been secured, the agents resumed the search for Thomas. Dorothy Cooksey, who was standing on her stoop in her bathrobe, told police that minutes before Thomas had tried to force his way into her house. Cooksey also told police that Thomas would "end up" at 2302 Bleker Street (catercorner to 3717 Campbell Street) where "Lamont with the afro" lived and drugs were sold.

At this point, more than 30 minutes after the execution of the Campbell Street warrant, the agents approached 2302 Bleker, knocked on the front door, identified themselves, and asked the inhabitants to come out and talk to them. Someone inside shouted "Who is it?" but no one opened the door.

An officer went to the rear of the house and found a window with a broken pane. Although a piece of plywood covered most of the opening, by leaning against the house and pressing his face within inches of a small gap in the plywood covering, the officer was able to see inside, where he saw defendant Donnie Lamont Blount handling a combination lock on a closet door.

After trying for 20 minutes to gain consensual entry into the house, the officer radioed for reinforcements and ordered electrical services to the house cut off. Meanwhile, Blount had called 911 and reported a burglary in progress. When a uniformed officer arrived, Blount opened the door and was immediately seized. Defendant Johnson also was seized.

After the defendants had been secured, the officers conducted a perimeter sweep to look for Thomas, who they believed, on the basis of Cooksey's statement, might be hiding within. In the kitchen, the officers observed a razor blade with a white residue that field-tested as cocaine.

An officer then secured and executed a search warrant at 2302 Bleker. The search turned up additional amounts of cocaine and firearms.

- *Was the officer's observation of Blount constitutional?*
  - *Can those observations form the probable cause for a search warrant? Explain.*
- *Were there exigent circumstances surrounding the search for Thomas so that a warrant was not needed?*
- *Were the police in "hot pursuit"?*
- *Are there other exigent circumstances present?*
- *Did police have probable cause to arrest Blount and Johnson for the crimes of harboring a fugitive (Thomas) and for possessing contraband? Explain.*
- *Were the warrantless search and protective sweep of the house constitutional? Explain.*

United States v. Blount (Fifth Cir. 1996): 60 CrL 1165

Open Fields

"Proceeding chronologically, we begin with Weston's *observation* of Blount through the small aperture in the rear window [emphasis added]. We conclude that when a police officer walks into the partially fenced back yard of a residential dwelling, using a passage not open to the general public, and places his face within inches of a small opening in an almost completely covered rear window to look into the house and at the inhabitants, that officer has performed a 'search' within the meaning of the 4th Amendment."

Exigent Circumstances

"The district court found that, due to the exigent circumstances surrounding the police search for Thomas, the officer's actions did not require a warrant. Any continuous police pursuit of Thomas had ended over 30 minutes before the police approached 2302 Bleker. Thus, this case does not involve the exigent circumstance of "hot pursuit." There is no evidence that the inhabitants of the house were aware of the police presence before the agents knocked on the door and introduced themselves. Aside from Cooksey's broad and uncorroborated statement, there was no indication that contraband would be found in the house and certainly no evidence regarding its 'ready destructibility' or the risk of its removal or destruction. While the prospect of danger attends every narcotics investigation, the police were unaware of any particular danger to themselves or others which might distinguish this case from the norm. (There is no record evidence that Thomas was armed when he fled the Campbell Street residence. The police suspicion that Thomas was armed stemmed entirely from a computer report, several months old, implicating Thomas in an offense involving a firearm.) An ATF agent was in a position to call in reinforcements which he subsequently did and seek a warrant while keeping the house under surveillance, a markedly safer course of action than brazenly confronting the unknown in 2302 Bleker. The district court's finding of exigent circumstances was clearly erroneous, and the officer's observations through the rear window must be excised from the warrant affidavit."

Probable Cause to Arrest

"The district court found that the police had probable cause to arrest Blount and Johnson for the crimes of harboring a fugitive (Thomas) and for possessing contraband. A precondition to the crime of harboring a fugitive under federal law is the issuance of an arrest warrant. The police were well aware that there was no extant arrest warrant for Thomas at the time the defendants were arrested. The analogous Texas statute requires knowledge of the fugitive's status and some affirmative action hindering police access to a felon. The police in this case simply arrested the defendants on first sight, inquiring about Thomas' whereabouts only after the defendants had been 'secured.' On these facts, we conclude that an objectively reasonable police officer would have had no probable cause to arrest the defendants for harboring a fugitive."

"We reach a similar conclusion regarding the 'possession of contraband' argument. The only factual basis for this theory is the statement of Cooksey, whom the police had spoken to only briefly and about whom they knew nothing. Her vague assertion that drugs were sold at 2302 Bleker was lacking in any indicia of reliability. Under the totality of these circumstances, we conclude that Blount's arrest was without probable cause and therefore violated the 4th Amendment."

Search of the Residence

"Finally, we turn to the warrantless search of the residence. The district court found that the search of the residence was justified due to exigent circumstances as a 'protective' sweep incident to lawful arrest. 'Exigent circumstances … do not pass 4th Amendment muster if the officers deliberately create them.' [*] We have already noted the absence of exigent circumstances at the time of the officer's rear window search. The only new circumstances present at the time the house was searched were those created by the agents' persistent efforts to question the defendants and search their house. We restate our conclusion that the district court's ruling on this point constitutes clear error. The 'protective sweep' rationale must also fail in light of the illegality of the arrests.

"Accordingly, all information obtained from the warrantless search of 2302 Bleker must be excised from the warrant affidavit. The information left in the warrant affidavit is insufficient to establish probable cause, and the defendants' convictions are reversed."

6.16   MIDDLETOWN, OHIO v. FLINCHUM (OHIO 2002)
(*Hot Pursuit*)

The defendant spun his tires leaving a traffic light, then accelerated rapidly, made a fishtailing right turn, and accelerated again when officers closed in. The officers did not activate their lights or siren. When they caught up with the vehicle, it was parked in front of the defendant's house and the defendant was standing outside it. When he saw the cruiser, he ran into his house through the back door, with the officers close behind yelling "Stop" and "Police." The officers entered the defendant's home without his permission and arrested him 5 feet inside the doorway on several traffic charges.

- *Is that arrest legal? Explain.*

Middletown, Ohio v. Flinchum (Ohio 2002): 71 CrL 106

The majority quoted the U.S. Supreme Court's statement in *United States v. Santana*, 427 U.S. 38 (1976), that "a suspect may not defeat an arrest which has been set in motion in a public place … by the expedient of escaping to a private place." Although *Santana* dealt with a warrantless felony arrest in a home, the majority saw "no reason to differentiate appellant's offense and give him a free pass merely because he was not charged with a more serious crime." The fact remains that he fled from police in lawful pursuit.

One judge dissented: "[T]he chief evil" at which the 4th Amendment is directed is the physical entry of the home. The dissenting judge said the officers' pursuit was no more than "lukewarm" and that "no recitation of the facts can change the truth that the police officer in this case burst into [the defendant's] home to arrest a mere tire spinner." He warned that as a result of the majority's decision, "we give up part of a right that has been jealously guarded for over 200 years."

chapter 7

Stop and Frisk Exception

We want police to be able to investigate suspected criminal activity in time to prevent it, in time to protect people and property from criminal intrusion if that is possible. The stop and frisk exception to the 4th Amendment protections was created in *Terry v. Ohio,* 392 U.S. 1 (1968), to allow early intervention short of an arrest or full search of a suspect. This kind of investigatory practice can be undertaken when the police do not have probable cause to arrest or search. Lacking probable cause, they nonetheless have facts to support a reasonable suspicion (for a stop) that criminal activity is afoot or (for a frisk) that the person is armed and dangerous. If police have reasonable suspicion that criminal activity is afoot and that the suspect is armed and dangerous, we want them to be able to do an immediate investigation, and we want to try to ensure their safety during that confrontation. With those policy goals in mind, the Court created the stop and frisk exception to the 4th Amendment mandate that we shall neither be seized nor searched without probable cause.

A stop is not an arrest. It is, however, sometimes very difficult to draw the line between the two. Indeed, this might be one of the most difficult factual determinations in criminal procedure. If police have a factual basis to believe that a person is engaged in criminal activity, that person can be detained for a reasonable period while police investigate their reasonable suspicion. The criminal activity that prompts police attention might be activity suggesting a current crime (as in *Terry,* where the suspects' behavior led police to believe suspects were casing a store, planning to rob it), or it might be a past felony or threat to public safety for which the suspect has not been tried or punished.

During a stop, police are entitled to engage in a fairly wide range of investigatory techniques, including, but certainly not limited to, interrogation of the suspect and detention

---

When the appellate court has cited and relied upon a U.S. Supreme Court opinion in reaching its decision, those citations are set out in full so you will know what Supreme Court authority the court relied upon. When you see an asterisk [*] in the court's opinion, that means the appellate court has referenced and relied upon a lower court case in reaching its decision. Those case citations are not included here.

for the purpose of allowing witnesses to make an identification. The detention of the suspect during these investigatory measures might appear to be an "arrest" and that is a common argument made by the defense in these cases. Whether the detention is a stop or an arrest will be measured by reasonableness. It is not simply a matter of time. It is a question of whether the police procedure was reasonable under the circumstances.

If police have facts to support a reasonable suspicion that a person is armed and dangerous, they are entitled to frisk that person. A frisk is not a search. It is a pat-down. If, during that pat-down, police feel a weapon in the suspect's clothing, they are entitled to seize it. This is in keeping with the policy underlying the creation of this exception: We want the police to be able to safely engage in early investigation of criminal behavior.

The purpose of the pat-down is to enable the police to find and seize weapons for their protection. It was not created as a means of allowing a search for evidence without probable cause. If, however, police feel something that is "immediately apparent" to them to be evidence of a crime, they can seize it under the authority of *Minnesota v. Dickerson,* 508 U.S. 366 (1993).

Perhaps in closing this summary it is helpful to consider two observations about the stop and frisk exception. First, stop and frisk are independent and the constitutional requirements for each are different. It is a little like bread and butter; although often found together, they are distinct. It is entirely possible that the facts known to police support a stop, but do not support a frisk of the person suspected of being engaged in criminal activity. In that case, only a stop is constitutionally permitted.

Second, this might well be the exception to 4th Amendment protections that is most often used unconstitutionally. If that is true, it might be true for all of the "right" reasons. It is easy to understand that police might be reluctant to place a suspect who has been stopped (a person who the police have a factual basis for reasonably believing is engaged in criminal activity) in the squad car for questioning without first ensuring that the person is not armed. If that caution prompts police to frisk the person without the requisite reasonable suspicion, factually based, that the person is armed and dangerous, it is an unconstitutional frisk. As the world works, that unconstitutional behavior might be invisible and it might never come to the attention of any court. It is only likely to become a part of a public record if the frisk results in the discovery and seizure of evidence that, at some point, becomes the subject of a motion to suppress. Otherwise, the cautionary and unconstitutional frisk might never be mentioned again. Courts have no direct supervisory power over the police. Courts can only respond to unconstitutional police practices when those practices are brought to the courts' attention, and that typically only happens when police have found and the government seeks to use evidence against the defendant.

7.1   STATE v. DUNCAN (WASH. 2002)
(*Stop and Frisk: Reasonable Suspicion*)

Two Seattle officers on patrol observed three men at a city bus shelter. On the bench was a brown paper bag with a glass bottleneck protruding from the top. In the officers' experience, bottles in paper bags often mean surreptitious consumption or possession of alcohol in public, a violation of the city's code. It is a violation of the civil code, not a criminal offense.

The officers investigated and found a half-empty bottle of beer approximately 6 inches from where the defendant was standing. Each of the three men denied drinking beer, but the bottle felt cold, and one of the officers testified he could smell alcohol on the defendant's breath. That same officer also recognized the defendant from a difficult arrest 9 months earlier in which he had to wrestle the defendant to the ground and relieve him of a firearm. He also recalled that the defendant had an arrest record for violent crimes, including murder. In light of this knowledge, the officer frisked the defendant and discovered a handgun in his waistband. A subsequent search incident to arrest turned up credit cards and a purse that did not belong to the defendant.

- *Was the stop justified? Explain.*
- *Was the frisk justified? Explain.*

State v. Duncan (Wash. 2002): 71 CrL 120

Noncriminal civil infractions, such as possession of an open container of alcohol in public, cannot justify a stop and frisk. Officers must have suspicion concerning criminal offenses.

The state contended that the stop and frisk was permissible as a *Terry* stop. The court disagreed, pointing out that *Terry* requires a reasonable, articulable suspicion, based on specific, objective facts, that the person seized has committed, is committing, or is about to commit a crime. Possessing an open container in public is a noncriminal civil violation of the Seattle code.

The court acknowledged that *Terry* has been applied to stops for noncriminal traffic violations. However, traffic stops are "[e]ssentially the only circumstance where, absent a reasonable articulable suspicion of criminal activity, *Terry* has been applied. The State would have us extend the *Terry* stop exception further to include all civil infractions. We decline to do so."

Reviewing case law, the court noted that the decisions turn on whether the interest in personal privacy is outweighed by public interests such as police officer safety and apprehending wrongdoers. The interest in preventing civil infractions might not deserve the same weight as the interest in arresting felons. In the same vein, the court noted that it has adopted the common law rule requiring a warrant to arrest for a misdemeanor committed outside the presence of the officer. This rule, the court said, "illustrates the higher burden this court imposes upon officers when investigating lesser crimes" and suggests that, given the lower risk to society occasioned by a mere civil infraction, "a less intrusive procedure would be more acceptable than with the commission of a felony or even a misdemeanor."

7.2 COMMONWEALTH v. HUFF (PA.SUPER.CT. 2003)
(*Stop: Reasonable Suspicion*)

An officer observed a female passenger in a car attempting to light a small pipe close to her face in a manner he believed was consistent with lighting a marijuana pipe. The officer based this belief on the proximity of the lighter and the pipe, the way she was holding the pipe, and the fact that the officer did not know "too many women who smoke pipes."

He stopped the car, and the stop led to the discovery of the pipe and marijuana.

- *What is required for a constitutional stop?*
- *Was this stop constitutional? Why?*

Commonwealth v. Huff (Pa.Super.Ct. 2003): 74 CrL 12

An officer's observation of a female passenger in a car attempting to light a small pipe did not provide reasonable suspicion to believe that she was smoking marijuana.

In a previous case [*] this court had found that the possession of a small pipe is not illegal per se and did not, in and of itself, provide probable cause because it could be used for the legal purpose of smoking tobacco.

In this case, the court extended that rule to cover the use of a small pipe as well. The facts that the user was a female and that the officer did not know many women who smoked pipes were "immaterial," the court said.

7.3   RANSOME v. STATE (MD. 2003)
(*Frisk: Reasonable Suspicion*)

Three plainclothes police offices were on patrol at 11:20 p.m. in an unmarked car in an area of Baltimore where the police had received numerous complaints about gunfire, narcotics activity, and loitering. One of the officers saw the defendant talking to another man on the sidewalk and noticed that the defendant had a bulge in his left front pants pocket. The defendant watched the officers as they slowed to a stop and approached him. An officer asked the defendant if they could speak with him, and the defendant stared at him without responding. The officer asked the defendant his name and address, and the officer noticed that when the defendant responded he stopped making eye contact and his voice sounded nervous.

The officer frisked the defendant and detected a soft packet at the defendant's waist that felt like controlled substances. The officer then turned to the pocket where he had seen the bulge and detected something hard. The officer lifted the defendant's shirt and found a plastic bag of marijuana. The pocket turned out to contain a roll of bills.

- *What is the standard that must be met before a frisk is constitutional?*
  - *Make the argument, based on these facts, that the frisk was proper.*
  - *Make the argument, based on these facts, that the frisk was not proper.*
    - *On these facts, what do you conclude?*

Ransome v. State (Md. 2003): 72 CrL 456

The Maryland Supreme Court said the officer needed to explain why he believed the bulge and other circumstances were suspicious. The fact that the defendant seemed nervous when he spoke to the officers was not enough. The majority stressed that the bulge was in the defendant's pocket, not at his waist, and that the officers failed to explain why the circumstances were suspicious.

In *Terry v. Ohio,* 392 U.S. 1 (1968), the U.S. Supreme Court said that "in justifying the particular intrusion the police officer must be able to point to specific and articulable facts which, taken together with rational inferences from those facts, reasonably warrant that intrusion." The majority of the Maryland court concluded that the totality of the circumstances surrounding the stop did not give rise to the reasonable suspicion that the 4th Amendment required to justify the officer's frisk.

Relying on *Pennsylvania v. Mimms,* 434 U.S. 106 (1977), the state argued that the officer's observation of the bulge, by itself, was enough to justify the frisk. The majority, however, "rejecte[ed] the notion that a bulge is a bulge is a bulge is a bulge, no matter where it is, what it looks like, or the circumstances surrounding its observation." The majority explained:

> We accept ... that a noticeable bulge in a man's waist area may well reasonably indicate
> that the man is armed. Ordinarily, men do not stuff bulky objects into the waist areas of
> their trousers and then walk, stand, or drive around in that condition; regrettably, the
> cases that we see tell us that those who go armed do often carry handguns in that fashion.
> We can take judicial notice of the fact, however, that, as most men do not carry purses,
> they, of necessity, carry innocent personal objects in their pants pockets—wallets, money
> clips, keys, change, credit cards, cell phones, cigarettes, and the like—objects that, given
> the immutable law of physics that matter occupies space, will create some sort of bulge.

Noting that *Mimms* involved a large bulge in the waist area of a man who was stopped for a traffic violation, the majority said "[t]o apply *Mimms* ... uncritically to any large bulge in any man's pocket, would allow the police to stop and frisk virtually every man they encounter."

The majority stressed that the officers in this case did not explain why they believed the bulge was a weapon or connected to criminal activity. Unlike defendants in other cases in which observed bulges were held to support a stop or frisk, the defendant here had not committed some other offense, attempted to hide the bulge, or done anything else to attract police attention, the majority said. It pointed out that the officer "never explained why he thought that petitioner's stopping to look at his unmarked car as it slowed down was suspicious or why petitioner's later nervousness or loss of eye contract, as two policed officers accosted him on the street, was suspicious." The majority concluded:

> If the police can stop and frisk any man found on the street at night in a high-crime area
> merely because he has a bulge in his pocket, stops to look at an unmarked car containing
> three un-uniformed men, and then, when those men alight suddenly from the car and ap-
> proach the citizen, acts nervously, there would, indeed, be little 4th Amendment protec-
> tion left for those men who live in or have occasion to visit high-crime areas.

The court acknowledged the rule set out in *United States v. Arvizu,* 534 U.S. 266 (2002), and other cases in which the U.S. Supreme Court has made it clear that courts determining the existence of reasonable suspicion should defer to police expertise. However, the majority explained:

> We understand the conduct that would seem innocent to an average layperson may properly be regarded as suspicious by a trained or experienced officer, but if the officer seeks to justify a 4th Amendment intrusion based on that conduct, the officer ordinarily must offer some explanation of why he or she regarded the conduct as suspicious; otherwise, there is no ability to review the officer's action.

One judge wrote a concurring opinion. She agreed that the officer lacked the justification to conduct a frisk, but she disagreed with the idea that a police officer must spell out why the circumstances surrounding a stop were suspicious. *Terry's* articulable suspicion standard is an objective standard, and "'[a]rticulable' does not mean articulated" she said.

Two judges dissented. They disagreed with the majority's statement that "an officer ordinarily must offer some explanation as to why he or she regarded the conduct as suspicious." The dissenters accused the majority of ignoring the context in which the officers observed the bulge in the defendant's pocket, and they contended that the circumstances provided justification for the frisk.

7.4   UNITED STATES v. TOWNSEND (SIXTH CIR. 2002)
(*Stop*)

Ohio highway patrolmen stopped the defendants' car for speeding on I-70 in the wee hours of the morning. During the stop, the officers questioned the defendants about their itinerary and the purpose of their trip, frisked the defendants, searched the car for weapons, and detained the defendants in a patrol car while a drug-sniffing dog was brought to the scene. The dog's positive alert prompted a search that turned up counterfeit bills hidden inside a CD changer in the trunk of the defendants' car.

The defendants complained that the stop was extended beyond what was required to issue a citation for speeding. The state relied on facially innocent facts that the officers said were indicative of criminal activity when viewed in light of their experience with drug couriers: The defendant who was driving raised his hands in the air and had his documentation ready to give to the officer without being asked; he readily admitted that he was driving faster than the speed the officer told him the police radar had shown; the defendant's statements that he was driving from Chicago to his sister's home in Columbus, Ohio; and the defendant did not know his sister's address, but intended to call her when he arrived in Columbus. Beyond that, the officers noted the presence in the passenger compartment of food wrappers, clothing, three cell phones, and a bible. In addition, one of the defendants had a prior arrest for a weapons offense, and an officer detected during frisks what felt like rolls of bills in the defendants' pockets. The officers also testified that the defendants behaved in a nervous fashion.

The district court suppressed the counterfeit bills, ruling that the officers lacked the reasonable suspicion necessary to detain the defendants for the dog sniff.

- *What is the standard for detaining people as a stop?*
- *Do these facts justify a stop? Explain.*

United States v. Townsend (Sixth Cir. 2002): 72 CrL 25

Law enforcement officers' experience with drug couriers was not enough to make facts that are not facially suspicious sufficient to justify prolonging a traffic stop.

In *United States v. Arvizu*, 534 U.S. 266 (2002), the U.S. Supreme Court reaffirmed its preference for an open-ended "totality of the circumstances" test for determining reasonable suspicion for investigative stops and chastised the Ninth Circuit for instructing courts to assign little or no weight to some factors in analyses of reasonable suspicion.

The court distinguished I-70 from the remote desert road at issue in *Arvizu*. "While it would be erroneous to hold that the defendants' travel plans are not suspicious simply because they are less odd than those in *Arvizu* ... we simply note that traveling from Chicago to Columbus, two large, mutually proximate Midwestern cities, is a more common occurrence."

As for the presence of the cell phones, which the officers said was typical of drug couriers, the court said the district judge did not hold that the presence of cell phones cannot contribute to reasonable suspicion. Rather, the court said, the judge explained that "cellular telephones are so much more common today than in 1992, when they were considered 'tools of the drug trade,' [*] that they are considerably less suspicious." Three cell phones in one car does seem slightly odd, the court admitted, but it decided that this factor "is weak and is not accompanied in this case by more substantially suspicious factors."

The defendants' cooperativeness and the officers' observations of the contents of the car were also properly treated by the district court as weak or very weak indicators of criminal conduct. It emphasized that the officer used the word "unusual" rather than "suspicious" in describing the defendants' cooperativeness. Although the officers attributed the defendants' efforts to expedite the stop to a desire to hide criminal activity, the court approved the district judge's inference that the earliness of the hour of the stop provided another innocent reason to want to speed the completion of the stop.

The officers testified that food wrappers and clothing littering the interior of the car is an indicator of drug trafficking because couriers are reluctant to leave their loads of drugs. The court—apparently requiring the officers to presume the truth of the defendant's assertions about his itinerary—pointed out that "it is not as if the defendants would have had to live in the car for days to drive from Chicago to Columbus. Given the context, the unkempt condition of the car is not terribly suspicious."

The rolls of bills felt during the frisk, which the officers said were indicative of drug trafficking because dealers carry large sums of cash, could just have easily have been rolls of one-dollar bills, the court said. The court also held that the district judge's determination that the officers' testimony regarding the defendants' nervous behavior was not credible was supported by the record. The prior drug arrest, although justifying a frisk and search of the car, carried very little weight once the officers satisfied themselves that the defendants were not armed.

What the officers had left was the defendants' dubious travel plans. The officer testified that they found that the defendant's lack of knowledge of his sister's address, and his asserted plan to call his sister at what would have been 4 or 5 a.m., unlikely and indicative of untruthfulness.

The court acknowledged that, in past cases, it has repeatedly recognized that motorists' far-fetched stories about their travel plans are indicative of criminal activity. It concluded, however, that the defendants' story lacked the indicia of the untruthfulness that the court has held particularly suspicious in the past. Here, both defendants gave the same story about visiting the sister, and the closest the officer came to providing a reason to doubt the story was noting that the trip was occurring in the middle of the night, which is "not inherently suspicious."

Affirming the district judge's ruling that the officers lacked reasonable suspicion to detain the defendants until the canine unit arrived, the court said "this case lacks any of the stronger indicators of criminal conduct that have accompanied these minor factors in other cases."

7.5 GALLEGOS v. LOS ANGELES (NINTH CIR. 2002) (*Stop v. Arrest*)

A woman reported that her father, who was the subject of a protective order, was attempting to break into her house. She described her father as a Hispanic male with a red shirt and blue pants. Police officers in a helicopter spied the plaintiff, wearing a red shirt, getting into a truck across the street. Other officers pulled the plaintiff over after a few miles and transported him back to the scene, where witnesses confirmed that he was not the man sought by police. The detention lasted between 45 minutes and an hour.

The plaintiff filed a civil rights suit, claiming the officers violated his 4th Amendment rights. He conceded that the police possessed the reasonable suspicion required for a stop, but he maintained that the officers' seizure amounted to an arrest requiring probable cause.

In a discovery deposition, the officers admitted to having "arrested" the plaintiff.

- *Did the stop become an arrest? Explain.*

Gallegos v. Los Angeles (Ninth Cir. 2002): 72 Crl 64

Officers were not required to choose the fastest, least intrusive means to dispel suspicion. Police officers with reasonable suspicion to believe that a man they observed was the person described in a broadcast about a burglary did not violate the 4th Amendment by stopping him at gunpoint, handcuffing him, placing him in the back of a patrol car, and driving him back to the scene without even checking his identification.

The majority observed that in past cases it has rejected the notion that circumstances involving officers' use of guns or handcuffs necessarily amount to arrests requiring probable cause. The majority said that the "whole point of an investigatory stop, as the name suggests, is to allow police to *investigate,* in this case to make sure that they have the right person" [emphasis in original]. Under the circumstances, the officers' actions in this case were not unreasonable ways of finding out whether the plaintiff was the person they were seeking.

> [I]t is unfortunate that an innocent man, in the wrong place at the wrong time, was inconvenienced for up to an hour. But by the same token, this investigative stop worked as it should. The detention was brief, calculated solely to make sure they had the right man, and resulted in [the plaintiff's] prompt vindication.

The officers' chosen course of action satisfied the 4th Amendment's requirements that police diligently pursue a means of investigation that is likely to confirm or dispel their suspicions quickly and that proceeds without any unnecessary delay.

The fact that the officers admitted during discovery to having "arrested" the plaintiff does not alter this conclusion. "Whether or not Gallegos' detention on July 4, 1999 was an arrest or an investigatory stop depends on what the officers *did,* not on how they *characterize* what they did" [emphasis in original].

One judge dissented, maintaining that the stop was unreasonable because the officers failed to take quicker and easier steps to confirm or dispel their suspicions, such as checking the plaintiff's identification, questioning him about the incident, or requesting more identifying information from the police dispatcher.

The majority responded to that by saying that the "4th Amendment does not mandate one and only one way for police to confirm the identity of a suspect. It requires that the government and its agents act *reasonably*" [emphasis in original].

7.6   STATE v. DELAROSA (S.D. 2003)
(*Stop: Canine Sniff*)

During a week-long motorcycle rally in Sturgis, South Dakota, the defendants were pulled over for failure to use a turn signal. The trooper who made the stop was on patrol with a drug-detection canine. After running a license and a warrant check, the trooper returned the driver's documentation and issued a warning for the signal violation. The trooper then had the dog sniff the defendant's truck for drugs. The dog alerted to the truck, and a search of personal effects in the truck turned up marijuana and peyote that resulted in drug charges against the defendant.

- *Was the drug dog sniff a "search" in violation of the 4th Amendment? Explain.*
- *Was it constitutional to hold the motorist while the drug dog sniffed the truck after the citation had been given? Explain.*

■ *Should the marijuana and peyote be suppressed?*

   ● *If so, why?*

   ● *If not, what exception to 4th Amendment protections justifies that search and seizure?*

State v. De La Rosa (S.D. 2003): 72 CrL 417

When the officer already has a drug dog with him, South Dakota declares the sniff after a traffic stop is constitutional. Neither the federal nor state constitution is violated "when a motorist's detention at a valid traffic stop is briefly extended for a canine sniff of the vehicle's exterior, when the officer has a drug canine at his immediate disposal." The U.S. Supreme Court held in *United States v. Place,* 462 U.S. 696 (1983), that a dog sniff of luggage in a public place is not a search for which the 4th Amendment requires probable cause. In that case, the Court noted that a dog sniff is limited both in the manner in which the information is obtained and in the content of the information revealed. The Court concluded, however, that the detention of the luggage required to conduct the dog sniff was a limited investigative seizure for which the 4th Amendment required reasonable suspicion.

Since *Place,* courts across the country have disagreed about many issues related to dog sniffs during traffic stops, including whether the sniff of the exterior of a car is a "search" requiring probable cause and whether a sniff extends a stop and transforms it into an arrest.

In this case, the trial court granted the motion to suppress the drugs, but the South Dakota Supreme Court reversed. The court rejected the defendant's argument that the officer needed reasonable suspicion to prolong the stop for the dog sniff. The majority said it would not "dissect the facts into two distinct events, those involving the normal checks of a driver's license and proof of insurance and second, the use of the drug dog to sniff around the exterior of the [d]efendant's vehicle."

The constitutional reasonableness of an extended detention to conduct a canine sniff after completion of a traffic stop depends on a balancing of the public's interest and the individual's right to personal security free from arbitrary interference by law enforcement officers. Weighing those interests in this case, the court concluded:

> Here, the officer had the dog at hand in his vehicle, and the defendants concede the sniffing activity was of a short duration. Had there been no "hits," the delay to the motorists would have been a matter of seconds. We cannot accept the premise that while the State's interest in drug interdiction is compelling, a few seconds delay for non-entry sniffing the exterior of a vehicle by a dog already on the scene is constitutionally unreasonable.

Motorists would be no more inconvenienced or delayed by a dog sniff in this case than they would be by a suspicionless roadblock to detect illegal aliens or verify drivers' licenses—which the U.S. Supreme Court has upheld as constitutional.

The court did not think the timing of the sniff (during the stop while the officer checked the paperwork or immediately thereafter) was significant: "Constitutional rights should be based upon reasonableness of the totality of the government intrusion, rather than a mere bright-line rule based solely upon a timing sequence. Either both must be constitutionally impermissible or both constitutionally permissible."

Note that in 2005 the U.S. Supreme Court held in *Illinois v. Caballes,* 543 U.S. ___ (2005) that a dog sniff conducted during a lawful traffic stop that reveals no information other than the location of a substance that no individual has any right to possess does not violate the 4th Amendment.

7.7   STATE v. WIEGAND (MINN. 2002)
(*Stop: Canine Sniff*)

An officer stopped the defendants for driving with a burned-out headlight. The officer decided to issue a warning and asked another officer to write it up while he walked his drug-detection dog around the defendant's car. The dog alerted three times to an area near the front of the passenger side. The officer searched the car's interior and found nothing. He then lifted the hood and found 4.5 ounces of marijuana. Searches of the defendants incident to their arrest turned up more drugs.

The defendants filed a motion to suppress, arguing that the drug dog sniff was improper as part of the stop.

- ■ *Analyze this. Should the police be able to do a drug dog sniff without any reason? Why?*
- ■ *Should reasonable suspicion be required? Why?*
- ■ *Should probable cause be required? Why?*

State v. Wiegand (Minn. 2002): 71 CrL 381

A police officer cannot have a drug-detection dog sniff the exterior of a vehicle during a routine traffic stop unless the officer has reasonable suspicion to believe that the vehicle contains drugs, according to the Minnesota Supreme Court. A dog sniff impacts on a reasonable expectation of privacy and extends the scope of the traffic stop.

In *United States v. Place,* 462 U.S. 696 (1983), the U.S. Supreme Court held that a dog sniff of luggage in a public place is not a search for which the 4th Amendment requires probable cause. In that case, the Court noted that a dog sniff is limited both in the manner in which the information is obtained and in the content of the information revealed by the procedure. The Court concluded, however, that the detention of the luggage required to conduct the dog sniff was a limited investigative seizure for which the 4th Amendment required reasonable suspicion.

Since *Place* was decided, state and federal courts across the country have disagreed about many issues related to dog sniffs during traffic stops, including whether a sniff constitutes a "search" requiring individualized suspicion and whether a sniff expands the "seizure" attendant to a traffic stop.

In this case, the majority of the Minnesota Supreme Court noted that the *Place* court "explicitly limited its ruling to the exposure of luggage in an airport, a public place, to a dog sniff, which suggests the possibility that a dog sniff under different circumstances might be treated differently." On the other hand, the court conceded that in another Supreme Court case, the Court indicated that the *Place* holding that a dog sniff is not a search would apply to a dog sniff conducted around the exterior of a motor vehicle because "an exterior sniff of an automobile does not require entry into the car and is not designed to disclose any information other than the presence or absence of narcotics," and that "[l]ike the dog sniff in *Place,* a sniff by a dog that simply walks around a car is 'much less intrusive than a typical search.'"

Deciding the case under both the federal and state constitutions, the court here noted that a motorist enjoys only a limited constitutional protection of privacy in automobiles. Nevertheless, the majority concluded:

> A dog sniff around a motor vehicle stopped only for a routine equipment violation is intrusive to some degree. A dog sniff detects something that the public generally cannot detect ... and something that, in this case, was purposefully hidden from view. Given that there is some intrusion into privacy interests by a dog sniff, we hold that an officer cannot conduct a narcotics-detection dog sniff around a motor vehicle stopped for a routine equipment violation without some level of suspicion of illegal activity.

Turning then to the question of how much suspicion is required, the court noted that the Court in *Place* likened the limited intrusion of a dog sniff to an investigative detention pursuant to a *Terry* stop. With this in mind, the court concluded:

> [W]e read *Place* and *Terry* and our recognized, albeit limited, privacy right in a motor vehicle to require a reasonable, articulable suspicion of drug-related criminal activity before law enforcement may conduct a dog sniff around a motor vehicle stopped for a routine equipment violation in an attempt to detect the presence of narcotics.

The majority also said it was basing its decision on the "changed scope of the investigation" in this case. The defendants in this case did not contend that the dog sniff prolonged the traffic stop. However, the court noted that "the reasonableness requirement in the 4th Amendment is not concerned only with the duration of a detention, but also with its scope." The court explained:

> We construe the reasonableness requirement of the 4th Amendment [and the corresponding section of the state constitution] to limit the scope of a *Terry* investigation to that which occasioned the stop, to the limited search for weapons, and to the investigation of only those additional offenses for which the officer develops a reasonable, articulable suspicion within the time necessary to resolve the originally-suspected offense.

"Thus, in order to lawfully conduct a narcotics-detection dog sniff around the exterior of a motor vehicle stopped for a routine equipment violation, a law enforcement officer must have a reasonable, articulable suspicion of drug-related criminal activity." The officers in this case had no such suspicion. The trial judge was correct in suppressing the evidence and dismissing the charges.

One judge submitted a concurring opinion, arguing that a dog sniff is a significant intrusion and should not be done absent probable cause.

7.8   UNITED STATES v. YOUSIF (EIGHTH CIR. 2002) (*Stop/Consent*)

The stop in this case was part of a so-called "ruse checkpoint" or "deceptive checkpoint" conducted by the Missouri Highway Patrol. Pursuant to this program, officers set up signs announcing a nonexistent drug interdiction checkpoint farther down the highway and then stopped cars leaving the highway at the next exit. The exits where the checkpoints were located were chosen for their remoteness and absence of services for motorists.

The defendant in this case pulled off I-44 after passing a ruse drug checkpoint sign. When he saw the uniformed officers and vehicles, he stopped halfway up the ramp and had to be waved on by one of the officers. The defendant had out-of-state plates on his car. During the stop, the defendant consented to a search that turned up evidence of a large quantity of marijuana.

- *Make the argument(s) that this is a proper stop.*
- *Make the argument(s) that this is not a proper stop.*
- *Which do you find more persuasive? Why?*
- *Was the defendant's consent to search good? Explain*

United States v. Yousif (Eighth Cir. 2002): 72 CrL 44

A defendant's act of exiting from a highway after passing a sign announcing a drug interdiction checkpoint did not, even when combined with other factors, give rise to the reasonable suspicion required by the 4th Amendment for a vehicle stop. The defendant's consent to a search during the stop was involuntary and the court suggested that consent to search in such circumstances will rarely be valid.

The checkpoint program was conducted prior to the U.S. Supreme Court's decision in *Indianapolis, Ind. v. Edmond*, 531 U.S. 32 (2000), that the 4th Amendment does not permit suspicious roadblocks conducted for the primary purpose of drug interdiction. After *Edmond,* the Missouri Supreme Court held [*] that a deceptive checkpoint scheme is fundamentally different from the actual drug checkpoint scheme struck down in *Edmond,* on the ground that a driver's decision to exit after passing a checkpoint sign generates the reasonable suspicion required by the 4th Amendment to justify an investigatory stop. Other courts disagree about the constitutionality of ruse checkpoint stops [*].

The court here rejected the purported suspiciousness of facts that the defendant's car had out-of-state plates and that drug couriers use I-44 in Missouri as a smuggling route. These facts apply to too many people to provide reasonable suspicion for a stop.

"As to the additional facts that [the defendant] took an exit just past the ruse checkpoint warning signs and then slowed down upon observing the actual checkpoint, we are chary to conclude that these provide sufficient additional circumstances to justify the intrusion." After emphasizing that "these circumstances never would have arisen but for the existence of the illegal checkpoint," the majority concluded that,

> because there is nothing inherently unlawful or suspicious about a vehicle (even one with
> out-of-state plates) exiting the highway, it should not be the case that the placement of

signs by the police in front of the exit ramp transforms that facially innocent behavior into grounds for suspecting criminal activity …. Reasonable suspicion cannot be manufactured by the police themselves.

While the checkpoint at issue in the present case differs from the checkpoint at issue in *Edmond* in that the MHP used signs to suggest to drivers that taking the Sugar Tree Road exit was a way to *avoid* a police checkpoint, the mere fact that some vehicles took the exit under such circumstances does not, in our opinion, create individualized reasonable suspicion of illegal activity as to every one of them. Indeed, as the government's evidence indicated, while some drivers may have wanted to avoid being caught for drug trafficking, many more took the exit for wholly innocent reasons—such as wanting to avoid the inconvenience and delay of being stopped or because it was part of their intended route [emphasis in original].

The Eighth Circuit was not impressed with data the state argued suggested the success of these ruse checkpoints. The court pointed out that of the 2,537 vehicles stopped at the checkpoint during a random sample of 54 days, only 1,644 (less than half), were driven by people not engaged in local traffic. Although the 644 stops yielded 501 arrests, only 42 loads of controlled substances in amounts apparently intended for distribution were discovered.

As for the defendant's stopping halfway up the exit ramp, the majority said that, because the checkpoint was not where the police signs indicated it would be, "any motorist would likely be surprised upon discovering it" and might be "inclined to hesitate out of surprise, annoyance, or nervousness." Accordingly, it distinguished the defendant's "hesitancy" from the "unprovoked flight" found adequate to provide reasonable suspicion in *Illinois v. Wardlow,* 528 U.S. 119 (2000).

The government argued that, even if the initial seizure of the defendant was not supported by reasonable suspicion as required by the 4th Amendment, the district court's finding that the defendant's consent was voluntary provided an independent basis for admitting the evidence of the drugs at the defendant's trial. The Eighth Circuit disagreed. The court employed the balancing test set out in *Brown v. Illinois,* 443 U.S. 590 (1975), which looks at (1) the temporal proximity between the illegal search or seizure and the consent, (2) the presence of intervening circumstances, and (3) the purpose and flagrancy of the official misconduct.

The majority noted that little time elapsed and no significant intervening event occurred between the stop and the officer's request for consent. The majority reiterated that the checkpoint program itself was unconstitutional and pointed out that the officers clearly exploited the illegal stop, even if they did not know the stop was illegal at the time. The trial court clearly erred in ruling the consent voluntary.

One judge dissented, arguing that the defendant's consent to search was voluntary.

7.9   STATE v. LOFFER (OHIO CT.APP. 2003)
(*Frisk: Plain Feel*)

An officer made a traffic stop of a suspected drug dealer. During the course of that stop, he frisked the driver. The officer felt loose pills in two places on the defendant and pulled them out.

The officer testified that he had probable cause to believe that the pills were illicit before he pulled them out of the suspect's jacket. He testified that in other investigations he had encountered loose pills that turned out to be illicit and that an informer had reported that the defendant in this case was a drug trafficker, specifically that the informant had purchased drugs from the defendant. The officer testified that it was immediately apparent to him that what he felt was pills, and it was not necessary for him to manipulate the objects to make that determination.

- *What is the test for a "plain feel" seizure?*
- *Was this a constitutional seizure under that test? Why?*

State v. Loffer (Ohio Ct.App. 2003): 74 CrL 14

The court held that the officer had probable cause to seize the pills under the 4th Amendment's plain feel doctrine as set out in *Minnesota v. Dickerson*, 508 U.S. 366 (1993).

The presence of the loose pills, combined with the knowledge that the defendant was a suspected drug trafficker, made the illicit nature of the pills apparent to the officer and gave him probable cause to seize them. Although the case was a "close call," the fact that the information about the defendant came from someone who purchased drugs from the defendant was significant. That, combined with the officer's detection of loose pills in two places on the defendant, was enough to enable the officer to possess a reasonable belief that the pills were illicit and justify their seizure.

7.10   MURPHY v. COMMONWEALTH (VA. 2002)
(*Frisk: Plain Feel*)

Police obtained a warrant to search a residence for drugs and items connected with drug sales, as well as one named individual. The defendant, who was not the person named, was on the scene when the warrant was executed. An officer conducted a weapons frisk and felt a bulge in the front pocket of the defendant's pants that he sensed was a plastic baggie. On the basis of his training and experience, the officer concluded that the baggie contained marijuana. The officer's retrieval of the baggie led to the defendant's arrest for marijuana possession, and a further search yielded other drugs.

The defendant was convicted on heroin and cocaine charges. He appealed, arguing that the character of the plastic bag's contents as contraband was not "immediately apparent" from the frisk, and that the officer therefore lacked probable cause to seize the bag.

- *To seize the baggie, was it necessary that the contents of it be "immediately apparent" to the officer? Explain.*
- *Were the contents "immediately apparent" when the officer felt the baggie? Explain.*
- *Is this seizure constitutional under the "plain feel" rule created by the Court?*

Murphy v. Commonwealth (Va. 2002): 72 CrL 122

An officer's detection of a plastic baggie during a lawful pat-down is not sufficient to justify a seizure of the baggie when it is the officer's experience and training, rather than the feel of the object, that leads the officer to believe the baggie contains contraband. The illegal nature of the object must be immediately apparent. Detection of the baggie during a pat-down did not permit seizure on plain feel theory.

Under the plain feel doctrine articulated in *Minnesota v. Dickerson,* 508 U.S. 366 (1993), an officer who, in lawfully patting down a suspect's outer clothing, feels an object with a contour or mass that makes its identity as contraband immediately apparent can seize the object without violating the 4th Amendment. In such a case, the Supreme Court reasoned, "there has been no invasion of the suspect's privacy beyond that already authorized by the officer's search for weapons." However, when the character of the item is not immediately apparent and the officer does not reasonably suspect that the item is a weapon, a further search of the item is unrelated to the justification for the frisk and, therefore, is not allowed.

The court in this case assumed without deciding that the execution of the search warrant permitted the officer to conduct a protective search of the defendant. However, the court concluded, the officer's actions exceeded the permissible scope of the pat-down.

The officer's testimony was a key factor in the court's decision. Significantly, the officer did not testify that he sensed from touching the defendant's pocket that the item he felt was a weapon; nor did he state that the character of the object as marijuana was immediately apparent to him. Instead, the officer testified only that it was immediately apparent that the pocket contained a plastic bag and that he knew from his training and experience that plastic bags are often used to package marijuana.

The information the officer had was insufficient under *Dickerson* to establish grounds for searching the defendant's pocket because the officer's conclusion about the contents of the bag was not based on his tactile perception of the bag's contents. The officer lacked probable cause to seize the bag from the defendant's pocket because the character of the bag's contents as contraband was not immediately apparent from the frisk.

It did not matter that the defendant was found in a residence that was the subject of a search warrant for illegal drugs. That fact contributed nothing to the probable cause equation in the absence of evidence linking the defendant to the suspected presence of the drugs sought under the warrant.

Other state courts have reached similar conclusions. For example, the Missouri Supreme Court held [*] that what an officer knew from his training and experience about crack dealers' penchant for carrying their wares in a particular kind of candy container did not justify seizure of such a container from a defendant's pocket.

Search Incident to Arrest

When the police make a lawful, custodial arrest, they are entitled to search the person arrested. This is a full search, for both weapons and evidence. It does not require search probable cause. It is a "free" search in that regard, constitutionally governed only by reasonableness.

The theory behind the search incident to arrest exception to 4th Amendment protections is simple: It is reasonable to believe that when a person is placed under arrest, that person, if armed, might seek to harm the police—hence it is reasonable to search for weapons. It is also reasonable to believe that when a person is placed under arrest, that person, if carrying evidence of crime, might seek to destroy it or otherwise get rid of it—hence it is reasonable to search for evidence. Although the search incident to arrest does not require search probable cause and although there are instances in which we allow a search incident to arrest to precede the arrest, it is absolutely clear that the product of the search incident to arrest cannot become the probable cause for the arrest. The search incident to arrest is only constitutional if it accompanies a lawful, custodial arrest—that is, an arrest for which there is good probable cause and an arrest that is custodial and not merely a detention for purposes of giving a traffic citation or doing a *Terry* investigation.

After the requisite lawful, custodial arrest has been made, there are two issues that arise with respect to a search incident to arrest. One is the scope of the arrest: How far beyond the person, if at all, are police entitled to search incident to the person's arrest? Police are entitled to search the person and that area within his or her immediate control. The rule reflects recognition that if a person under arrest has a weapon close at hand (e.g., in the desk drawer or under the seat of the car), the person might be inclined to use that weapon

---

When the appellate court has cited and relied upon a U.S. Supreme Court opinion in reaching its decision, those citations are set out in full so you will know what Supreme Court authority the court relied upon. When you see an asterisk [*] in the court's opinion, that means the appellate court has referenced and relied upon a lower court case in reaching its decision. Those case citations are not included here.

against the police, hence it is reasonable to allow the police to discover that weapon and seize it before it can be used against them. Likewise, police are entitled to secure evidence that is within reach of the arrestee. The "area of immediate control" is a term of art and its interpretation in any given set of facts will be governed by reasonableness.

The second issue that arises in a search incident to arrest is intensity: How intrusive can this search be? The search incident to arrest is a full search, not limited to outer clothing, and it is designed to protect the police and to protect evidence. Those policy considerations suggest that, as we apply the constitutional standard of reasonableness, we should not be too narrow or restrictive in our application.

The most recent expansion to the search incident to arrest is the protective sweep, created by the U.S. Supreme Court in *Maryland v. Buie,* 494 U.S. 325 (1990), allowing a "properly limited" sweep of the property when the police have a reasonable belief, factually based, that someone might be on the premises who could pose a danger to the police. In *Buie,* police suspected a co-defendant, but the danger to police could come as reasonably from a friend or family member. If the facts justify a protective sweep, police are entitled to search the property for a person or people who might constitute a threat to them; they are only entitled to look in places where a person might reasonably be found.

8.1   UNITED STATES v. BOOKHARDT (D.C.CIR. 2002) *(Search Incident to Arrest)*

A police detective in an unmarked car observed the defendant driving recklessly on an expressway and decided to pull him over only after the defendant took the detective's exit. A check of the defendant's driver's license revealed that it had expired a month earlier. The officer told the defendant he was being arrested for driving on an expired license, searched the defendant's car incident to the arrest, and found guns that the government relied on to charge the defendant with a federal firearms offense.

Under local law, the license violation does not become an arrestable offense until after 3 months have passed. A district court ordered the guns suppressed, relying on *Knowles v. Iowa,* 525 U.S. 113 (1998), in which the U.S. Supreme Court rejected a "search incident to citation" exception to the 4th Amendment's probable cause requirement.

- *For what crime(s) did the officer have probable cause to arrest the defendant?*
  - *If the officer had probable cause to arrest the defendant for more than one offense, how does that play into the search incident to arrest analysis?*

United States v. Blookhardt (D.C.Cir. 2002): 70 CrL 390

A police officer with probable cause to believe that a suspect has committed both an arrestable and a nonarrestable offense does not violate the 4th Amendment by conducting a search incident to arrest after arresting the defendant for the nonarrestable offense.

The appeals court reversed the suppression order. The court observed that reckless driving is an arrestable offense and said the question to be answered in this case is "whether, if a police officer arrests a defendant on a ground that proves invalid, the arrest is nonetheless lawful if the same officer had probable cause to arrest the defendant for a different offense."

The court explained that "the key point" in *Knowles v. Iowa,* 525 U.S. 113 (1998), was that the justifications for the search incident to arrest exception do not come into play unless the defendant is actually arrested. In contrast, "[w]hen an officer does take a defendant into custody, the historical justifications for the search incident to arrest exception apply regardless of whether the officer articulates the wrong reason for making the arrest."

This case is governed by *Whren v. United States,* 517 U.S. 806 (1996), in which the Supreme Court held that an officer's subjective motivations for making a pretextual stop do not invalidate the stop so long as it is supported by probable cause. It does not matter that the officer in this case was making a mistake rather than a pretextual stop, the court decided. "We fail to see ... why the police should be in a better position if they prevaricate about the reason for arresting a defendant than if they make an honest mistake of law. As long as [the detective] had an objectively valid ground upon which to arrest [the defendant], the fact that he articulated an invalid one does not render the arrest unlawful."

8.2   STATE v. HARDAWAY (MONT. 2001)
(*Search Incident to Arrest/Federalism*)

Blood found at the scene of a burglary suggested that the perpetrator had cut his hand while breaking a window. The defendant was arrested after being stopped by an officer who noticed that he matched a description of the perpetrator and that he had fresh wounds on his hands. The officer frisked the defendant and transported him to a detention facility, where the blood on his hands was photographed and swabbed for testing. The test results were used to convict the defendant.

- *Was taking a swab of blood a "search" for 4th Amendment purposes? Explain.*
- *If this was a search, was this a constitutional search incident to the defendant's arrest? Explain.*

State v. Hardaway (Mont. 2001): 70 CrL 258

The majority confirmed that, like a fingernail scraping at issue in *Cupp v. Murphy,* 412 U.S. 291 (1973), the swabbing and testing of the defendant's hands constituted a "search." There was "little doubt" that the search in this case would fall within the search incident exception to the 4th Amendment warrant requirement as interpreted in *United States v. Robinson,* 414 U.S. 218 (1973).

Swabbing blood detected on an arrestee's hands for testing to match it to blood found at the scene of a crime did not fall within the search incident to arrest exception to the Montana constitution's warrant requirement, however. That requirement is stricter than the federal requirement. The defendant was in custody, and the officers could have bagged his hands and kept him under surveillance while a warrant was obtained, the majority noted. It also said that the photographs of the defendant's hands sufficed to preserve evidence of the presence of blood on his hands.

Two judges concurred in the decision. One disagreed with the majority's conclusion that the warrantless swabbing of the defendant's hands was permissible under the 4th Amendment. The other added that the warrantless swabbing was not conducted at the time of arrest as required by a state statute.

One judge dissented, arguing that swabbing should be treated like photographing.

8.3   UNITED STATES v. TOBON-SIERRA (D.C.N.Y. 1997)
(Search Incident to Arrest)

Tobon arranged to purchase cocaine from a confidential informer at a McDonald's restaurant. While DEA agents watched, the pair met and were joined at various times by others. One member of the party left and then returned, followed by the defendant, who was driving a Buick. The informer left the restaurant and spoke to the defendant. Soon afterward, the DEA agents began to arrest the conspirators. Two or three agents wearing identifying jackets approached the Buick from behind. The defendant turned around in the car, looked out the rear window, and then immediately moved to the passenger side and exited the Buick. He began moving "quickly" away from the Buick. He was stopped and arrested some distance from the car—"approximately 5 feet" away according to the agents, "probably more than 5 feet" according to the defendant.

After the defendant was arrested and handcuffed, an agent immediately searched the Buick and found a hidden compartment above the glove compartment in the dashboard. Another agent found a calculator and a scale in the glove compartment. The agents impounded the car. The glove compartment was later found to contain traces of cocaine.

The defendant moved to suppress the physical evidence discovered during the search of the car, arguing that it was not a proper search incident to arrest because he was not an occupant of his vehicle when he was arrested.

- *What is the purpose of allowing a search incident to arrest?*
- *Does it matter here that the defendant was not actually in the car that was searched at the time of his arrest?*
- *Was this a proper search incident to arrest? Explain.*

United States v. Tobon-Sierra (D.C.N.Y. 1997): 60 CrL 1425

In *Chimel v. California,* 395 U.S. 752 (1969), the U.S. Supreme Court held that when a police officer lawfully arrests a suspect, that officer can conduct a search of the suspect and the area within the suspect's immediate control. This rule ensures the protection of law enforcement officials by removing any weapons the suspect might have and prevents the destruction of evidence. In *New York v. Belton,* 453 U.S. 454 (1981), the Court developed the general rule that "when a policeman has made a lawful custodial arrest of the occupant of an automobile, he may, as a contemporaneous incident of that arrest, search the passenger compartment of that automobile." The search may extend to any containers, open or closed, found within the passenger compartment, including glove compartments.

Courts have consistently held that the defendant need not be in the car when the search is conducted [*].

If the agents had arrested the defendant while he was still sitting in the Buick, removed him, and then searched the Buick, the search would clearly be covered by the *Belton* rule. Instead, the defendant left the car when he knew that the DEA agents, who were clearly identified by their jackets, were closing in on him. Under both scenarios, however, the defendant left his car as the result of contact initiated by law enforcement officers. There is no reason why a search that is permitted when the officers make it to the car window to ask the defendant to get out of the car should not be permitted when the officers' approach to the vehicle prompts a swift-moving defendant to exit in an attempt to escape. In both instances, the defendant was in the vehicle immediately prior to being apprehended, thus establishing that he had access to the "grab" area inside the car. In [*] the Sixth Circuit said, "Where the officer initiates contact with the defendant, either by actually confronting the defendant or by signaling confrontation with the defendant, while the defendant is still in the automobile, and the officer subsequently arrests the defendant (regardless of whether the defendant has been removed from or has exited the automobile), a subsequent search of the automobile's passenger compartment [is] reasonable." The court contrasted such a situation to that "where the defendant has voluntarily exited the automobile and begun walking away from the automobile before the officer has initiated contact with him."

Agents were entitled to search the glove compartment. Once they found a hidden compartment, a calculator, and a scale in their initial search, they had probable cause to impound the vehicle for the subsequent drug testing.

8.4   STATE v. WELLS (UTAH CT.APP. 1996)
(Search Incident to Arrest: Scope of Search)

Police officers went to the home of Stephen Wells to execute drug-related arrest warrants for Wells and his girlfriend. Detective Russo, who knew Wells, stayed out of view while another officer knocked on a sliding glass door. When the defendant appeared, the officer asked if he was Steve Wells; the defendant replied, "No Steve is here." Detective Russo then identified the defendant, who recognized Russo and immediately ran downstairs. When Wells refused to open the door, the officers entered by force. Wells was arrested at the bottom of the stairs; his girlfriend was found hiding in a downstairs closet and was arrested. While sitting with the girlfriend in a bedroom adjacent to where she was arrested, an officer observed a baggie of marijuana and two marijuana pipes. He then asked her "where the cocaine was" and she replied that Wells had hidden cocaine in the lining of a jacket lying on a bed. Russo recognized the jacket as one belonging to Wells. The officers retrieved the cocaine from the jacket lining.

According to Russo, the basement was divided into three adjoining rooms and the defendant was "down in the basement just several feet from us" at the time of the seizure. The record reflects that at the time the cocaine was seized, both defendants were handcuffed and in custody. The record further reflects that after the arrests, but before the search, officers had done a protective sweep of the home and knew that only the appellant and his girl-friend were present.

- *Was the seizure of cocaine within the scope of the search incident to arrest? Explain.*

State v. Wells (Utah Ct.App. 1996): 60 CrL 1277

The state argued that officers had not determined whether third persons were in the home until after the arrests were made. The officers, however, never indicated any belief that oth-ers inside or outside the home were likely to seize the contraband. The state had to show more than a mere possibility that evidence might be removed [*]. The state failed to pre-sent evidence "that even intimated that the officers reasonably believed that destruction, re-moval or concealment of contraband material was imminent or threatened" [*].

Alternatively, the state argued the cocaine was lawfully seized incident to Wells' law-ful arrest. Under the search incident to arrest exception in *Chimel v. California*, 395 U.S. 752 (1969), an officer may search the area within the arrestee's "immediate control" to prevent the arrestee from obtaining weapons or destroying evidence. The Court relied on the fol-lowing factors to determine if items seized were within a defendant's control: (1) whether or not the arrestee was placed in some form of restraints; (2) the position of the officer vis-à-vis the defendant in relation to the place searched; (3) the ease or difficulty of gaining ac-cess to the searched area or item; and (4) the number of officers present in relation to the number of arrestees or other persons.

Applying the relevant factors to the facts of the present case demonstrates that the co-caine in the jacket's lining was not within the appellant's control. First, the appellant was in handcuffs when the search took place. Second, in determining the officers' and appellant's proximity to the item searched, the state relied on one officer's testimony that the appellant was in the basement "several feet away." Taken in the context of the officer's entire response, this testimony is too ambiguous to support the search. In response to a question asking where the appellant was as the two officers searched the jacket, Russo initially replied, "I can't tell you for sure," before he stated the appellant was "several feet" away in the base-ment. More important, the officer's testimony never defines "several feet" more accurately, and "in the basement" was not defined to mean within the same room, in an adjoining room, or in the hallway. Several feet could mean 3 or 20. Furthermore, the two police offi-cers were between the appellant and the jacket.

Another factor supporting the court's conclusion was the appellant's relative difficulty in accessing the evidence—in a different room and in the lining of the jacket. It is difficult to see how the appellant could gain access to the evidence to destroy it while handcuffed with two police officers between him and the evidence.

Additionally, there were four police officers at the appellant's home when the search took place. After the arrests but before the search, officers had done a protective sweep of the home and knew that only the appellant and his girlfriend were present. Moreover, there was no evidence of any safety concerns as to the jacket and no evidence that the appellant had requested to wear the jacket or take it with him, or had made any motion toward the jacket.

8.5 STATE v. SPENCER (CONN. 2004)
(*Search Incident to Arrest: Protective Sweep*)

Officers conducted a controlled delivery of a Federal Express package containing marijuana that was addressed to a house that contained several apartments. The defendant answered the door and said he would accept the package on behalf of the addressee. When the defendant started to leave the building without the package, an arrest team moved in and brought the defendant into the first-floor common hallway. From there, they could see that the defendant's second-floor apartment door was ajar.

The defendant said he did not know the addressee of the package or the package's contents and that he accepted it merely as a courtesy. He did not respond when he was asked if there was anyone in his apartment. The officers then entered the defendant's apartment and observed a crack pipe in plain view.

The defendant argued that there was no justification for the officers to enter his home and that the drug evidence was therefore not admissible in court.

- *Was this a constitutional protective sweep? Explain your thinking.*

State v. Spencer (Conn. 2004): 75 CrL 6

The protective sweep doctrine established in *Maryland v. Buie,* 494 U.S. 325 (1990), which allows police officers to make a warrantless sweep of a residence to protect themselves from danger, applies even when the arrest giving rise to officers' safety concerns was made without a warrant and even when the arrest occurs outside of the residence. The court held, however, that the sweep in this case was not based on articulable facts supporting a reasonable concern for officer safety.

In *Buie,* officers were in a home to execute an arrest warrant. The *Buie* court relied on the officer safety rationale expressed in *Terry v. Ohio,* 392 U.S. 1 (1968), and *Michigan v. Long,* 463 U.S. 1032 (1983), to authorize officers' cursory search of areas of the home that might harbor dangerous persons. The *Buie* court said:

> [A]s an incident to the arrest the officers could, as a precautionary matter and without probable cause or reasonable suspicion, look in closets and other spaces immediately adjoining the place of arrest from which an attack could be immediately launched. Beyond that, however, we hold that there must be articulable facts which, taken together with the rational inferences from those facts, would warrant a reasonably prudent officer in believing that the area to be swept harbors an individual posing a danger to those on the arrest scene.

Courts disagree as to whether an arrest is a prerequisite to a *Buie* sweep [*]. In the instant case, the Connecticut court framed the questions before it as whether an arrest warrant is a prerequisite for a sweep and whether a sweep is justifiable when the arrest takes place outside of the arrestee's home.

The court rejected a per se rule that protective sweeps are unreasonable when incident to a warrantless arrest. The court noted that the federal courts that have addressed the issue uniformly have held that *Buie* applies to warrantless arrests. It added that officer safety interests are no less weighty when a suspect is arrested without a warrant. Nor does the fact that the arrest occurred just outside the home preclude a sweep, because dangerous persons could easily emerge from the home to attack the arresting officers.

Here, however, the court said the warrantless search of the defendant's apartment could not be justified. The court read *Buie* as authorizing two tiers or searches: (1) sweeps of the area immediately surrounding arrestees, and (2) sweeps of areas beyond those spaces immediately adjoining the place of arrest. To satisfy the 4th Amendment, the court said, a second-tier protective sweep must, in *Buie's* words, be supported by "articulable facts which, taken together with the rational inferences from those facts, would warrant a reasonably prudent officer in believing that the area to be swept harbors an individual posing a danger to those on the arrest scene."

The search in the instant case was a second-tier sweep because the search included the defendant's apartment one floor up from the scene of the arrest. The officers here, however, lacked the factual basis required to support their protective sweep.

The court stressed that the officers testified that they were unaware of whether the defendant had any accomplices and that their investigation revealed no persons living in the building who might have been armed or involved in the drug trade. The court added that the defendant's failure to respond to the officers' questions as to the presence of anyone in his apartment might have stemmed from a desire to invoke his rights under *Miranda v. Arizona*, 384 U.S. 436 (1966).

The generalized possibility that an unknown, armed person might have been lurking nearby did not constitute an articulable fact sufficient to justify a protective sweep. The court said that allowing a warrantless search of home on the basis of officers' lack of information about dangers would encourage officers to remain ignorant of the facts when faced with the possibility of an arrest inside or just outside of a home.

The court concluded that the search of the defendant's home was not justifiable under *Buie* and that the evidence gained therefrom had to be suppressed.

One judge dissented, arguing that the majority wrongly focused on what the officers did not know, when focusing on what they did know permitted a reasonable inference that a person posing a danger to the officers could have been hiding behind the partly open apartment door. The officers possessed knowledge sufficient to justify a sweep under the second tier of *Buie* according to the dissent.

c h a p t e r   *9*

Consent Exception

The constitution guarantees that the government will not search us, nor will it search our property or effects without probable cause and (preferably) a warrant. We are entitled to give up those protections and consent to a search without probable cause or a warrant, and we do that in remarkable numbers. The consent search may well be the backbone of criminal investigation; indeed, Dressler and Thomas (1999: 314, n. 1) reported that "as many as 98 percent of warrantless searches" are consent searches. More cases are included in this section than in others, reflecting the reliance placed on this exception by police.

Two things are required for a good consent: The person giving consent must have requisite authority over the property or place to be searched to justify giving consent to its search, and the consent must be voluntary.

Authority to consent to search is not simply a matter of ownership. The owner of property most likely is entitled to consent to its search, but ownership is not determinative and others might also have authority to give consent. If we give possession of our property to another, an argument can be made that we have assumed the risk that the holder will examine the property and allow others, including the government, to search it as well. The contrary argument is that we retain an expectation of privacy, an expectation that just because someone else is in control of our property, it is not reasonable to think they would search it or allow someone else to do so. Each of those philosophical positions is a legitimate one and courts are split on whether one is more constitutionally acceptable than the other.

A doctrine of apparent authority was developed, set out most clearly in *Illinois v. Rodriguez,* 497 U.S. 177 (1990), allowing police to rely on consent of a person that police

---

When the appellate court has cited and relied upon a U.S. Supreme Court opinion in reaching its decision, those citations are set out in full so you will know what Supreme Court authority the court relied upon. When you see an asterisk [*] in the court's opinion, that means the appellate court has referenced and relied upon a lower court case in reaching its decision. Those case citations are not included here.

reasonably, but mistakenly, believe has the authority to consent to a search. The doctrine of apparent authority essentially allows the government to use the evidentiary products of a search that was conducted without probable cause and without authoritative consent of the person who actually controls the property if, under the circumstances, it was reasonable for the police to believe that the person who gave consent was entitled to do so.

Whether one has authority to consent to a search is often hotly contested. It is well established that co-tenants can consent to search of any common area in the home that is shared. That authority is not grounded on mutual access to the property; it is grounded instead on a more restrictive standard of "mutual use" of the property, as stated in *United States v. Matlock,* 415 U.S. 164 (1977).

The second requirement for a constitutional consent is a voluntary consent. The Court made it clear in *Schneckloth v. Bustamonte,* 412 U.S. 218 (1973), that consent may be voluntary even though the person did not know that he she was not required to cooperate with the officers and give consent; that is, the waiver of constitutional rights in this case need not be a "knowing" waiver. Consent in this context means that police cannot coerce the consent by making promises or threats to induce it.

If the facts demonstrate that the person giving consent to search had the authority to do so and gave consent voluntarily, the last issue that is commonly encountered in consent cases focuses on the scope of the consent given relative to the scope of the search conducted. That is, did the police search areas or items that they did not have permission to search?

Cases focusing on authority to consent and scope of the consent are emphasized in this section.

9.1   MAXWELL v. STATE (TEX.CRIM.APP. 2002) (*Consent: Authority*)

Police pulled over a tractor-trailer rig for following too closely. An officer asked the driver to get out of the cab and asked for his commercial license, registration, bill of lading, and log book. The driver told the officer that the defendant, the rig's owner and the driver's employer, was in the cab's passenger seat. The officer then obtained permission from the driver to inspect the trailer. The defendant moved to suppress the marijuana found behind a load of limes on the ground that the officer knew that the defendant had a superior property interest in the vehicle and should have obtained consent from him.

- *Did the driver have authority to consent to the search? Explain.*
- *Was this a constitutional consent search? Explain.*

Maxwell v. State (Tex.Crim.App. 2002): 71 CrL 130

A third party can properly consent to a search of a vehicle over which he or she shares equal control with the owner despite the presence of the owner and the owner's superior property interest.

A legal property interest is not dispositive in determining whether a third party has the authority to consent to a search. Instead, common authority derives from the mutual use of the property. Others with an equal or greater interest in the property assume the risk that, through the grant of permission to use, the third party might permit the property to be searched. The defendant conceded mutual use and control at the suppression hearing when he testified that when the rig is in operation, the driver is "in charge of the truck." It was therefore reasonable for the officer to believe that the driver, as the defendant's employee, had mutual control of the rig and authority to consent to the search, and the defendant's superior property interest did not give him a superior privacy interest.

9.2   STATE v. WEST (GA.CT.APP. 1999)
(*Consent: Authority*)

A mother's 19-year-old son resided rent-free in her home. Police asked the mother if they could search the home after receiving a tip that the son was growing marijuana there. The mother, who owned the house along with the defendant's stepfather, enthusiastically agreed to root out any contraband that might be on the premises. The stepfather gave police a key to unlock the bedroom door. Once inside, police found marijuana plants. The son argued that the marijuana should have been suppressed, on the ground that his mother did not have authority to consent to a search of his room.

- *What test do you use to decide whether this consent search was constitutional?*
  - *Common authority?*
  - *Other?*
- *If you use a common authority analysis, what do you conclude?*
- *If you do not use that doctrine, what do you conclude?*
- *What is your final conclusion? Why?*

State v. West (Ga.Ct.App. 1999): 65 CrL 72

Permission to search can be obtained by anyone who has "common authority" over a premises or "other sufficient relationship" to it. The common authority idea is not applicable in this case, however. The court framed the issue as whether a resident homeowner has authority to permit a search of her own home, including an adult child's bedroom that he is permitted to use for free. As owner and authority figure, the mother possessed a sufficient relationship to the home to allow the search. Concepts such as access and mutual use, which are relevant in a common authority analysis, are not relevant here, so it did not matter that the son locked the bedroom door, or whether the mother had been reluctant to breach his assertion of privacy. The mother had the right to enter the room, and properly assigned that right to police.

Dissenting judges believed the nature of the familial relationship dictated a common authority analysis, under which the mother did not have sufficient use of or access to the room to have authority to consent to its use.

9.3   STATE v. BRAUCH (IDAHO 1999)
(*Consent: Authority*)

Assume that circumstances indicate to a reasonable person that the tenant has abandoned the apartment or house that he had rented.

- *Can a landlord consent to search of a tenant's apartment or house when the circumstances indicate to a reasonable person that the tenant has in fact abandoned the premises?*
  - *If not, why not? Explain fully.*
  - *If so, what circumstances or facts would have to be present to permit that result? Be specific in the examples you offer.*

State v. Brauch (Idaho 1999): 65 CrL 511

According to the Idaho Supreme Court, "a landlord has apparent authority to consent to a search where the totality of the circumstances indicates to a reasonable person that the tenant has in fact abandoned the premises."

Indicators of abandonment "may include nonpayment of rent, removal of furniture, clothes, foodstuffs, and personal items, nonpayment or disconnection of utilities, statements to landlords or neighbors, and any other acts inconsistent with a tenant's control or occupation of the leased premises." However, nonpayment of rent is not enough by itself, the court said.

In the instant case, the owner of a house rented by the defendant told officers that the tenants had moved out, that there was no furniture or goods inside, that she was cleaning the house for sale or re-rent, that she had come across suspicious items during the cleanup, and that she wanted the officers to inspect the premises. She used a key to unlock the house and garage, and the officers found the house empty. The court said that even if the officers had conducted an investigation before entering, as the defendant contended they should have done, and had learned that the tenants retained keys and had not yet tried to retrieve their security deposit, the officers would still have been justified in concluding that the tenants had abandoned the premises.

9.4   KRISE v. STATE (IND.CT.APP. 1999)
(*Consent: Authority*)

Police came to the defendant's home to serve a warrant on the defendant. She let them in to discuss the validity of the writ. While inside, officers saw a pipe and detected the odor of burning marijuana. The defendant was taken to jail on the strength of the writ, which turned out, as she claimed, to be no longer active.

Meanwhile, officers who remained at the home obtained permission to search the premises from the defendant's male housemate. In the bathroom, an officer found and opened a purse located on top of the commode. Inside the purse were the defendant's driver's license and a small, closed case containing two bags of drugs. The drugs were admitted at the defendant's possession trial, and she was convicted.

The defendant contended that her housemate had no authority to consent to a search of her personal effects, and that the police could not have reasonably believed that he had the common control or access over the purse that would give him such authority. She stressed the absence of any evidence that the officers had seen the housemate carry or otherwise have contact with the purse.

There was testimony that the housemate shared the bathroom, along with the rest of the residence, with the defendant.

- *Was the housemate's consent good? Can this evidence be used against the defendant? Explain.*

Krise v. State (Ind.Ct.App. 1999): 66 CrL 92

The police officer's warrantless search was justified by the male co-habitant's consent to a search of their home, where the purse was found. Reasonableness inquiry must focus on the consenting party's authority over the premises, not over particular containers.

Citing *United States v. Matlock*, 415 U.S. 164 (1974), the majority noted that "the authority which justifies the third-party consent rests on the mutual use of the property by persons generally having joint access or control for most purposes, so that it is reasonable to recognize that each of the co-inhabitants has the right to permit the inspection in his or her own right and that the others have assumed the risk that one of their number might permit the common area to be searched." Once valid consent is obtained, the police "need not separately request permission to search each container."

In *Florida v. Jimeno*, 500 U.S. 248 (1991), a defendant's consent to a search of the vehicle he was driving was held to cover a folded paper bag on the floor of the passenger side. In [*], the state supreme court held that a search consent given by a defendant's live-in girlfriend validated officers' seizure of personal effects from the bedroom the couple shared. The lesson of these cases, the majority said, is that "although the standard for measuring the scope of a suspect's consent under the 4th Amendment is that of objective reasonableness …, the determination of reasonableness pertains to the third person's authority over the premises in question and not any particular container within a common area of such premises."

In this case, there was testimony that the housemate shared the bathroom, along with the rest of the residence, with the defendant. Therefore, the majority said, it was reasonable for the officers to conclude that the housemate had authority over the purse and its contents. The majority also pointed out that the housemate did not explicitly limit the scope of his consent in any way.

In a footnote, the majority acknowledged a recent decision of the court [*] holding that a male motorist's consent to a search of his vehicle did not extend to a woman's handbag therein.

One judge dissented, saying that the officers could not reasonably believe that the housemate could consent to the search of the purse and the closed container within it. Citing Justice Breyer's concurring opinion in *Wyoming v. Houghton*, 526 U.S. 295 (1999), the dissenting judge remarked that a purse "is a unique and special type of container in which a person possesses the highest expectation of privacy." He also said that [*] is distinguishable from this case in view of the fact that it did not involve a search of a container belonging solely to the defendant.

9.5   UNITED STATES v. ELLIOTT (2D CIR. 1995)
(*Consent: Authority*)

Robin Elliott lived at 26 Garden Street in a building containing four legal dwelling units. Within each single legal unit, there were four bedrooms, each opening onto a shared hallway and kitchen area. The building's owner operated the building as an illegal boarding house, renting a legal unit's four bedrooms individually.

The owner, concerned about trespassing and criminal activity at the building, wrote to the police department and authorized the police to enter the premises to make arrests. The letter stated, "We hereby give the police our permission and enthusiastic support to arrest anyone on these properties (who is not a tenant or guest of a tenant) for trespassing." The owner also allowed the police to have keys to the external doors at 26 Garden and urged police to patrol the shared areas inside the building. The officers routinely entered the building and made numerous arrests.

At the time of the defendant's arrest, three of Unit A's four bedrooms were unrented, with two tenants, one of whom was the defendant's sister, residing in Bedroom 1. The owner allowed the two tenants to keep some of their belongings in one of the vacant bedrooms. The owner removed the door of Bedroom 3, and boarded up the other. The owner told the tenants that they could use all of Unit A's rooms until they were rented.

During a routine visit by officers, tenant Carrington allowed the officers into Unit A's kitchen area. From there, the officers noticed Elliott and a woman sleeping on a mattress on the floor of the doorless, and otherwise empty, Bedroom 3. Although Carrington later testified that he told the officers that Elliott was a guest, the officers knew that Elliott was not a tenant and they questioned him for that reason. In the course of that questioning, a gun and ammunition were discovered in the defendant's possession.

At the suppression hearing, the officers testified that they thought 26 Garden was run as a rooming house, with tenants in each unit renting individual rooms and sharing the kitchen and bathroom, and that they had customarily entered the units of 26 Garden, either without objection from tenants who answered the door or by using the keys.

- *Did the owner have authority to consent to search of any areas in 26 Garden?*
  - *If so, which ones?*
- *Was the consent given to police by the owner constitutional? Explain fully.*
- *If police did not have actual consent, could they rely on the doctrine of apparent authority? Explain.*
- *Should the evidence be suppressed?*

United States v. Elliott (2d Cir. 1995): 57 CrL 1059

"The trial court found, relying primarily on *Illinois v. Rodriguez,* 497 U.S. 177 (1990), that the entry did not violate the 4th Amendment because the officers reasonably believed that the owner had given valid consent to their entry. It also found that for years 26 Garden had been operated as an unlicensed rooming house, and that until just prior to February 19, 1993, the owner had retained control of the common areas of the building, including the kitchen and the common entry into the kitchen area. Although the owner testified that the building was in transition to its lawful use as an apartment building, the district court rejected Elliott's contention that the owner lacked the authority to consent because the building was licensed as an apartment building, and landlords generally lack authority to consent to a search of a leased apartment on the tenant's behalf.

"The question with respect to a third-party authorization to search is whether the third party possessed 'a sufficient relationship to the searched premises to validate the search.' A third party may validly grant the requisite consent if he or she has joint control of the property for most purposes. Under *Rodriguez,* even if the third party did not have the requisite relationship to the premises, official reliance on his or her consent may validate the search if it was reasonable for the officers to believe he or she had the requisite relationship. *Rodriguez,* however, validates only searches that are based on a reasonable mistake as to the facts, not those based on an erroneous legal conclusion drawn from the known facts.

"Although in general a landlord does not have common authority over an apartment or other dwelling unit leased to a tenant, a landlord does have authority to consent to a search of dwelling units that are not leased. Further, if the landlord has joint access or control over certain areas of the apartment building for most purposes, he or she may validly consent to a search of those areas.

"The officers correctly concluded that the owner's representations, if true, authorized their entry into common areas and unleased rooms. The officers simply committed a reasonable mistake of fact because, unbeknownst to them, the owner did not actually possess a license to operate 26 Garden as a rooming house.

"Elliott contends the search should be invalidated because the trial court found that, at the time of arrest, Unit A was being operated as a single apartment rather than four separate dwelling units. The owner of a building that has unleased dwelling units has the right to authorize the police to search the unleased units. Whether or not a given unit is unleased, however, is a question of fact. Any error of the officers with respect to the owner's authority to consent to their entry into and search of the common kitchen of Unit A and bedroom 3 was a mistake of fact since it turned on what arrangements the owner and the tenant had made with respect to those areas. The officers, having for years been given authority by the owner to enter the common areas and vacant bedrooms of 26 Garden had no basis on which to suspect that on the day of the arrest the owner could not validly authorize their entry into either Unit A or bedroom 3. The police had no reason to know of any change in the operation of the building from rooming house to apartment house, and they reasonably believed their authorization to enter remained intact."

The dissent contended that consent given by the landlord was no good at the time of the entry because of the change in the configuration of the building to apartment units. Even if the single-room occupancy configuration still prevailed and the kitchen remained an area common to unrelated tenants, the landlord lacked joint exercise or control of the kitchen. The officers who entered the bedroom where the defendant was sleeping lacked the requisite objectively reasonable belief that the landlord could give them permission to be there.

9.6   STATE v. BENSON (IDAHO 1999)
(*Consent: Authority*)

Officers responded to a tip about drugs at a residence. On the officers' arrival, the woman who rented the home greeted them and informed them that her daughter resided in the house's detached garage. The mother accompanied the officers to the garage and knocked on the door. The daughter answered, became upset, and asked the officers to leave the premises. The daughter's boyfriend soon came out and also told the officers to leave. Officers decided to separate the agitated daughter and her boyfriend. While the daughter was being led away, she screamed at her mother not to speak with the officers and not to give permission for a search. The officers asked the mother if the garage was hers, if she had access to it, and if she had "stuff" inside; she answered "Yes" to each question. After receiving her permission to search the garage, the officers discovered drugs inside and arrested the boyfriend, the defendant in this case. He argued that the drugs should have been suppressed as fruits of an unlawful search.

Facts at trial included these: The daughter did not pay her mother rent for the garage, but she babysat her brother's children, who lived in the house. The daughter used a padlock on the garage door when she and the defendant were absent and the mother did not have a key to that lock.

- *Did the mother have common authority over the garage to allow her to give consent to search? Explain.*
- *Will the apparent authority doctrine work here to justify the police search? Why?*

State v. Benson (Idaho 1999): 65 CrL 505

The court analyzed the mother's consent to the search under both the common authority and apparent authority doctrines. The court pointed out that although the daughter did not pay her mother rent for the garage, she babysat her brother's children, who lived in the house, in lieu of rent. The court also deemed it significant that the daughter used a padlock on the garage door, which was locked when she and the defendant were absent, and to which only she and the defendant had keys. Therefore, the mother was unable to enter the garage without the permission of either her daughter or the defendant, regardless of the fact that she stored some of her own items inside. The mother also testified that she considered the garage to be her daughter's residence.

Although the trial court held that these facts established common authority over the garage, the appellate court disagreed. The U.S. Supreme Court, it noted, in *United States v. Matlock,* 415 U.S. 164 (1974), described common authority as stemming from "mutual use" and "joint access and control for most purposes, so that it is reasonable to recognize that any of the co-inhabitants has the right to permit the inspection in his own right and that others have assumed the risk that one of their number might permit the common area to be searched." A state case [*] held that a landlord did not have common authority over his tenant's home and could not consent to its search. These cases compel the conclusion that the mother did not possess common authority over the garage, the court concluded. The relationship between mother and daughter in this case was more akin to that between landlord and tenant than that between a parent and a child in residence. Furthermore, the retention of the keys to the garage by the daughter and the defendant demonstrated that they did not assume the risk that the mother would allow others to enter it.

Turning to the doctrine of apparent authority as set out by the U.S. Supreme Court in *Illinois v. Rodriguez*, 497 U.S. 177 (1990), the court concluded that the information known to the officers did not give them grounds for a reasonable belief that the mother had common authority over the premises and could therefore validly consent to a search. In reaching this conclusion, the court stressed the presence of the garage's inhabitants and their strenuous objections to the search.

If there were nothing but the mother's assertion that the garage belonged to her, that she had "access" to it, and that she had property inside it, a belief in her authority to consent to a search might have been reasonable. However, the officers' awareness that the daughter and the defendant lived there and their demands that the police leave the premises rendered unreasonable any belief they might have had about the mother's authority. At a minimum, the court said, the presence of the nonconsenting parties put the officers on notice that further inquiry into the parties' relationship to the premises was in order. The importance of an "active objection" to a search was implicitly acknowledged in a recent case [*] that used the failure of an individual with a possessory interest to object to a search as justification for applying the apparent authority doctrine.

Under the facts of this case, the officers consciously ignored or were deliberately indifferent to the possessory interests of the garage's inhabitants. The officers' intentional bypassing of persons with a superior possessory interest rendered application of the apparent authority doctrine unreasonable.

9.7   STATE v. FRANK (MINN.CT.APP. 2002)
(*Consent: Authority*)

The defendant was one of two passengers in a car that was stopped for having only one working headlight. The officer questioned the driver about the group's destination and became suspicious on learning they were going to visit an individual known for drug activity.

Out of the defendant's range of hearing, the officer asked the driver for permission to search the vehicle for "multiple things, bodies, weapons, guns, drugs." On receiving the driver's consent, the officer searched the vehicle and found two suitcases in the trunk. The officer opened one suitcase without inquiring into its ownership or requesting permission from the passengers. The search uncovered controlled substances and a handgun, and more drugs were found in a subsequent search of the car's backseat area.

At trial, the defendant moved to suppress all the drug evidence obtained from the search of the vehicle. The trial court denied the motion, citing *Wyoming v. Houghton,* 526 U.S. 295 (1999), for the proposition that the search of the suitcase was proper in light of the driver's consent. The defendant was convicted of a drug crime.

Houghton was an automobile exception case in which the U.S. Supreme Court held that officers with probable cause to believe that there is contraband in a vehicle may search any containers in the vehicle that are capable of holding the contraband, regardless of their ownership.

- *What do you think? Was this consent search constitutional? Why?*

State v. Frank (Minn.Ct.App. 2002): 71 CrL 660

A driver's consent to a search of his vehicle does not justify police in searching items belonging to passengers according to the Minnesota Court of Appeals. This rule requires police to inquire about the ownership of items that are not clearly owned or controlled by the consenting party. In reaching this conclusion, the court made a sharp distinction between vehicle searches based on consent and those based on probable cause.

The court concluded that *Houghton,* a case decided under the "automobile exception" to the 4th Amendment's warrant requirement, does not apply to searches based on consent. Some courts have relied on *Houghton* to hold that a driver's consent to a vehicle search permits police to search any container in the vehicle, no matter who owns it [*]. This court rejected that idea, however, stressing that the automobile and consent exceptions are separate and distinct doctrines. The trial court's reliance on *Houghton* to uphold a search based on consent was clearly erroneous.

The decisive issue in this case was whether the driver had or appeared to have authority to consent to the search of the defendant's suitcase. The court ruled that he did not have either actual or apparent authority to permit such a search. Deciding the case on this basis, the court did not address whether the driver meant his consent to extend to the suitcase or whether the officer reasonably understood the driver to intend the consent to go that far.

Quoting *United States v. Matlock,* 415 U.S. 164 (1974), the court noted that if a warrantless search of an individual's personal possessions is based on consent by a third party, the government must show that the consenting party had "common authority over or other sufficient relationship to the premises or effects sought to be inspected." Common authority exists when multiple persons exercise joint control of property, with each assuming the risk that another might permit the property to be searched.

Courts in other jurisdictions that have examined factual scenarios similar to this one are split over the scope-of-authority issue, the court reported. For example, the Fifth Circuit held [*] that a driver may consent to a search of a passenger's belongings by consenting to a search of the vehicle. On the other hand, other courts [*] have held that a driver does not have authority to consent to a search of passenger's personal items. The Minnesota court concluded that it is "more consistent with constitutional limits on warrantless searches" to hold that a driver's consent to the search of a vehicle does not authorize police to search property owned by passengers who are present and available to give consent themselves.

It was undisputed in this case that the driver lacked actual authority to consent to a search of the defendant's suitcase. Furthermore, the officer did not present facts to support a reasonable belief that the driver had authority to consent. The officer's mistake in believing that the driver's consent to search the vehicle constituted legal authority for him to search any containers in the vehicle that might hold the contraband he sought was a mistake of law, not fact, and thus could not support a finding of apparent authority even if it was reasonable.

When a vehicle search is based solely on consent and the circumstances do not clearly indicate that the consenting person owns or controls the items to be searched, the police have an obligation to ascertain ownership of those items before searching them. The officer in this case acted unreasonably by failing to find out who owned the suitcase before searching it.

9.8 WELCH v. STATE (TEX.CRIM.APP. 2002)
(*Consent: Authority*)

A police officer pulled over the defendant's truck for speeding and the officer asked her permission to search it. The defendant avoided responding to the request. She was arrested on an outstanding warrant and requested that the car be turned over to her companion, a passenger in the truck. The officer agreed to this request after warning that the passenger would become responsible for everything in the vehicle.

The defendant gave the keys to the officer, who gave them to the passenger. The officer then requested and obtained the passenger's consent to a search of the truck. The search yielded drugs, and the defendant was convicted of possession. The defendant argued on appeal that the consent was invalid.

- ■ *Was it? Analyze the problem.*
  - • *Does it matter that the owner did not actually refuse consent, but just avoided giving it? If so, how does that play into the analysis?*
  - • *Does it matter that the owner who had not consented to the search was present when the passenger gave consent? Explain your thinking.*
- ■ *Can you think of any other exceptions to the warrant requirement that might work in this case to support admission of the evidence against the defendant?*
- ■ *If the passenger had not given consent, what would have happened to the truck after the defendant's arrest? Would that have led to discovery of the evidence? If so, could the evidence then have been used against the defendant?*

Welch v. State (Tex.Crim.App. 2002): 72 CrL 11

In giving control of the car and its keys to the passenger, the owner assumed the risk that the recipient of the keys would consent to search of the vehicle. When the owner entrusts the vehicle to another with no limitations, that includes an assumption that the other person will consent to a search of the vehicle, even when the owner has actively avoided a search request.

The court said the defendant's ownership of the vehicle alone was insufficient to trump the passenger's consent and that her superior privacy interest in the truck was not controlling. Under *United States v. Matlock,* 415 U.S. 164 (1974), property rights are not dispositive in determining whether a third party has joint access and control; nor is the defendant's presence or absence at the time of the search. On that point it declined to follow a Ninth Circuit case [*] that held *Matlock* inapplicable to cases in which the party contesting the search is present when the third party's consent is obtained.

Rather, the court observed, *Matlock* teaches that the relevant inquiry in this case is whether the passenger had joint access and control over the truck for most purposes at the time she granted consent and whether the defendant assumed the risk in turning the truck over to her passenger that the latter would consent to a search. The court answered both questions in the affirmative.

Once the passenger had the keys to the truck, she had control over, as well as access to, the truck for most purposes. The defendant's decision to turn over the keys despite the officer's statement that the passenger would then become responsible for the vehicle's contents contributed to the conclusion that the defendant assumed the risk of a third-party consent.

The court also said that because the defendant did not actually refuse consent, this case does not present the issue of whether a third-party's consent is sufficient when the owner is present and refuses consent. A reasonable interpretation of the defendant's actions is that she sought to avoid answering the officer's request to search by turning the truck over to the passenger.

The court suggested that if the passenger had heard the exchange in which the defendant avoided answering the officer's request for consent, the defendant might have been able to argue that her release of the truck contained a limitation regarding consent to a search and, therefore, that she did not assume the risk of such a consent. However, the court said the facts indicated that the passenger could not have heard the defendant's failure to consent.

In conclusion, this court declared that the rule of third-party consents set out in *Matlock* applies "even when the defendant is present at the scene and does not consent to a search."

One judge concurred, adding that a search incident to arrest theory could support admission of the evidence found in the truck.

9.9   UNITED STATES v. PATTEN (TENTH CIR. 1999)
(*Consent: Voluntariness*)

The officer stopped the defendant for speeding and gave him a warning ticket. After some conversation about tourist attractions and the defendant's travels, the officer asked the defendant how many suitcases he was carrying. The defendant said he had two, one of which was in the trunk. The officer then asked if there was anything illegal in the trunk. When the defendant did not respond, the officer asked, "Well, do you think we could take a look at your suitcase there? I don't want to necessarily look in it, but—nor do I want to read any letters necessarily, but maybe we could just take a look?" The defendant said "Okay" and opened the vehicle's trunk.

The officer pushed down on the large, soft-sided suitcase in the trunk and, by trying to slide it with his hand, determined that it was very heavy. After making a comment to which the defendant did not respond, the officer said, "Well, let's just unzip it." The defendant partially unzipped the suitcase to a point where straps surrounded it. The officer told him, "To unzip it more, you just got to squeeze the prongs there. Just squeeze them together there and it will open up." When the defendant hesitated, the officer repeated the instruction to squeeze the prongs. The defendant unbuckled the straps, and the officer said, "Well then, we'll just have to unzip it." The defendant did so and began shuffling a jacket that lay atop the suitcase's contents. The officer asked him to identify a green plastic sack underneath the jacket, but the defendant did not respond. The officer then pulled out the sack and saw several clear plastic baggies of a white powdery substance. In response to the officer's question about the substance, the defendant said the suitcase was not his and he thought the substance was dextrose or steroids. It turned out to be ephedrine, a controlled substance.

- *Was this search constitutional? On what theory do you base your conclusion? Explain fully.*

United States v. Patten (Tenth Cir. 1999): 65 CrL 487

The words a law enforcement officer used in requesting consent for an inspection of a defendant's suitcase, combined with the facts that the defendant did not object to opening the suitcase and ultimately did so himself, led the U.S. Court of Appeals for the Tenth Circuit to conclude that the defendant validly consented to the officer's viewing of the inside of the suitcase.

The trial court had upheld the search as consensual in reliance on two factors: First, it pointed out that the officer's initial disclaimer of a desire to look into the suitcase was qualified by the word "necessarily." With the inclusion of that word, the district court said, the officer's language "alerts the hearer that there is a possibility of looking into the suitcase, although it may not be necessary to do so." A reasonable person would thus understand "that the officer may, or may not, want to look into the suitcase." Second, the defendant showed that he understood the request in this way by maintaining silence and cooperating with the officer in opening the suitcase. The appellate court saw nothing wrong with that finding of voluntariness.

The court distinguished this case from [*] in which the officer asked permission to "look through" the trunk of a defendant's car but added, "I don't want to look through each item" and said he just wanted to see how things were "packed" or "packaged." The court held in that case that the consent the defendant gave did not extend to opening the luggage in the trunk.

Whereas the officer's statement in [*], discussed in the paragraph above, would have informed a reasonable person that the officer was interested only in a visual inspection of the trunk, his statements in this case "left open the distinct possibility that he might wish to view the inside of the defendant's suitcase," the court said. It also stressed that the defendant was with the officer when the trunk was opened, that the defendant unzipped the suitcase himself, that the officer made no coercive show of authority toward the defendant, and that the defendant did not object to unzipping the suitcase.

9.10   STATE v. MCCORD (FLA.DIST.CT.APP. 2002) (*Consent: Voluntariness*)

A detective suspected the defendant of being the perpetrator of an armed robbery during which blood had been left at the scene. The defendant was in jail on other charges when the detective told the defendant that he was investigating a rape and asked the defendant for a DNA sample that could be used to exclude him as a suspect. The defendant consented and provided a saliva sample. The detective was not actually investigating rape.

- *Did the detective's trickery render the defendant's consent involuntary? Explain.*

State v. McCord (Fla.Dist.Ct.App. 2002): 72 CrL 244

A police detective's fabrication of an investigation into a nonexistent crime rendered involuntary a defendant's consent to give a DNA sample according to a majority of the Florida District Court of Appeals.

The majority agreed with the lower court that the detective's deception undermined the voluntariness of the defendant's consent to the search and that the procurement of the DNA sample violated the defendant's 4th Amendment rights. Unlike the suspect in *Frazier v. Cupp*, 394 U.S. 731 (1969), in which the U.S. Supreme Court held that a confession was voluntary despite officers' fabrication of a story that a relative of the suspect had confessed to a crime, the defendant in this case did not know what crime the detective was investigating. Nor is this case like an earlier Florida case [*], in which officers were investigating two crimes and simply did not tell the defendant about one of them.

"Unlike the officers in *Frazier* and [*], who did not lie to the defendants regarding the crimes for which they were suspects, the detective in this case fabricated a rape charge to obtain [the defendant's] consent." The majority therefore agreed with the trial court that "this deception, while [the defendant] was in jail, was so manipulative that his 'consent' did not 'validate the search.'"

One judge concurred, agreeing that the deception was unfair and rendered the defendant's consent involuntary.

9.11   UNITED STATES v. RICH (FIFTH CIR. 1993) (*Consent: Voluntariness*)

Defendant William Rich's pickup truck was stopped by Texas State Trooper Crais because of a burned-out license plate bulb. Rich volunteered an explanation of where he was going and said he would be there "just for the day." While Rich looked for his insurance papers, the trooper radioed Rich's driver's license number to the dispatcher and asked for various checks to be performed. Back at the pickup, the trooper shined his flashlight into an open side window and saw several items of luggage. He also detected the odor of fabric softener, which he knew was often used to mask the scent of marijuana. He asked Rich again how long he planned staying at his destination; this time Rich said "a couple of days." Rich's hands trembled when he gave the trooper the insurance papers.

The trooper went to his car and learned that no checks could be run because the computer was down. After he asked Rich to stand by the patrol car, the trooper tried to look through the back window of the pickup to see what was underneath the suitcases in the extended cab portion of the truck. He was unable to see through the tinting on the window. He again smelled fabric softener.

The trooper then asked Rich whether he had any narcotics or weapons in the vehicle. Rich said "No." The trooper then asked "Can I have a look in your truck?" Rich did not respond to this question or to the trooper's first repetition of it. The trooper put the question a third time and added, "I either need a yes or a no." Rich said "Yes," and the trooper told him to stand near the patrol car. The trooper first opened the driver's side door, then the passenger side door, pulled out one of the suitcases from behind the passenger seat, opened it, and found marijuana packed in fabric softener tissues. He placed Rich under arrest. Apparently no more than 5 minutes elapsed between the initial stop and the arrest.

- *Did the officer ask to search the vehicle? Explain.*
- *Did Rich give good consent to the search? Explain.*
- *Was the officer entitled to open the luggage? Justify your answer.*
- *Should the marijuana be suppressed?*

United States v. Rich (Fifth Cir. 1993): 53 CrL 1247

"The key inquiry in determining the scope of a consent to search is what the 'typical reasonable person [would] have understood by the exchange between the officer and the suspect.' *Florida v. Jimeno,* 500 U.S. 248 (1991).... Here the defendant argues that the trooper's request to 'have a look in' the truck was only a request to 'see inside' the vehicle, especially since the trooper had tried to 'see inside' but had been foiled by the tinted window. Somewhat similarly, the court below relied in part on the trooper's failure to use the more precise term 'search' in his request.

"We decline the defendant's invitation to establish a list of specific terms from which an officer must select the most appropriate for each individual situation and/or defendant. To so hamper law enforcement officials in their everyday duties would be an unjustifiable extension of the 4th Amendment's requirement that searches be 'reasonable.'

"It is not necessary for an officer specifically to use the term 'search' when he requests consent.... [A]ny words, when viewed in context, that objectively communicate to a reasonable individual that the officer is requesting permission to examine the vehicle and its contents constitute a valid search request for 4th Amendment purposes.

"Rich asserts that the general request to search his truck was unaccompanied by an express declaration of the item or items that were being sought; thus, it was not objectively reasonable for the officer to assume that Rich had consented to the search of his luggage.... When the conversation between [the trooper] and Rich is considered in toto, it is indisputable that Rich knew that the object of [the trooper's] search was illegal weapons or narcotics. [The officer had asked if the defendant had any weapons or narcotics; the defendant said no; officer then asked three times if he could "have a look in" the truck.] In light of the fact that the entire scenario was played out in a matter of minutes ... it is unreasonable to assume a period of silence ensued that was long enough to disassociate the two sentences from each other.

"The defendant argues that from where the officer had instructed him to stand he was unable to observe the search, hence could not object to or limit the search of his luggage.... We are unwilling to require that all consent searches be conducted in the plain view of the suspect and in a manner slow enough that he may withdraw or limit his consent at any time. Rich, knowing the contents of the vehicle and its various containers at the time he gave his consent, had the responsibility to limit the scope of the consent if he deemed it necessary to do so.

"We think that under the facts of this case, it was objectively reasonable for [the trooper] to conclude that Rich's consent to search the vehicle included his consent to search containers found within the vehicle that could hold illegal narcotics or weapons, the expressed object of [the trooper's] search."

9.12   EDWARDS v. COMMONWEALTH (VA.CT.APP. 2002) (*Consent: Scope of Search*)

A police officer had a tip that someone known as "E" was selling narcotics from a hotel room. As the officer was completing search of the room, the defendant came in carrying a bag of tube socks; he identified himself as "E." The officer explained what he was doing there and requested consent to search the defendant's person. The defendant said "Sure, no problem," and placed the bag of tube socks on the bed. The officer patted down the defendant and found nothing. The officer then searched the bag of tube socks and found crack cocaine. The cocaine was used to convict the defendant of a drug offense.

For purposes of this exercise, you can presume that the officer had proper authority to search the hotel room.

■ *Did the defendant's consent to search of his person extend to search of the bag of tube socks he had placed on the bed? Explain.*

Edwards v. Commonwealth (Va.Ct.App. 2002): 71 CrL 661

A suspect's consent to a police officer's search of his person includes permission to search any bags or purse the suspect is carrying at the time.

This was a case of first impression in Virginia, but the majority agreed with the Seventh Circuit, which decided in [*] that a suspect's "person" includes a purse or bag carried by the suspect because the human anatomy does not naturally have containers, and people wear pockets and purses to remedy this anatomical deficiency. The Seventh Circuit had observed: "Containers such as these, while appended to the body, are so closely associated with the person that they are identified with and included within the concept of one's person." A Ninth Circuit case, [*], was in accord, holding that search of a backpack constituted a search of the defendant's person; likewise, the court cited cases in accord from Wisconsin and Minnesota.

The defendant in this case was holding the bag of tube socks when he consented to a search of his person, hence "the bag was 'appended to' or intimately connected with, his person." Accordingly, the majority held that the trial court's finding that the officer reasonably concluded that the consent included the bag was not plainly wrong.

To the extent that the scope of the consent is made less clear by the defendant's act of placing the bag on the bed before the pat-down, "his passive acquiescence while the officer searched the bag affirmed that the bag was within the scope of his consent."

One judge dissented, arguing that placing the bag on the bed was a demonstrable withholding of his permission for a search of that bag and, therefore, he did not acquiesce to its search.

9.13   UNITED STATES v. MENDOZA-GONZALES (FIFTH CIR. 2003) (*Consent: Scope of Search*)

Border Patrol agents at a permanent immigration checkpoint stopped the defendant's truck and questioned him about his citizenship and his cargo. The defendant answered that he was a Mexican citizen residing in the United States and was hauling cheese. An agent asked for permission to "take a look in the back" of the truck, and the defendant said "Okay."

The truck's trailer contained a load of white cardboard boxes wrapped in plastic on pallets; however, there were also a few brown cardboard boxes on top of the white boxes. The agent used a pocket knife to slice a piece of tape that closed a brown box and found marijuana.

The defendant argued that agents should not have been permitted to slice the tape from the box and look inside. the defendant also objected to the scope of the search, arguing that it was reasonable for a person in his position to think the agents wanted to look in the truck for illegal aliens, not to search places that were too small to hide a person.

For purposes of this analysis, presume that Border Patrol agents are held to the same constitutional standards as any other law enforcement officers.

  ▪ *Did the defendant consent to opening the box that was taped shut? Explain.*

United States v. Mendoza-Gonzales (Fifth Cir. 2003): 72 CrL 332

Border Patrol agents at an immigration checkpoint who obtained a defendant's unqualified consent to "take a look in the back" of a commercial truck did not violate the 4th Amendment by slicing open the adhesive tape that closed a small cardboard box the agents saw inside the truck. In the circumstances of this case, the agents' actions were more like un-screwing an access panel than breaking open a locked container.

Box Was Not Like a Locked Container

Under *Florida v. Jimeno,* 500 U.S. 248 (1991), a court determining the scope of a suspect's consent to search is to ask, "What would the typical reasonable person have understood by the exchange between the officer and the suspect?" In *Jimeno,* the U.S. Supreme Court held that a paper bag with its top rolled closed could be searched pursuant to a consent to search a car for drugs. The court explained that a reasonable person would know that drugs are not kept strewn about openly in vehicles and thus the consent necessarily included per-mission to look inside closed containers in the vehicle. The Supreme Court commented, however, that "[i]t is very likely unreasonable to think that a suspect, by consenting to the search of his trunk, has agreed to the breaking open of a locked briefcase within the trunk."

The defendant in this case argued that the cardboard box was "sealed" with tape and thus was like the locked container that the *Jimeno* dicta would treat as outside the scope of a general consent. The government argued that a cardboard box held shut with a piece of tape should be treated as merely a "closed" container, like the paper bag in *Jimeno.* The court found the distinction between "closed" and "sealed" containers to be an unnecessary se-mantic squabble and did not engage in it. *Jimeno's* distinction between a rolled paper bag and a locked briefcase was enough by itself to decide that slicing open the tape on the card-board box and looking inside did not exceed the scope of the defendant's consent.

The court concluded that *Jimeno* "likely differentiated between a reasonable and un-reasonable search of a container premised upon general consent to search the vehicle in which it was found by the varying impact that such a search has upon two interests: (1) the owner's expectation of privacy as demonstrated by his attempt to lock or otherwise secure the container; and (2) the owner's interest in preserving the physical integrity of the con-tainer and the functionality of its contents."

The defendant's expectation of privacy with regard to the cardboard box was not com-parable to the privacy expectation people have with regard to locked containers, the court concluded. "Locked containers require specific knowledge of a combination, possession of a key, or a demonstration of significant force to open." In contrast, "[a] single piece of tape is commonly used on a cardboard box not to send any particular message of privacy, but rather to keep the stiff side flaps closed to prevent the contents from spilling out and being damaged during transit."

As for the physical integrity of the box, the agent's slicing of the single piece of tape did not damage the box or render it unusable, the court noted. It likened the search of the box to a case [*] in which a search was upheld after troopers who had obtained consent for a search of a car unscrewed vent covers from the interior panels of the vehicle. "In each case, with minimal effort, the structure of the vehicle, and the boxes opened by [the agent] can be restored to their original condition." In a footnote, however, the court left open the ques-tion "whether a package can ever be so well bound with tape that it is tantamount to a 'locked' container for purposes of the 4th Amendment."

Scope of the Search

The court also rejected the defendant's argument that a reasonable person in his situation would have understood the agent to be asking for consent to search the truck for illegal aliens—not to search cardboard boxes that were too small to hide a person. The defendant pointed out that he had been stopped at an immigration checkpoint and that the agents asked him about his citizenship. He also observed that while he was opening the back of the truck, the agent asked him if he had any passengers.

The court decided that the questions asked by the agent would lead a reasonable observer to believe that the agent was interested in the contents of the truck generally. It also stressed the unqualified nature of the agent's request and the defendant's expression of consent. In addition, the court cited case law upholding consent searches of containers in vehicles on the basis of defendants' failure to object on the scene when the officers turned their attention to the containers in question.

The court said that *Jimeno* should not be interpreted "to hold ... that enforcement officials must conduct all searches in plain view of the suspect, and in a manner slowly enough that he may withdraw or delimit his consent at any time during the search."

9.14   UNITED STATES v. AL-MARRI (S.D.N.Y. 2002) (*Consent: Scope of Search*)

The defendant, a graduate student in computer science, arrived in the United States from Qatar on September 10, 2001. In the wake of the September 11 attacks, the FBI visited the defendant at his home and obtained his permission to conduct a search of the premises. They also asked permission to take his computer to their office for a more thorough examination than they could perform on the scene. He agreed and gave them the computer's carrying case.

In examining the computer, agents made copies of the hard drive, identified deleted as well as current files, and examined the defendant's Internet bookmarks. This scrutiny, along with an inspection of the carrying case, yielded evidence of credit card fraud.

The defendant was charged with unauthorized possession of access devices with intent to defraud. He moved to suppress on the ground that the agents' search exceeded the scope of his consent.

- *Did the defendant consent to the government making copies of his files? Explain.*
  - *To identification and examination of deleted files? Explain.*
  - *To seizure of the computer to enable officers to inspect it at their offices? Explain.*

United States v. Al-Marri (S.D.N.Y. 2002): 72 CrL 175

A defendant's unqualified consent to searches of his home and laptop computer authorized agents to seize the computer and conduct an extensive search of its hard drive. The court added that even if the defendant did not voluntarily hand over his computer, his consent to the search of the home encompassed a search of the computer as a closed container.

The court concluded that the exchange between the defendant and the agents would lead a reasonable person to understand that the agents asked for and received permission for an extensive search of the computer.

On being asked to allow the computer to be taken away, the defendant agreed without placing any explicit limitation on the scope of the search. The agents told him that they did not have the skills or the time to perform the examination at his home. That comment must have made the defendant realize that the examination of his computer would be more than superficial.

Furthermore, given the defendant's educational background, he would have clearly understood the technological resources of the FBI and its ability to thoroughly examine his computer. On the basis of this knowledge, he could have provided specific instructions to the FBI about the scope of the search he had permitted—in particular, whether there were any files or programs he wanted kept private. He did not do so. Therefore, it was objectively reasonable for the agents to conclude that the defendant's unrestricted grant of access to them indicated that he had no qualms about an extensive search of his computer.

Finally, the defendant did not ask for the computer to be restored to him within a specific time frame. A reasonable person could reasonably understand the failure to make such a request as demonstrating that the consent was open-ended.

Even if, as the defendant contended, he did not voluntarily surrender his computer, the search of the device was covered by the rule that a lawful search of premises generally extends to the entire area where the object of the search could be found, including closed containers. In this case, the object of the search was not made explicit, but the totality of the circumstances would have made it clear to any reasonable person that the agents' questioning of the defendant related to the investigation of the recent terrorist attacks. Therefore, a reasonable person would have recognized the agents' request to search the defendant's home and computer as a search for evidence of possible criminal activities.

Because a computer can be searched without damaging it, courts treat computers as closed but not sealed containers, the court noted. Computers are thus covered by the general rule that police with consent for a premises search do not need separate consent to search closed containers where evidence can be found. Accordingly, the defendant's consent to a search of his home covered the agents' seizure and search of the computer.

9.15   STATE v. TROXELL (TENN. 2002)
(*Consent: Scope of Search*)

After concluding a traffic stop, a state trooper issued a warning but asked the driver whether he had "any weapons in the vehicle." When the driver replied in the negative, the trooper asked for permission to "take a look" and the driver agreed.

After an extensive 20-minute search of the cab of the defendant's truck and luggage located there, as well as a sweep of the truck by a narcotics-detection dog, the trooper examined the undercarriage of the truck and observed signs that the gas tank had recently been altered. A later search of the interior of the gas tank revealed 300 grams of cocaine.

- *What arguments are available to the state that this was a constitutional search?*
- *What arguments are available to the defendant that this was not a constitutional search?*
- *Was this a constitutional consent search? Explain fully.*

State v. Troxell (Tenn. 2002): 71 CrL 304

A defendant's consent to have a law enforcement officer search his vehicle for weapons did not include permission to inspect the gas tank and undercarriage of the vehicle.

A majority of the Tennessee Supreme Court held that the trooper's examination of the undercarriage exceeded the scope of the defendant's consent in violation of both the state and federal constitutions. Emphasizing that the trooper asked about weapons "in" the defendant's vehicle, the majority said that a reasonable person would have understood the consent given by the defendant to include "only the interior of the vehicle and any containers that may have contained weapons." From this it follows that "it was *not* objectively reasonable to believe that the consent to search 'in the vehicle' would permit [the officer] to examine the undercarriage and gas tank of the vehicle while continuing and prolonging the detention of the defendant" [emphasis in original].

The majority also rejected the state's argument that the defendant's failure to object to the continued search rendered reasonable the trooper's expanded view of the defendant's consent. "Although a defendant's later expressed language, coupled with silence, may be evidence of an expansion of the scope of the consent, a defendant's silence alone cannot expand the scope of the initial consent or allow a prolonged and continued detention."

One judge dissented, arguing that the undercarriage and gas tank are "in" a vehicle and that the defendant's silence during the search supported the reasonableness of the trooper's conclusions that the defendant's consent extended to a search of those areas.

9.16   UNITED STATES v. PIERRE (FIFTH CIR. 1991)
(*Consent/Automobile Exception/Plain View Exception/Search Incident to Arrest*)

Otis Harris, Derrick Turner, and Terry Pierre were traveling from Los Angeles to New Orleans in a GMC Jimmy. Harris was driving when he and Pierre smoked some marijuana. About an hour later, the men reached a border patrol checkpoint at Sierra Blanca, Texas, where Agent Hillin stopped them. Harris was driving, Turner was in the passenger seat, and Pierre was resting in the back. Harris rolled down his window. Hillin asked Harris and Turner if they were citizens, and both said, "Yes." Hillin then inserted his head through the window into the car, purportedly to get a clear view of Pierre in the back seat. At that moment, Hillin smelled burned marijuana. He directed Harris to pull the vehicle into the secondary inspection area. There, Harris consented to a search of the luggage in the vehicle, which revealed 13.8 pounds of cocaine inside one suitcase. All three men were arrested.

- *Analyze the officer's search of the car.*
- *Should the contents of the luggage be admissible? Were they found in a lawful search?*
- *If so, what exception applies?*
  - *Search incident to arrest?*
  - *Plain view?*
  - *Consent?*
  - *Automobile exception?*
- *As always, justify your answers.*

United States v. Pierre (Fifth Cir. 1991): 49 CrL 1246

"The central concern of the 4th Amendment is to protect people from 'unreasonable government intrusions into their legitimate expectations of privacy.' That Harris had a reasonable and legitimate expectation of privacy in the interior of the GMC Jimmy is not disputed.

"The Government's contention that this was not a search turns, therefore, on whether Agent Hillin 'intruded' upon Harris' reasonable expectation of privacy. In *New York v. Class* [475 U.S. 106 (1986)], a police officer reached into the defendant's car to move some papers on the dashboard that obscured the vehicle identification number, and in the process of doing so saw the handle of a gun protruding from beneath the driver's seat. The [Supreme] Court held 'that the intrusion into that space [the car's interior] constituted a search.' The fact that the officer in *Class* made physical contact with objects inside the car, whereas Agent Hillin did not, is immaterial; it was the officer's act of reaching into the automobile, not his shuffling of papers, that allowed him to see the gun handle and that the Supreme Court held to be a search.

"The Government argues that Agent Hillin's intrusion in this case is no different from the practices sanctioned in the so-called 'flashlight' cases, holding that it is not a search for the police to use artificial illumination, aerial photography electronic tracking devices, binoculars, or other technology to aid their perception of objects in 'plain view.' That invocation begs the question. These cases uniformly rest on the axiom that one has no reasonable expectation of privacy in what one exposes to public view (or public smell). They presuppose, and it is integral to the plain view doctrine as it relates both to defining searches and to regulating seizures, that the viewer (or smeller, as the case may be) is where he lawfully has a right to be. These cases, therefore, are relevant only if Agent Hillin's head was lawfully within the vehicle—but that, of course, is the very question before us.

"In this case, the district court found on the record that Agent Hillin 'stuck his head through the driver's side window.' The agent thus effected a physical intrusion into the vehicle. While an officer's act need not constitute a physical intrusion to be a 'search' we are aware of no case holding that an officer did not conduct a 'search' when he physically intruded part of his body into a space in which the suspect had a reasonable expectation of privacy. Agent Hillin's physical intrusion allowed him to see and to smell things he could not see or smell from outside the vehicle, and indeed, that was his declared purpose: He 'ducked [his] head in to get a clear view of the backseat.' In doing so, his inspection went beyond that of the vehicle which may be viewed from outside the vehicle by either inquisitive passersby or diligent police officers.

"We do not decide the reasonableness of searches by 'balancing the need to search against the invasion which the search entails' on an ad hoc basis. 'The intrusiveness of the search is not measured by its scope, but by the expectation of privacy upon which the search intrudes.' [*] The Supreme Court recently made this point quite clear, albeit in the context of a dwelling-place search in *Arizona v. Hicks*, 480 U.S. 321 (1987): 'The distinction between 'looking' at a suspicious object and 'moving' it even a few inches is much more than trivial for purposes of the 4th Amendment.... A search is a search, even if it happens to disclose nothing but the bottom of turntable.'

"Agent Hillin had no objectively justifiable suspicion warranting a search of the Jimmy, so the search was unreasonable under the 4th Amendment. Furthermore, the illegal search tainted Harris' subsequent consent to the search of the luggage."

Plain View Exception

Presume the officer does not have a search warrant and he observes something in plain view that he reasonably believes is evidence of a crime. If that officer is in a place where he is lawfully entitled to be when he makes the observation, and if he has not impermissibly moved or manipulated anything to see the object, the observation is a constitutional plain view observation. If there is probable cause to believe the item is evidence of a crime, it can be seized without a warrant. That is the essence of the plain view exception to the 4th Amendment protections.

Plain view requires the police to be in a place where they are lawfully entitled to be when the "plain view" observation is made. If police are in a public place, the plain view exception can operate. If police have a search warrant to look for cocaine and they find illegal weapons during the course of that search, the plain view exception can operate. If police have consent to be in a home and they observe drugs, the plain view exception can operate.

If police, however, are not lawfully in the place from which they make their observation, the observation is not in plain view for constitutional purposes and it is unlawful.

If police make their observations from a lawful vantage point, but the evidence observed is in a protected area, the police must find a lawful way to get into the area to seize the evidence. The plain view observation does not get them into a protected area. The plain view observation can serve as the factual basis to find probable cause for a warrant, or there might be exigent circumstances that would permit entry, or someone authorized to give consent can consent to their entry. However, the plain view observation, in and of itself, is

---

When the appellate court has cited and relied upon a U.S. Supreme Court opinion in reaching its decision, those citations are set out in full so you will know what Supreme Court authority the court relied upon. When you see an asterisk [*] in the court's opinion, that means the appellate court has referenced and relied upon a lower court case in reaching its decision. Those case citations are not included here.

not sufficient to justify police entry into a constitutionally protected area to seize the evidence observed.

Plain view typically refers to the observation of items that appear to be evidence of a crime. For an item to be observed in plain view, the police not only need to have observed it from a lawful vantage point, but they must not have moved the item. The item and that part of it that gives police probable cause to believe it is evidence of a crime must, literally, be in plain view.

Once police have made a plain view observation, they are entitled to seize the item if they have probable cause to believe it is evidence of a crime and, as just discussed, if they can physically get to the item lawfully.

Traditionally, we thought a plain view seizure required police to show that the evidence they had observed in plain view had been discovered inadvertently, or by surprise. In 1990, the U.S. Supreme Court made it clear that inadvertence is not a requirement for a plain view seizure in *Horton v. California*, 496 U.S. 128, reasoning that if "an officer is interested in an item of evidence and fully expects to find it in the course of a search, [that fact] should not invalidate its seizure if the search is confined in area and duration by the terms of a warrant or a valid exception to the warrant requirement." So if the police are executing a lawful search warrant for drugs and they also suspect the home contains illegal gambling paraphernalia (but have no probable cause to justify a warrant to search for gambling paraphernalia), they can seize any gambling paraphernalia they find if they were in a place where they were lawfully entitled to be when they observed the gambling paraphernalia (in this hypothetical they were, because they are entitled to search any place where drugs could be found) and if they have probable cause to believe the gambling paraphernalia is evidence of a crime. The fact that they fully expected to find it during the course of their search for drugs and the fact that they were actually looking for it during the course of their search for drugs are quite irrelevant. Before 1990, they could not have seized the gambling paraphernalia under the plain view exception; now that inadvertence is not a requirement, the exception permits that seizure.

10.1   COMMONWEALTH v. BALICKI (MASS. 2002)
(*Plain View Exception: Inadvertent Discovery/Federalism*)

Police officers suspected that school officials had taken household items purchased with public funds for their personal use. After reviewing invoices, they obtained a warrant to search the defendants' home for 17 specific items. While executing the warrant, they saw other items that they remembered were mentioned in the invoices and seized them.

A trial judge suppressed these items after ruling that they were not discovered inadvertently.

- *What is the social policy argument supporting the inadvertence requirement in plain view?*
- *What is the social policy argument supporting the position that a plain view discovery need not be made inadvertently?*
- *Under the federal constitution, would this plain view seizure be lawful? Explain fully.*

Commonwealth v. Balicki (Mass. 2002): 70 CrL 434

The inadvertence requirement of the plain view doctrine was jettisoned for 4th Amendment purposes by the U.S. Supreme Court in *Horton v. California,* 496 U.S. 128 (1990). However, the inadvertence requirement remains part of the Massachusetts Declaration of Rights.

In *Horton,* the Supreme Court reasoned that an officer's subjective expectation of finding an item does not create any greater impact on privacy than the officer's lawful presence in the area where he discovers the items. The *Horton* court said that prior decisions' statements that the inadvertence requirement was necessary to keep police from converting lawful searches into general searches were not persuasive because that privacy interest is already protected by the requirements that (1) a warrant particularly describe the place to be searched and the items to be seized, and (2) a warrantless search be circumscribed by the exigencies that justify it.

The state court here agreed with the dissent in *Horton* that, even if the inadvertent discovery requirement furthers no privacy interests, it is still necessary to protect possessory interests. The court made clear, however, that the inadvertence requirement is satisfied so long as police do not have probable cause to suspect the items' presence. Here, the officers generally anticipated that they would find items not mentioned in the warrant, but the record shows that the investigations into these items were on-going and that the officers did not yet have probable cause, the court decided. Accordingly, it reversed the suppression order.

10.2   STATE v. GREEN (N.C.CT.APP. 2001)
(*Plain View: Observation/Seizure*)

Officers were in an area, and specifically at an intersection, known for drug activity. It was late at night. They came on the defendant and two other individuals; as the officers approached, the defendant bent down and then began to walk away. Spotting an overturned beer bottle on the ground, the officers suspected that the defendant, who appeared to be under 21, might have been drinking illegally. When asked by an officer to return to where he had been standing, the defendant immediately placed his hand in his front pants pocket, prompting the officer to order him to remove his hand for safety reasons. When the defendant raised his arms in response to the officer's request for consent to a pat-down, the officer saw in plain view approximately 2 inches of a plastic baggie protruding from the pocket. The officer testified that his experience and training supported his conclusion that such a package would contain drugs.

- *Was that a constitutional plain view observation? Explain.*
- *What is required for a constitutional plain view seizure?*
- *Was this a constitutional plain view seizure? Explain.*

State v. Green (N.C.Ct.App. 2001): 70 CrL 152

A plastic baggie protruding from a defendant's pants pocket fulfilled the requirements for a warrantless seizure under the 4th Amendment's plain view doctrine, including the requirement that it be immediately apparent that the object was contraband or evidence of a crime. This court, in a previous case [*], adopted a totality-of-the-circumstances test for determining whether a container can be immediately apparent as contraband.

The circumstances in this case, considered in their totality, provided probable cause for the officers to conclude that the baggie contained drugs. Therefore, the facts were sufficient to satisfy the "immediately apparent" prong of the plain view doctrine.

10.3   UNITED STATES v. $557,933.89 (2D CIR. 2002)
(*Plain View: Observation/Search Probable Cause*)

A briefcase was inspected during a routine airport security inspection. The briefcase was observed to contain a large number of unsigned, undesignated money orders in amounts less than $1,000. After the airport security personnel observed the money orders, they closed the briefcase and detained it for a few minutes while a police detective was summoned to investigate. When the police detective arrived, he opened the briefcase and observed the same things the airport security person had seen.

- *The money orders were all issued within a few days of each other. Is that fact significant with respect to the observations made by the airport security personnel?*
- *Was the observation of the money orders by the airport security personnel legal? Why?*
- *Was the subsequent detention of the briefcase by the airport security personnel legal (holding it for a few minutes until the police detective arrived)? Why?*
- *Was the search by the police detective a legal search? Explain.*

United States v. $557,933.89 (2d Cir. 2002): 71 CrL 52

Observations that a briefcase carried by a traveler contained a large number of unsigned, undesignated money orders in amounts less than $1,000 was enough to give airport security personnel reasonable suspicion to detain the briefcase and to give a police detective probable cause to seize it.

The court concluded that the incriminating characteristics of the money orders were, in the language of the plain view doctrine, "immediately apparent" to the airport personnel during the security inspection. The fact that airport security personnel are laymen was irrelevant.

The court declined to find, however, that the observation that the money orders were issued within a few days of one another was immediately apparent. The judges suggested that the kind of search that would have been necessary to reveal this fact "almost certainly would have exceeded the permissible scope of a weapons/explosives check."

Because the airport security personnel detained the briefcase for only a few minutes until the detective arrived to investigate what they had found, their detention of the briefcase required only reasonable suspicion to justify it because the U.S. Supreme Court had suggested in *Arizona v. Hicks,* 420 U.S. 321 (1987), that a plain view seizure based on less than probable cause might be permissible in some circumstances. "Even to the layman, untrained in the ways of narcotics traffickers and the details of currency transactions reporting requirements, the presence at the airport of a person carrying a briefcase full of blank money orders of small (at least relative to the total value of the money orders) denominations would give rise to a well-founded suspicion that some kind of 'criminal activity' [was] afoot."

The same observations by the trained police detective gave rise to probable cause to believe the defendant was violating currency reporting laws or was engaged in illegal structuring of transactions. That the airport security personnel closed the defendant's briefcase before the detective arrived is irrelevant in light of the fact that the detective's search of the briefcase did not exceed the scope of the airport personnel's security inspection.

chapter   1 1

Automobile Exception

If police have probable cause to believe there is evidence of a crime in a car, they can search the car. If there is probable cause to believe the evidence is in the trunk, they can search the trunk. If there is probable cause to believe the evidence is in a coffee can, they can search the coffee can. If there is probable cause to believe the evidence is in the car (exactly where in the car unknown), they can search anywhere in the car that this evidence may be found. The exception takes the place of a warrant; it allows police to search as far as their probable cause will take them.

The rationales offered by the U.S. Supreme Court in support of the automobile exception are primarily two: the mobility of the automobile, and a reduced expectation of privacy in an automobile. Clearly, mobility of the automobile favors a rule that allows police to search with probable cause alone, as the car can be so easily moved while the warrant is being secured. The reduced expectation of privacy rationale recognizes that automobiles are regulated in any number of ways, and those regulations reduce the extent to which one might reasonably expect privacy in the car, especially relative to the expectation of privacy in one's home.

The most recent extension of the automobile exception deals with probable cause to believe evidence is in the car (exact location unknown), possibly in a container belonging to a passenger in the automobile. If police have probable cause to believe evidence of a crime is in the car, can they search for it in a container (e.g., a purse or luggage) belonging to a passenger? Yes, according to *Wyoming v. Houghton,* 526 U.S. 295 (1999). If that was not the rule, every thinking person with evidence of crime in the car would have a passenger, complete with purse or other container containing the evidence!

When the appellate court has cited and relied upon a U.S. Supreme Court opinion in reaching its decision, those citations are set out in full so you will know what Supreme Court authority the court relied upon. When you see an asterisk [*] in the court's opinion, that means the appellate court has referenced and relied upon a lower court case in reaching its decision. Those case citations are not included here.

142

11.1   UNITED STATES v. MERCADO (TENTH CIR. 2002)
(Automobile Exception: Probable Cause/Automobile Exception: Mobility)

Late at night, the defendant had his minivan towed to a repair shop, where the mechanic said the vehicle would have to be left overnight to be repaired. When the defendant suggested that he return the next morning with the keys, rather than leave the keys overnight with the mechanic, the mechanic told the defendant he would have the minivan repaired by the time the defendant arrived the next morning. A highway patrolman who happened to be at the repair shop and who observed the defendant's interaction with the mechanic developed probable cause to believe the minivan contained contraband. After the defendant left the shop, the officer used the defendant's keys to conduct a search that turned up drugs.

- *Assume for the sake of argument that there is probable cause to believe evidence of crime is in the vehicle. Does the automobile exception apply in light of the fact that the car is temporarily immobile due to its engine trouble? Explain.*

United States v. Mercado (Tenth Cir. 2002): 72 CrL 56

The fact that the car was temporarily immobile due to engine trouble did not dispel the "inherent mobility" of the vehicle that justifies the automobile exception to the 4th Amendment's warrant requirement.

The automobile exception is based on the diminished expectation of privacy that people enjoy in their automobiles and the idea that automobiles' "inherent mobility" makes it impractical to get a warrant before a car is driven away. The issue in this case was "whether the automobile exception applies to an inoperable car."

Answering this question in the affirmative, the court relied on *Michigan v. Thomas,* 458 U.S. 259 (1982), in which the Supreme Court said, "the justification to conduct ... a warrantless search does not vanish once the car has been immobilized; nor does it depend on the reviewing court's assessment of the likelihood in each particular case that the car would have been driven away, or that its contents would have been tampered with, during the period required for the police to obtain a warrant." Although the car in *Thomas* was immobile due to officers' impoundment rather than mechanical problems, the vehicle in this case "had not lost its *inherent* mobility" [emphasis in original]. It also pointed out that the repair shop was open all night and that the mechanic said he would have the minivan repaired by morning.

A prior decision [*] by the Tenth Circuit that held that the automobile exception did not apply to a vehicle with a partially disabled engine did not apply here, because the vehicle in that case "had no prospect of being made mobile in a matter of hours."

11.2   BLACK v. STATE (IND.APP.CT. 2003)
(Automobile Exception: Probable Cause/Automobile Exception: Mobility)

Police received information that the defendant was dealing cocaine from a 1972 gold Chevrolet Caprice on Central Avenue in Indianapolis. Detective Farrell, who had had previous contact with the defendant, drove to Central Avenue and observed the defendant standing near a 1972 gold Caprice. The detective watched for approximately an hour, during which time he observed six to eight people walk up and talk to the defendant, who would then briefly enter the car, exit and return to the person, then appear to shake hands or exchange something with the person, who would then leave. The detective concluded this was street-level narcotics dealing.

Detective Farrell knew that the defendant's license was suspended. He asked a uniformed officer in a marked vehicle to pull the defendant over. Before that happened, the defendant pulled into a parking lot and got out of the vehicle. Police arrived immediately thereafter and placed the defendant under arrest for driving while suspended.

An officer conducted a cursory search of the Caprice, but did not discover any contraband. Detective Farrell, however, had received information that the defendant had concealed cocaine under the steering column of the car. When Detective Farrell arrived on the scene, he looked under the steering column and found what immediately appeared to be cocaine.

The defendant was charged with dealing in cocaine, possession of cocaine, and driving while suspended. The defendant moved to suppress the cocaine found in his car.

- *Was there probable cause to search the car? Explain.*
- *The car was impounded at the time it was searched, hence it was not "mobile." Does that take this case out of the purview of the automobile exception?*
- *Was the search of the car constitutional? Justify your answer.*

Black v. State (Ind.App.Ct. 2003): 74 CrL 4

The automobile exception to the 4th Amendment's warrant requirement applies to impounded vehicles that officers have probable cause to believe hold evidence so long as the vehicles were "readily mobile" when they were seized.

One of the original justifications for the automobile exception was the "inherent mobility" of cars; that mobility makes it impractical to require police to get warrants to search before a car is driven away. In [*] the Indiana Court of Appeals recognized that and concluded that the automobile exception does not apply to impounded vehicles because a vehicle in police custody and control is no longer "inherently mobile" and is not likely to disappear. It also noted that, under those circumstances of impoundment, there was no chance of evidence tampering.

By contrast, other Indiana cases [*] reached the opposite conclusion, holding that the justification for a warrantless search does not depend on whether the car has been immobilized and is no longer likely to be driven away, or whether evidence is likely to be tampered with.

Here, the court sided with the latter group of cases, holding that a warrantless search can be made of an impounded car and no exigent circumstances are required to justify that search.

The court noted that the U.S. Supreme Court has offered two justifications for the automobile exception, in addition to the "inherent mobility" of the car. First, there is a reduced expectation of privacy in an automobile (as opposed to a dwelling). Second, the entitlement to search under the authority of the automobile exception arises at the time the automobile is seized; if the vehicle was readily mobile when it was first seized and if there was probable cause to believe it contained evidence of a crime, the 4th Amendment allows a warrantless search of that automobile.

These two requirements were satisfied in this case. The trial court was correct in denying the defendant's motion to suppress.

One judge dissented, arguing that an impounded car is no longer "inherently mobile" and likely to disappear before a proper warrant can be issued.

11.3   STATE v. BRANHAM (ARIZ.CT.APP., DIV. 1 1997)
(*Automobile Exception: Probable Cause/Consent*)

William Branham was stopped for speeding and the officer asked him to produce his driver's license and registration. Branham gave the officer his license but said he had cleaned his car and had left the registration at home. The officer asked Branham twice to look in the car for the registration and, when none was produced, he ordered Branham and his wife out of the car so the officer could search the car himself for the registration. The officer said that Branham said, "Okay." At the motion to suppress, the officer further testified that failure to produce the automobile registration was justification to search the car for it, and he admitted he had no other basis for searching the car. The officer said he conducted similar searches in approximately 85 percent of cases in which a driver did not produce a registration. The search turned up methamphetamine and drug paraphernalia.

The defendant was charged and convicted of possession of dangerous drugs. On appeal, he admitted that the officer made a legitimate traffic stop, but complained that it was unconstitutional for the officer to conduct a limited search for the automobile registration on the sole basis of the driver's failure to produce it.

The trial court had rejected this argument, reasoning that if a person had stolen the car, he might turn over his driver's license but not the registration because it would show another's name.

- *Was this limited search constitutional as an automobile exception search? Defend your answer.*

- *Assume for purposes of this exercise that you find the search unconstitutional. Under what circumstances would this search be a proper automobile exception search (i.e., what facts, not present here, would save this search)?*

- *Was this limited search justified by Branham's consent? Explain.*

State v. Branham (Ariz.Ct.App., Div.1 1997): 62 CrL 1330

The Arizona Court of Appeals cited a line of cases [*] stating the rule that if a driver is unable to produce proof of registration, the officer can conduct a limited search of the car for evidence of automobile ownership. In those cases, however, probable cause to believe the car was stolen was supported by more than the defendant's failure to prove ownership. For example, the car was parked in an area where stolen cars were typically abandoned; the defendant tried to elude police; or the defendant had no driver's license and did not know the name of the car's owner or the name of the person who loaned it to him. In each of those cases, there was probable cause to believe that the vehicle was stolen, based only in part on the driver's failure to produce the registration. In this case, the officer admitted and the court found that the search was based entirely on the driver's failure to produce proof of registration; indeed, this officer had a policy of searching cars under this circumstance.

In [*], the California Supreme Court said, "It would not be unreasonable for a thief to remove or destroy the registration card of an automobile he has taken; his purpose in doing so might be to prevent the true owner from being traced, to eliminate the discrepancy between the owner's name and his own, or to facilitate substitution of a forged card.... [I]t is also true that being a stranger to the vehicle he might not be able to present the card to an officer simply because he did not know where to find it." The trial court in this case adopted that reasoning and found the search to be constitutional. However, the California court also observed that failure to produce the registration card "could equally well be entirely innocent," as when a person renews or transfers registration, or when a driver might innocently be unable to locate the registration. The California court concluded that the failure to produce registration, without more, does not provide probable cause to believe that a car has been stolen.

The Arizona Court of Appeals reached the same conclusion. The failure to produce registration is not a criminal offense. It is as consistent with innocent behavior as with supposed criminal behavior. Therefore, that failure, by itself, does not provide probable cause to believe that a car is stolen and it does not permit the limited search conducted here.

"This decision does not mean that failure to produce registration is irrelevant in all cases.... [O]ther facts, in combination with the failure to provide registration, may provide probable cause to believe that a car is stolen, or is involved in some other criminal activity. We hold that because the state did not provide any additional evidence that the vehicle in this case might be stolen or involved in some other criminal activity, the search was not supported by probable cause under the automobile exception."

The case was remanded for ruling on whether the driver had given consent for the search.

Open Fields Exception

The exception to 4th Amendment protections that might be most difficult for students of criminal procedure to accept is the open fields exception. This development allows police to go onto property belonging to a citizen, without notice or permission, and to seize evidence of crime found on that property—all without probable cause or a warrant.

The open fields exception began innocently enough as an observation without elaboration in a case in which the government had entered privately owned land, in *Hester v. United States,* 265 U.S. 57 (1924). Officers opened containers found on the ground and discovered evidence of crime in the containers. They seized the evidence and the U.S. Supreme Court ultimately declared that this trespass onto private land was not a search for constitutional purposes because the government had not trespassed on the curtilage, the area immediately surrounding the house.

The exception, as it developed, distinguished between two areas: first, the curtilage, the land immediately surrounding the house, which enjoys 4th Amendment protection; and second, open fields, the area beyond the curtilage that does not enjoy 4th Amendment protection.

Open field is a term of art. It should not be interpreted literally because an open field for constitutional purposes need neither be "open" nor a "field." It is simply the area on the property that is not curtilage.

This exception expands warrantless police activity without any doubt. Under the open fields exception, police are allowed to search private property without probable cause or a warrant. However, it offers an important protection as well, because it defines an area beyond the confines of the house that is protected by the 4th Amendment. That is, the 4th

---

When the appellate court has cited and relied upon a U.S. Supreme Court opinion in reaching its decision, those citations are set out in full so you will know what Supreme Court authority the court relied upon. When you see an asterisk [*] in the court's opinion, that means the appellate court has referenced and relied upon a lower court case in reaching its decision. Those case citations are not included here.

Amendment by its terms protects our "houses" and the Court in these cases makes it clear that our "house" extends some reasonable distance beyond its exterior walls.

How far that protection extends is a little difficult to determine, because the test offered by the court to ascertain where the curtilage ends and the open field begins is not precise. The test was set out in *United States v. Dunn,* 480 U.S. 294 (1987), and directs us to define this boundary by considering how close this spot is to the home, whether it is fenced, what the space is used for, and what the resident has done to protect it from observations by others who might be passing by. The last two elements of the test are very subjective and invite dispute with respect to which facts are relevant and how they should be interpreted. Nonetheless, it is clear that our homes enjoy 4th Amendment protection that includes the house itself as well as a reasonable space beyond and surrounding it. The area beyond that protected curtilage, however, can be entered, and evidence found there can be seized without probable cause or a warrant.

12.1   PEOPLE v. PITTMAN (ILL. 2004) (*Open Fields Exception*)

A relative of the defendant who lived on a farm with him notified police that the defendant was growing marijuana on the farm. Without obtaining a warrant, police went to the farm and knocked on the front and back doors of the house. Receiving no answer, they walked to a barn located about 50 yards from the house. The barn was open in the sense that it had only three walls: In place of a south wall, it had a canopy covering a feedlot. The officers entered the barn through a large door that stood open on the east side and observed marijuana plants that could not be seen from outside the barn. The defendant was arrested when he arrived at the barn shortly thereafter.

The farm was owned by the defendant's mother. The defendant had the authority to manage the entire farm.

The defendant moved to suppress the evidence of the marijuana plants, arguing that the warrantless search was unconstitutional. The state contended that the defendant did not have a legitimate expectation of privacy in the barn because it was in the open fields outside the curtilage of his home.

- ■ *Analyze this open fields exception case.*
  - • *Was the barn in an open field?*
  - • *Were the police constitutionally entitled to approach it?*
  - • *Were the police constitutionally entitled to search it? Explain fully.*

People v. Pitman (Ill. 2004): 75 CrL 449

The defendant possessed a reasonable expectation of privacy protected by the 4th Amendment in an open barn outside the curtilage of his home. Through his mother, the owner, the defendant had a possessory interest in the entire farm and the ability to exclude others from it; thus, a warrantless search of the barn was unlawful. The court rejected the state's open fields argument, stating that the 4th Amendment protects buildings other than dwellings.

The U.S. Supreme Court ruled that a person does not have a legitimate expectation of privacy in open fields outside the curtilage of his home. In *United States v. Dunn,* 480 U.S. 294 (1987), the court set out factors for determining whether an area is within the curtilage. Applying those factors here, the Illinois court concluded that because the barn was 50 yards from the farmhouse, outside of the enclosure surrounding the dwelling, used chiefly for carpet storage, and open to the observation of anyone standing in the open field, it was not within the curtilage of the dwelling.

Nonetheless, the court said, citing [*], the 4th Amendment protects structures other than dwellings, and those structures need not be within the curtilage of the home. *Dunn* held that officers without a warrant could stand outside a barn that was outside the curtilage and look inside the barn's front door, but *Dunn* did not hold that police could enter the barn itself.

In deciding whether the defendant possessed a reasonable expectation of privacy in the barn, the court turned to state precedents. The court in [*] said that relevant factors in the analysis are: (1) the ownership of the property, (2) whether the defendant was legitimately on the premises, (3) whether the defendant had a possessory interest in the property searched, (4) prior use of the area searched, (5) whether the defendant had the ability to exclude others, and (6) the defendant's subjective expectation of privacy.

Those factors were satisfied here. Although the defendant did not own the barn, he had a possessory interest in it, the right to be there, and the ability to exclude others, all by virtue of the owner's conferring on him legal authority to manage the entire farm. "These rights are sufficient to establish defendant's reasonable expectation of privacy in the barn."

One judge dissented. He said that courts that have addressed whether a defendant has a reasonable expectation of privacy in a barn outside the curtilage have looked to whether the barn was being put to a business purpose for the farm and whether the defendant took measures to effectuate privacy, such as closing and locking the doors.

12.2   UNITED STATES v. HATFIELD (TENTH CIR. 2003) (*Open Fields Exception*)

Acting on an anonymous tip that the defendant was growing marijuana behind his house, police officers went to the house and requested consent for a search. When permission was denied, one officer entered an adjacent pasture that was owned by the defendant and separated by a fence from the backyard, dwelling, and various outbuildings of the curtilage. The officer walked along the pasture side of the fence toward the back of the house and sighted what appeared to be marijuana growing inside a chicken coop. A warrant was issued, and police seized marijuana plants growing in various places in the backyard.

In a motion to suppress the evidence, the defendant argued that the warrantless search of his backyard from his adjoining open field was unconstitutional.

- *Did the officer trespass? Does that matter constitutionally?*
- *Was the officer's observation constitutional? Why?*
- *Was this a constitutional search? Explain.*

United States v. Hatfield (Tenth Cir. 2003): 73 CrL 429

A defendant lacked a reasonable expectation of privacy protected by the 4th Amendment in areas within the curtilage of his home that were viewable from an adjoining open field. The fact that an officer was trespassing in the open field when he made a warrantless observation does not affect the privacy analysis.

There is no reasonable expectation that a home and its curtilage exposed to public view will be free from ordinary visual surveillance. In *California v. Ciraolo,* 476 U.S. 207 (1986), the U.S. Supreme Court held that police officers did not conduct a warrantless search in violation of the 4th Amendment when they made naked-eye observations of a fenced yard within the curtilage of a home from a plane flying at a 1,000-foot altitude over the property. Although the fencing around the yard prevented ground-level surveillance, the fact that the property could be viewed from above, either in a plane or by a worker on a utility pole, meant that the yard was "knowingly expose[d] to the public," the *Ciraolo* court said.

The court pointed out that, under *Ciraolo,* the defendant in the instant case would clearly not have had an expectation of privacy if the pasture from which the officer viewed his backyard had been owned by a neighbor, because in that situation the defendant would have been exposing the marijuana to the view of his neighbors and their guests. The court, therefore, framed the question in this case as whether the facts that the defendant owned the pasture and the officer was a trespasser changed the result by creating a reasonable expectation of privacy from observations made of the curtilage.

Answering this question in the negative, the court relied on *United States v. Dunn,* 480 U.S. 294 (1987) and [*]. In *Dunn,* the Supreme Court upheld a search by trespassing officers who, while standing in the defendant's open field, were able to view drug paraphernalia within the defendant's barn. Assuming without deciding that the interior of the barn, although not part of the residence's curtilage, was protected by the 4th Amendment, the court said there was no difference between observations police made in a public place and observations they made while standing in an open field.

[*] involved observations made while officers were trespassing on the defendant's open fields. The court held that the officers' observation of an illegal distillery in a shed located within the curtilage was not a search prohibited by the 4th Amendment. Had the officers physically breached the curtilage, however, their observations would have constituted a search. Similarly, in the instant case, the officer's observation of illegal activity was made from outside the curtilage and without physically breaching it. Following these cases, the court held "that police observation of a defendant's curtilage from a vantage point in the defendant's open field is not a search under the 4th Amendment."

The defendant made much of the fact that the officer's presence in his pasture violated a state criminal trespass statute. Despite the law having been in effect for some 90 years, the court said it had "never found it to be relevant to 4th Amendment analysis of whether an officer was properly in an open field in cases arising in [that state]." The court went on to explicitly hold that "the fact that a state may have chosen to protect interests of its citizens by making trespass a crime under state law" does not affect the analysis of the individual's 4th Amendment interests.

Admissions and Confessions

There are basically three constitutional protections that might come into play with respect to admissions and confessions. The due process clause in the 5th Amendment essentially requires that the government treat us fairly. In the arena of admissions and confessions, this test has been confusing because the test for a due process violation is "voluntariness" and that became an umbrella term having little to do with what most people think of as voluntary. The due process protection is valuable, however, because it is not limited in time; it is always available to the defendant whether he has been arrested or not, whether she is in custody or not, and whether he is being interrogated or otherwise questioned. The most salient elements to consider in determining if a due process violation is present (if the admission or confession is "involuntary") are the conduct of the police and the characteristics of the defendant that might make him more vulnerable and that might contribute to an involuntary confession.

The right to counsel guaranteed by the 6th Amendment is the second constitutional provision protecting admissions and confessions. This guarantee is not very helpful to defendants in the earliest stages of police investigation because the 6th Amendment right to counsel only becomes operative after criminal prosecution has begun (because the 6th Amendment refers specifically to rights adhering in "all criminal prosecutions" and the Court determined in *Kirby v. Illinois,* 406 U.S. 682 [1972] that "criminal prosecutions" begin with arraignment or indictment). The major case in this area is *Massiah v. United States,* 377 U.S. 201 (1964), holding that police may not deliberately elicit information from a

---

When the appellate court has cited and relied upon a U.S. Supreme Court opinion in reaching its decision, those citations are set out in full so you will know what Supreme Court authority the court relied upon. When you see an asterisk [*] in the court's opinion, that means the appellate court has referenced and relied upon a lower court case in reaching its decision. Those case citations are not included here.

defendant who is represented by counsel without counsel being present. Although the "deliberately elicit" standard is fairly generous, it nonetheless functions in a restricted time frame and is not helpful to the suspect who has been arrested but not yet arraigned or indicted—for example, the defendant who is arrested on Friday evening and not arraigned until Monday.

At that early stage, the suspect is not only protected by due process, but also by the 5th Amendment right to be free from self-incrimination, as set out most clearly in *Miranda v. Arizona*, 384 U.S. 436 (1966). *Miranda* is designed to protect us during "custodial interrogation." Both words are important. Before *Miranda* is operative, we must find that the suspect is "in custody" for 4th Amendment purposes and is being "interrogated." Interrogation for these purposes means direct questioning by the police, whether or not that questioning is likely to elicit any information, or the "functional equivalent of questioning" if that is likely to produce information from the defendant.

Because the *Miranda* warning is compound, it would generally be to a defendant's benefit to use a compound sentence and clearly announce, for example, "I do not want to talk with you and I want a lawyer." However, many defendants do not express themselves that clearly and cases are abundant in which we examine what the defendant said, trying to determine whether the defendant chose to exercise or waive his or her rights. Cases are selected in this section to illustrate.

If a suspect elects to exercise the right to remain silent and the right to counsel, it is clear that the police must stop interrogating and they cannot begin again until counsel is present. However, if the defendant has only exercised the right to remain silent, police must stop questioning, but they can ask later if the suspect wants to talk. Beyond that, if the defendant has only exercised the right to remain silent (and not the right to counsel) and if the defendant thereafter initiates conversation with the police, that initiation of conversation can be considered a waiver of the right to silence and police can continue their conversation or interrogation.

A suspect can waive his or her *Miranda* rights and choose to talk with the police without the benefit of counsel. In many cases, the constitutional issue has switched from whether the interrogation was constitutional to whether the waiver was constitutional. Ironically enough, the test here is whether the waiver was made knowingly and voluntarily. We are back to the box from which we began, the imprecision of the "voluntariness" standard. *Miranda* did not eliminate it; it simply changed its focus.

13.1   STATE v. ANSON (WIS.CT.APP. 2002)
(*Admissions and Confessions*)

The defendant had been charged with sexual conduct with a child, and the police had a warrant for his arrest. While the defendant was still unaware of both of these facts, officers contacted him in the hopes of getting a statement from him. The officers assured the defendant that he was not under arrest, and they lied to him when he asked whether any charges had been filed. Without giving *Miranda* warnings, they questioned the defendant and his answers were used to convict him.

- *The defendant complained that the interrogation was unconstitutional. Was it? Explain.*

State v. Anson (Wis.Ct.App. 2002): 72 CrL 104

The defendant should have been informed of charges that had been filed against him and should have been informed of his right to counsel. A defendant who was unaware that charges had been filed against him could not have given a valid waiver of his 6th Amendment right to counsel.

The U.S. Supreme Court has not decided whether an accused must be told that he has been charged before a postindictment waiver of right to counsel will be valid.

The Wisconsin Supreme Court in an earlier case [*] decided that a defendant who has already been charged and who does not have counsel must invoke the right to counsel to prevent interrogation. In that case, the court also concluded that a defendant who had already been charged and who had counsel did not have to again assert his 6th Amendment right to counsel when detectives arrived to question him at the jail. In the course of rendering that opinion, the court said that, after the right to counsel has attached:

> [t]he right [to counsel] must be "invoked" by the accused to terminate police questioning before an attorney has been retained or appointed for those specific charges, provided the accused has been fully alerted to the right to have an attorney and the right not to answer questions. This normally would entail *Miranda* warnings.

In this case, the court was guided by that language and was led to conclude that a defendant cannot knowingly waive his 6th Amendment right to counsel unless he is aware that charges have been filed. The court explained:

> Although *Miranda* warnings may not be necessary at the onset of all noncustodial police interrogations, [it is logical to conclude] that an accused must be aware that the right to counsel is available in order to decide whether to invoke it and request the presence of counsel or to waive it and proceed without counsel.

The court concluded:

> At the onset of postcharge pretrial police interrogations, the accused must be made aware that the adversarial process has begun and that he or she can request the assistance of counsel at the onset of postcharge police interrogations.

This can be accomplished by informing the accused that he or she has been formally charged, or by reading *Miranda* warnings to the suspect, or by anything else that would inform the suspect that the adversarial process has begun. "Any uncounseled statements made after that knowledge or after a *Miranda* warning can constitute a valid waiver of the 6th Amendment right to counsel."

In this case, the defendant's uncounseled statements did not constitute a valid waiver of the right to counsel because he was not aware that he had been charged. Accordingly, the interrogation violated his right to choose to deal with the state through the intermediary of counsel once formal adversarial proceedings had begun.

13.2   IN RE D.F.L. (COLO. 1997)
(*Admissions and Confessions/Search*)

Officer Shires received information that certain named individuals were selling narcotics out of an apartment in Aurora. The officer obtained a "no-knock" warrant authorizing a search of the apartment, the persons found therein, and "such vessels, implements, and furniture used in connection" with the manufacture, storage, or dispensing of marijuana or LSD. The warrant also authorized seizure of any "articles of personal property tending to establish the identity of the persons in control of the contraband."

On executing the warrant, officers found three males and a juvenile female, D.F.L., in the living room area. The officers secured the apartment, patted down the individuals, and placed them in custody. D.F.L. was searched for weapons or contraband, but none was found at that time. Officer Shires then entered the master bedroom and found a purse near the bed. She brought the purse back to the living room, where the individuals had been handcuffed, and asked to whom it belonged. D.F.L. said, "That's mine." She had not been advised of her rights under *Miranda* prior to the officer's inquiry. After the individuals were taken to the police station for identification, the officers conducted a thorough search that extended to the purse. The purse was found to contain a cigarette package containing a psilocybin mushroom.

- *Were police entitled to search the purse? Explain.*
- *Was the statement admissible? Explain.*

In re D.F.L. (Colo. 1997): 60 CrL 1449

Search of the purse was included within the four corners of the warrant because the purse was found within the apartment and is a container capable of holding the drugs and paraphernalia identified in the warrant. The U.S. Supreme Court commented in *United States v. Ross,* 456 U.S. 798 (1982), that a lawful search of a building or dwelling generally extends to the entire area in which the object of the search may be found and is not limited by the possibility that separate acts of entry or opening might be required to complete the search. Federal courts have consistently applied the proposition that a container found in a dwelling or residence that is subject to a validly issued warrant can be searched if it is large enough to contain the contraband or evidence the officers are looking for.

D.F.L. said these cases are not controlling because she did not live in the apartment and she was not named in the warrant. She relied on [*], holding that the purse of a guest in an apartment was not subject to a search under a warrant, the terms of which were not disclosed in the case. However, here the terms of the warrant granted a broad scope of authority including the search of all persons found within the premises and any vessels used for the storage of drugs. Furthermore, the notion that one's status as a guest, without more, vitiates the otherwise legal search of a container is not supported by law.

The Question of Suppression of the Statement

The parties agreed that D.F.L. was in custody. The question is whether the officer's inquiry constituted interrogation. Interrogation includes "any words or actions on the part of the police (other than those normally attendant to arrest and custody) that the police should know are reasonably likely to illicit an incriminating response from the suspect," as cited in *Rhode Island v. Innis,* 446 U.S. 291 (1980).

Given the valid search warrant for drugs and paraphernalia, the officers had probable cause to believe that drugs were in the apartment or in containers found therein. Officer Shires clearly intended to search the purse after discovering it in the bedroom. The fact that the officers were searching for drugs supports the conclusion that any question concerning the ownership or control of illegal drugs or containers that might hold those drugs clearly was designed to elicit an incriminating response. The argument that the officers did not actually know that drugs would be found does not obviate the fact that the officers should have known that such a question could elicit an incriminating response. Therefore, the court found that Officer Shires' question concerning ownership of the purse constituted "interrogation" without the benefit of a *Miranda* advisement.

The suppression of D.F.L.'s statement was affirmed.

13.3   STEARNS COUNTY, MINN. v. HANNON (MINN. 2001) (*Admissions and Confessions/Federalism*)

The defendant was arrested for the murder of a woman with whom he lived. Her badly burned body had been found in the apartment.

The defendant was read his rights under *Miranda v. Arizona,* 384 U.S. 436 (1966), and agreed to talk to police. The interrogators did not immediately state that the victim was dead. When they did so, the defendant asked what they were saying; they responded, "We're saying that you took [the victim's] life." This statement was followed by several exchanges in which the defendant said, "You think I killed her?" or words to that effect, and the interrogators assured him they knew he had killed the victim but wanted to know why. The following exchange then took place:

> *Defendant:* Can I have a drink of water and then lock me up—I think we really should have an attorney.
>
> *Detective:* We'll get you a drink of water.
>
> *Defendant:* I don't want to talk anymore please. (Pause). This is—this is really wrong. This woman has scars all over her from this Paul Mackey. He's callin' her 50 times a week.
>
> *Detective:* 'Kay. If you want to talk to an attorney, you understand that we have to stop talking to you. OK? And—and then your side of this story will never be known. That's your choice. That's a choice you're making.

The defendant asked what the detective meant, and the detective answered that the police would "put this thing together and ... convict you of murder." The interrogation continued, and the defendant made incriminating statements that were recorded on video or audiotape. He then gave a formal statement to the officers.

The defendant moved to suppress all the statements he made after his remark about having a lawyer. The trial court ruled that the remark was only an equivocal request for counsel and that the officers were permitted to ask questions tailored to clarify the defendant's true desire with respect to counsel. The trial court concluded that the detective's comment about the defendant's story remaining untold was permissible and that the defendant's response amounted to reinitiation of the interrogation. The suppression motion was therefore denied.

- *Was the statement equivocal? Or was it clear? Was the trial court correct? Explain your reasoning.*

Stearns County, Minn. v. Hannon (Minn. 2001): 70 CrL 329

A murder defendant undergoing custodial interrogation clearly invoked his right to counsel when, after being told by detectives that they knew he was a murderer, said, "I think we really should have an attorney."

The Minnesota Supreme Court said the defendant's remark was an unequivocal request for counsel within the meaning of the test established in *Davis v. United States*, 512 U.S. 452 (1994). Under that standard, a defendant must "articulate his desire to have counsel present sufficiently clearly that a reasonable police officer, in the circumstances, would understand the statement to be a request for an attorney."

The court began by pointing out that the remark was preceded by three exchanges in which the defendant asked if the officers believed he had killed the victim, and the officers assured him that they knew he had done so. The court then indicated that, in terms of its objective sufficiency as an unequivocal request, the defendant's remark was equivalent to a statement—"I think I'd rather talk to a lawyer"—that was held to be an unequivocal request for counsel in [*]. Furthermore, the court said, the detective responded to the remark in a way that showed he did not consider the request for counsel to be equivocal.

Even if the defendant's request for counsel was equivocal, the detective's response was not an appropriate "clarifying" question under Minnesota law—which, the court noted, is more protective of defendants' rights than federal law as established in *Davis*. The detective's response improperly implied that the defendant "had to make a choice between either talking to an attorney and never having his side of the story known or continuing to talk with the officers," the court said.

Because that response was improper, the court added, the defendant's subsequent question as to what the detective meant could not be considered a reinitiation of the interrogation under *Edwards v. Arizona*, 451 U.S. 477 (1981). The detective's remark about the consequences of invoking the right to counsel and his statement that the police would put the case together and convict the defendant of murder "were designed to induce appellant to continue talking and were improper." The mere fact that the defendant made a further statement does not show a waiver, the court concluded.

13.4   ALVAREZ v. GOMEZ (NINTH CIR. 1999)
(*Admissions and Confessions:* Miranda)

The petitioner was warned of his rights under *Miranda* and he said he understood them. A detective then asked him whether he wanted to give up the right to remain silent and speak about the incident under investigation, a fatal shooting. In response, the petitioner asked, "Can I get an attorney right now, man?" After the detective said "Pardon me?" the petitioner asked, "You can have attorney right now?" The detective said, "Ah, you can have one appointed for you, yes." The petitioner responded, "Well, like right now you got one?" The detective and his partner then told the petitioner there was no attorney currently present and that one would be appointed for him at arraignment if he could not afford one. The petitioner then said he would talk to the detectives and answered "Yes" when asked if he wanted to talk without a lawyer.

In this jurisdiction, "*Miranda* duty lawyers" were available around the clock to arrestees.

- *Was there a violation of the petitioner's constitutional rights? Explain.*

Alvarez v. Gomez (Ninth Cir. 1999): 65 CrL 510

The three questions asked by this interrogation target concerning the availability of an attorney amounted to an invocation of his right to counsel and triggered an obligation on the part of police officers to stop questioning him. The three questions the petitioner asked "considered together" could constitute an unequivocal request for an attorney and thus call for a halt to questioning. The court rejected the trial court's conclusions that the officers interpreted the petitioner's inquiries as mere "clarifying questions regarding his right to counsel" and that their answers to those questions were made in good faith. "The correct answer to each of [the petitioner's] three questions, after all, was a simple unambiguous 'yes,'" the majority said, noting that *Miranda* duty lawyers were available around the clock to arrestees in the jurisdiction where the interrogation took place. The detectives' failure to honor the rule that questioning must cease if a suspect invokes his right to counsel made the petitioner's subsequent incriminating statements inadmissible.

13.5   PEOPLE v. GONZALES (COLO. 1999)
(*Admissions and Confessions:* Miranda)

The defendant was charged with murdering his girlfriend. He was being transported back to his jail cell after a hearing on his pretrial motions. The defendant had invoked his interrogation rights when he was Mirandized; at the time of this encounter, he was being escorted by a deputy.

The in-custody defendant asked the deputy, "Can I be up front with you?" The deputy answered, "Sure." After the deputy's one-word response, the defendant told him, "I didn't intentionally kill her," and "It was an accident."

The deputy reported those comments made by the defendant. When the state sought to use that evidence against him, the defendant moved to suppress, arguing that his rights to be free from custodial interrogation had been violated.

- *Were they? Analyze the problem and explain.*

People v. Gonzales (Colo. 1999): 66 CrL 91

The deputy did not violate the defendant's rights under *Miranda v. Arizona,* 384 U.S. 436 (1966). *Miranda's* protections of the 5th Amendment's privilege against self-incrimination require that, when a suspect invokes his right to counsel, police-initiated "interrogation" must cease. Under *Rhode Island v. Innis,* 466 U.S. 291 (1980), interrogation includes not only express questioning but also its "functional equivalent"; that is, words or actions that the officer knows or should know are "reasonably likely to elicit an incriminating response from the suspect."

The Colorado Supreme Court pointed out that *Innis* also reaffirmed the idea that the *Miranda* rules do not apply to "volunteered" statements that are not the product of interrogation. In [*] a suspect asked an officer if he could explain why he had pointed a gun at another driver and then went on to make incriminating statements when the officer did not respond. In [*] a suspect began spontaneously to explain the circumstances of his offense to an officer who asked no questions concerning what had happened. In both cases, the court held that the officers' reaction did not amount to interrogation for *Miranda* purposes.

The deputy's response in the instant case "differs little from the silent authorizations at issue in [the other cases cited above]."

"A police officer may allow a suspect to make a statement by expressly voicing his consent or by remaining silent. A response explicitly permitting a defendant to make an inculpatory statement does not rise to the level of police interrogation…. Moreover, unlike the examples of psychological ploys provided in *Miranda* and *Innis,* the facts here contain no suggestion that the deputy used deception, intimidation, coercion, or lengthy harangues to obtain the defendant's statements."

The court acknowledged that "it may well be that [the deputy] knew or should have known that the defendant was about to make an incriminating statement and that, by responding 'Sure' such a statement would in fact be made." Even so, the court said, "we cannot conclude that [the deputy's] response *compelled* the defendant to make a statement, much less that, based on the totality of the circumstances, [the deputy] should have anticipated his response would be perceived by the defendant as an interrogation and overcome his desire not to speak about his case" [emphasis in original].

The court, after noting that the 5th Amendment does not protect suspects from "their own impulses to speak," concluded that "even assuming, arguendo, that [the deputy] knew the defendant was asking whether he could make a voluntary, perhaps inculpatory statement, [the deputy] did nothing improper by acquiescing."

13.6   HILL V. BRIGANO (SIXTH CIR. 1999)
(*Admissions and Confessions:* Miranda)

The petitioner in this habeas corpus case was convicted in state court in connection with his participation in murders in Belmont County, Ohio. He was arrested on a warrant in Franklin County where, in response to interrogation, he asserted his right to counsel. The officers ceased their interrogation for approximately 2 hours while they obtained a confession from a codefendant. After the codefendant admitted his role and implicated the petitioner, the officers put them both in the same room for 45 minutes. The officers then resumed their interrogation of the petitioner. The petitioner again asserted his right to counsel, and the officers ended the interrogation, although not immediately.

The next morning, the petitioner was taken to an arraignment hearing before a Franklin County magistrate, where he was represented by counsel. That evening, as he was being transported back to Belmont County, an officer asked the petitioner whether he wanted to talk to anyone and advised the petitioner that his cooperation would be beneficial. Again, the petitioner invoked his right to counsel.

On the morning of his second day of custody, the petitioner had his initial appearance. He was not represented by counsel at this hearing, but the court appointed counsel for him at the end of the hearing and informed him of his *Miranda* rights.

After the hearing, as the petitioner and his codefendant were being transported back to jail by the sheriff, the co-defendant asked whether the officers had found the victims' wallets and other evidence about which the codefendant had told them. When the sheriff responded that they had not, the petitioner stated that he knew where the evidence was located. When the petitioner arrived at the jail, he asked to speak with the sheriff and told the sheriff that he could take the officers to the location of the evidence. The sheriff advised the petitioner that neither he nor the other officers could initiate a conversation with the petitioner and that the petitioner was entitled to be represented by his attorney. The petitioner stated that he understood and was willing to proceed to the site of the evidence without his attorney. The petitioner then led the officers to the evidence.

- *Had police violated the defendant's* Miranda *rights? Explain.*
- *Should the evidence be suppressed? Explain.*

Hill v. Brigano (Sixth Cir. 1999): 66 CrL 264

Despite prior *Miranda* violations, the suspect's inquiry lifted the bar to interrogation. Police officers' repeated violations of the suspect's rights under *Miranda* did not prevent his request, the following morning, to talk to police from allowing further interrogation. Ordinarily, a suspect who has invoked his right to counsel under *Miranda* but subsequently initiates contact with police cannot be questioned if his initiation was preceded by a *Miranda* violation. Here, however, enough time had passed between the *Miranda* violations and the suspect's initiation of further questioning to trigger an exception to that rule.

Under *Edwards v. Arizona,* 451 U.S. 477 (1981), police must cease all police-initiated interrogation when a suspect invokes his *Miranda* right to counsel. If the police, rather than the suspect himself, initiate contact with a suspect who has invoked his right to counsel, any waiver of that right is invalid.

The petitioner contended that his 5th and 6th Amendment rights were violated because the officers never honored his request for interrogation to cease until his attorney was present. He argued that the cumulative effect of the numerous *Miranda* violations coerced him into providing the officers with information about the location of the evidence, and that he did not voluntarily waive his right to counsel.

The last impermissible interrogation of the defendant occurred as he was being transported back to Belmont County, the court observed. "Taking into account both the time lapse between the impermissible interrogation and the incriminating statements by the defendant and the fact that the defendant was aware that he had been assigned counsel, we believe the trial court was correct in analyzing the admissibility of this evidence under the initiation exception to *Edwards*.... In addition, prior to the discovery of any of the challenged evidence, the defendant stated numerous times that he understood that he had the right to have his lawyer present."

13.7 CLARK v. MURPHY (NINTH CIR. 2003)
(*Admissions and Confessions:* Miranda)

A suspect was in custody, having been arrested in connection with his sale of a car stolen from a murdered relative. He was advised of his *Miranda* rights several times, acknowledged that he understood those rights, and admitted to stealing the victim's car. When a homicide detective told the petitioner that he doubted the petitioner's version of events, the petitioner said, "I think I would like to talk to a lawyer." The detective responded by saying that, if the petitioner wanted a lawyer, the detective would call one but that it would probably mean the end of their conversation. The detective then left the petitioner alone for a few minutes to decide what he wanted to do.

When the detective returned, the petitioner stated that he did not want a lawyer, and the interrogation continued. The petitioner soon confessed to the murder.

The defendant contended that his statement, "I think I would like to talk to a lawyer," represented a clear request for a lawyer that should have precluded additional questioning.

- *Has the defendant clearly invoked his right to counsel? Should the confession be suppressed? Explain.*

Clark v. Murphy (Ninth Cir. 2003): 72 CrL 351

A homicide suspect's statement during a custodial interrogation that "I think I would like to talk to a lawyer" did not unambiguously invoke the right to consult with counsel. The officer's continued questioning did not violate the rule from *Edwards v. Arizona,* 451 U.S. 477 (1981), that all questioning must cease once a suspect requests counsel.

In *Davis v. United States,* 512 U.S. 452 (1994), the Supreme Court held that a suspect does not trigger the *Edwards* rule unless the suspect "unambiguously request[s] counsel";

that is, a suspect "must articulate his desire to have counsel present sufficiently clearly that a reasonable police officer in the circumstances would understand the statement to be a request for an attorney." In *Davis,* the Supreme Court found the statement, "[m]aybe I should talk to a lawyer," to be ambiguous.

A majority of the court reported that decisions in the circuit are, like decisions from other jurisdictions, "somewhat inconsistent on what qualifies as unequivocal and what constitutes an equivocal request for a lawyer." Returning to *Davis,* the majority identified a possible distinction between the statement there and the petitioner's statement—the petitioner's use of the qualifying clause "I think I would," instead of "maybe I should." Dictionaries define "to think" to mean "to reflect on" or "to ponder," and the majority said that the words "I think" used by a suspect could render a request for counsel equivocal. However, it concluded that "without knowing [the petitioner's] tone of voice, inflection, and more about the context in which the statement was made, it is difficult to tell just *how* equivocal his statement was" [emphasis in original].

The majority found guidance in a Fourth Circuit case [*] in which that court held that the statement "I think I need a lawyer" was too equivocal to amount to an invocation of the right to counsel. The majority said that the statement at issue in the instant case is even more ambiguous "since [the petitioner] stated that he *thought* he would *like* to talk to an attorney" [emphasis in original].

The majority called the question "a close one" but concluded that the petitioner "failed to 'articulate his desire to have counsel present sufficiently clearly that a reasonable police officer' standing in [the detective's] shoes would have understood the statement to be a request for counsel." Quoting from *Michigan v. Mosley,* 423 U.S. 96 (1975), the majority said that "[i]f a questioning officer is reasonably unsure as to whether or not the suspect wants a lawyer, then to require the cessation of questioning would 'transform the *Miranda* safeguards' into 'irrational obstacles to legitimate police investigative activity,' ... and this we may not do."

Because the state court did not err when it admitted the petitioner's confession, the petitioner could not show that the state court's decision merited habeas corpus relief.

13.8   COOPER v. STATE (GA.CT.APP. 2002)
(*Admissions and Confessions:* Miranda)

The defendant was arrested after police found drugs in his car. At the scene, he was given *Miranda* warnings and he invoked his right to silence.

The defendant was transported to a police station, where officers placed him in an interrogation room and, according to testimony from one officer, asked him if he wanted to "help hi[m]self"—a phrase the trial court found to mean "become an informer." The defendant repeated that he did not want to talk about anything. The officers and the defendant then engaged in general conversation, primarily concerning the defendant's girlfriend. About 30 minutes after the defendant's initial invocation of his right to silence, an officer told the defendant the crime with which he was going to be charged and asked the defendant whether he had "anything to say." The defendant responded with a statement about the drugs, which was used to convict him of a drug offense.

- *After a person invokes the right to silence, what are the police required to do?*
- *Did the police behave constitutionally? Explain.*
- *Can the defendant's statement be used against him at trial? Why?*

Cooper v. State (Ga.Ct.App. 2002): 72 CrL 242

Police officers did not violate the 5th Amendment rule barring continued custodial interrogation following a suspect's invocation of the right to silence by asking a suspect whether he had "anything to say" after the defendant had engaged the officers in some general conversation.

The majority of the court stressed that the conversation preceding the defendant's statement did not address his case, that the defendant denied that he felt compelled to answer the officers' questions when he was taken to the interrogation room, and that he denied even making the statement. "Surely, we will have gone far afield, when, after [the defendant] willingly conversed with law enforcement in contradiction of his right to silence, an officer's simply asking him if he has anything to say becomes the 'coercive police practices' against which *Miranda* was designed to protect," the majority said.

The majority also suggested that the officer's question falls within the general booking questions exception to *Miranda* and that the question did not amount to "interrogation." Quoting in part from *Rhode Island v. Innis*, 446 U.S. 291 (1980), the court explained: "[A]n open-ended, 'Do you have anything to say,' is a phrase normally attendant with arrest, custody, and processing, and nothing in the record supports a determination that the officers '*should have known* [such a general question] was reasonably likely to elicit an incriminating response' from [the defendant]" [emphasis in original].

Two judges dissented, arguing that the officer's testimony showed that he knew his question was likely to elicit an incriminating response and that the defendant's invocation of the right to silence was not "scrupulously honored" as required by the 5th Amendment.

13.9   WILSON v. STATE (GA. 2002)
(*Admissions and Confessions:* Miranda)

The defendant was a suspect in the murder of his girlfriend when he was taken into custody for probation violation. During interrogation about the murder, he was given his *Miranda* warnings. He initially agreed to answer questions, but police continued questioning him after he stated that he was through answering questions.

The next day, the defendant indicated a desire to see the autopsy photographs of the bludgeoned victim, and an officer brought them to him. The officer again advised the defendant of his *Miranda* rights and, again, the defendant waived them. When the defendant, looking at the photographs, asked what had happened to the victim's head, the officer stated that he would like the defendant to answer that question.

The defendant's statements during the first interrogation were suppressed. His statements during the second interrogation were admitted into evidence and were used to obtain a murder conviction.

- *Were police entitled to continue questioning the defendant after he stated he was through answering questions in the first interview? Explain.*
- *Were police entitled to talk with the defendant the next day after he indicated a desire to see the autopsy photographs? Explain.*
  - *Were police entitled to give him his* Miranda *rights again that second day?*
  - *Were police required to give him his* Miranda *rights again that second day?*

Wilson v. State (Ga. 2002): 71 CrL 50

Police are entitled to reinitiate interrogation concerning other crimes arising out of the same incident after a significant period of time. "[A] person's right to silence is not protected by any per se rule of 'permanent immunity' against further police-initiated interrogations," the court said. Here, there was a 16- to 17-hour break between the end of the first interview and the beginning of the second. That was not enough. That period of time "fails to reflect the 'significant period of time' required by [*Michigan v. Mosley,* 423 U.S. 96 (1975)] to warrant reinterrogation by police on the same crime that was the subject of the first interrogation."

Nevertheless, the majority of the Georgia Supreme Court decided that the defendant's statements during the second interrogation were admissible on the ground that he "indicated his willingness to talk with police" on the second occasion by initiating further dialogue with them over the autopsy photographs.

Three judges concurred in the decision but argued that the interaction involving the autopsy photographs did not open the door to further interrogation or cure the *Miranda* violation of the day before. However, the defendant's statements in both interrogations were voluntary and evidence derived from voluntary statements obtained in violation of *Miranda* need not be suppressed.

13.10 UNITED STATES v. CLEMONS (D.D.C. 2002) (*Admissions and Confessions: Custody*)

Patrolling police officers heard what sounded like an automobile accident and observed the defendant driving with two flat tires. The defendant stopped when he saw the officers following him, and his passenger exited and attempted to flee. The officers ordered the defendant to stay in the car until the passenger was apprehended, at which time they forcibly removed the defendant from the car, handcuffed him, and ordered him to sit on the ground.

Without advising the defendant of his *Miranda* rights, an officer asked the defendant about the ownership of the car and about two handguns the officers found under the front seat.

- *Was the defendant in custody at the time the officer asked those questions? Explain.*
- *Was the questioning by the officer constitutional? Why?*

99978789780131700444

United States v. Clemons (D.D.C. 2002): 71 CrL 243

The officer's questioning during this *Terry* stop was "custodial interrogation" for purposes of complying with *Miranda v. Arizona,* 384 U.S. 436 (1966). The officer's questions went beyond routine investigatory questions that an officer can ask without advising the defendant of his rights. The fact that this encounter was a valid investigatory detention under *Terry v. Ohio,* 392 U.S. 1 (1968), rather than an arrest, does not mean that the suspect was not "in custody" for purposes of *Miranda.*

The government argued that the stop and restraint of the defendant was a permissible investigatory stop under *Terry,* not an arrest, and therefore *Miranda* was not implicated.

The court, however, ruled that "[e]ven if the stop and detention were permissible under *Terry,* the court cannot agree with the government that *Miranda* is not implicated merely because there was no formal arrest." A suspect can be in police custody for purposes of *Miranda* before he or she has been arrested in the 4th Amendment sense and "[i]t simply is not accurate to say that because a person has been 'reasonably detained' on less than probable cause for good and sufficient reason under *Terry,* it necessarily follows that there is no 'custodial interrogation' triggering the procedural safeguards and the warnings mandated by *Miranda.*"

Times have changed since *Terry* and *Miranda* were decided. The court explained that "the traditional post-*Terry* view" was that *Miranda* warnings are not implicated in a valid investigative stop because the typical police–citizen encounter envisioned by *Terry* usually involves no more than a very brief detention, no weapons or handcuffs, and a few questions relating to identity and the suspicious circumstances. In a similar case [*], the Tenth Circuit observed that the atmosphere during such an encounter would be "substantially less police-dominated than that surrounding the kinds of interrogation at issue in *Miranda.*" However, that is not necessarily the case today. Quoting from the Tenth Circuit case, this court observed:

> [P]olice officers confront situations more fraught with danger than in the past, including circumstances that sometimes justify—even under the rationale of *Terry*—the use of handcuffs, the placing of suspects in police cruisers, the drawing of weapons and other measures of force more traditionally associated with the concept of "custody" than with "brief investigatory detention." ... In such contexts, detention without probable cause may still be permissible for 4th Amendment purposes, while at the same time creating a 'custodial situation' under *Miranda* because a reasonable person so detained would feel that he has been deprived of his "freedom of action in [a] significant way," or that he was "completely at the mercy of the police."

In such cases, suspects must be advised of their constitutional rights before they are interrogated.

Removing the suspect from the car, handcuffing him, and putting him to the ground clearly deprived him of his freedom of action in a significant way, and any reasonable person would have understood that he was in custody and not free to leave.

The government argued that the officer in this case merely asked generic questions necessary to determine the facts of the situation. The government relied on [*], a case in which officers stopped a car and noticed that a passenger was bleeding and appeared to have been beaten. When the officers asked the passenger who had beaten him, the passenger, who was drunk, mumbled something unintelligible and appeared to point to the driver. Without providing a *Miranda* advisory, the officers asked the driver about the ownership of the car, and whether he had beaten the passenger. The court in [*] upheld the admissibility of the driver's responses, reasoning that "some inquiry can be made as part of an investigation notwithstanding limited and brief restraints by the police in their effort to screen crimes from relatively routine mishaps." The [*] court added that "[t]he courts must look to the essence of the situation and it seems to us clear that the essence here was not an officer staging an interrogation that had focused on a subject but an officer reacting to a street scene and trying to run down the facts."

The court in the instant case interpreted [*] as standing for the proposition that "the police may ask generic preliminary questions to ascertain the facts of a situation without violating *Miranda*." In this case, however, the officers questioned the defendant after they had removed him from the car, placed him in handcuffs, forced him to the ground, and discovered two handguns in the car. In these circumstances, "[t]he questions posed to [the defendant] went beyond the kind permitted by [*] and were intended to elicit incriminatory responses about the weapons just seized from the vicinity of a suspect in custody."

13.11   STATE v. STOTT (N.J. 2002)
(*Admissions and Confessions: Custody/Privacy*)

The defendant had been involuntarily committed to the state psychiatric hospital, where he shared a room with another patient. Patients on his ward were not permitted to leave the ward without an escort. Rooms on the ward were subject to search by hospital personnel. The hospital had its own police and a police station in the basement.

The defendant and his roommate shared some heroin and Xanax before bed. The next morning, the defendant's roommate was found dead, apparently from a drug overdose. All patients were moved to the day room while the death was investigated. A detective from the prosecutor's office interviewed a patient who said that the defendant had offered to sell him Xanax tablets the night before. When the detective interviewed the defendant, the defendant admitted using drugs with his roommate and said that Xanax could be found in the hem of the curtain. The detective and a hospital police officer immediately conducted a warrantless search of the defendant's room, which had been locked and guarded by a police officer since removal of the body, and found four Xanax pills in the hem of the curtain.

The defendant was taken downstairs to the basement police station for questioning, where he gave a tape-recorded account of the preceding evening. After a 2-week stint in a drug rehabilitation program, the defendant was returned to the hospital with a police escort. He was immediately taken to the basement police office where an officer again questioned him. On neither occasion was the defendant given the warnings prescribed by *Miranda*.

The pills and the defendant's statements were introduced at his trial on drug charges.

- *Were police required to Mirandize the defendant? If so, when? If not, why not?*
- *Was search of the curtain and discovery of the pills legal? Explain.*

State v. Stott (N.J. 2002): 71 CrL 62

Regarding the search of the curtain, a police officer's warrantless search for illicit drugs in a defendant's room at a psychiatric hospital intruded on a reasonable expectation of privacy and was not justified by exigent circumstances.

The court observed that the defendant's room "had many of the attributes of a private living area." Under the circumstances, the defendant had a reasonable expectation of privacy in it. Patients in long-term care enjoy a greater expectation of privacy than those rushed to the emergency room and released the same day. Although the staff must enter a private or semiprivate hospital room regardless of the patient's wishes, the patient can at least restrict access of visitors and nonmedical personnel and control the degree of privacy.

The majority of the court attached no significance to the fact that the search was limited to the hem of the curtain. "It is the room as a whole that implicates the expectation of privacy in this setting." Therefore, the inquiry shifts to whether the search fit within a valid exception to the warrant requirement.

In this case, there was no objectively reasonable basis to believe that the evidence was about to be lost, destroyed, or removed from the defendant's room. The trial court found that the defendant's room had been secured, guarded, and locked before the search. Moreover, the detective who conducted the search acknowledged at the suppression hearing that the room could have been secured until the police got a warrant. The majority found the argument that a rogue employee with a key could have entered the room and tampered with the evidence to be too speculative to be objectively reasonable.

Therefore, the majority concluded the warrantless search was impermissible under the federal and state constitutions. This disposition would not unduly hamper law enforcement according to the majority: "As is true of so much of our search-and-seizure jurisprudence, the analysis that we have employed is fact sensitive and offers no sure outcome in future cases."

Regarding the statements made by the defendant to the police, the defendant's statements were ordered suppressed on the ground that, under the circumstances, he was in custody during questioning.

Every member of the court agreed that the defendant's 5th Amendment right against compelled self-incrimination was violated by the interrogation sessions without *Miranda* warnings.

There is no serious dispute that the police interrogated the defendant. At least one officer acknowledged at the suppression hearing that his questions were likely to elicit incriminating responses. The question then was whether the defendant was in custody when he was questioned.

Several factors led the court to conclude that he was in custody. Police questioned the defendant in a secluded basement area of the hospital that was reserved solely for police use. Under the circumstances, it was reasonable for the defendant to conclude that he was a suspect in a criminal investigation.

Beyond that, the defendant was an involuntarily committed patient; as such, his freedom of movement was limited on a daily basis. Involuntary commitment to a treatment facility is a "massive curtailment of liberty" [*]. The record included testimony that the defendant was not permitted to leave the ward or walk the hospital grounds without an escort. "We are satisfied that a patient subjected to that level of restriction would not feel free to leave an interrogation conducted in the hospital's basement police office."

Although the officers told the defendant that he was free to leave or terminate the interrogation at any time, that statement was belied by the circumstances. The severe restrictions already imposed on the defendant provide the context for evaluating the officers' assurances. The court concluded "the defendant was in custody during his interviews for purpose of *Miranda* because the interrogations took place in a police-dominated atmosphere, there were objective indications that defendant was a suspect, and his movements were circumscribed as a result of his commitment status."

One judge concurred in the suppression of the defendant's statement, but dissented as to the search. She argued that confinement in a mental hospital is much different than a stay in a general-care hospital because of the close supervision that psychiatric patients receive. Thus, any expectation of privacy a psychiatric patient might have is greatly diminished. Moreover, because of the danger the pills presented to patients who might have discovered and ingested them, exigent circumstances existed at the time to justify the warrantless search.

13.12   STATE v. SPAULDING (OHIO CT.APP. 2002)
(*Admissions and Confessions: "Interrogation"*)

An officer arrested the defendant on outstanding warrants, searched him, and took him to the local jail. Just outside the jail, the officer asked the defendant "if there was anything in his shoes or socks, something like a pill that he would not want to transport into the jail because they will find it and charge him." The defendant disclosed that he was carrying cocaine in his shoe and was charged and prosecuted for possession of the drug.

- *Was that "interrogation"? Explain.*
- *Was that proper?*
- *Can discovery of the drug under these facts be used against the defendant? Explain.*

State v. Spaulding (Ohio Ct.App. 2002): 72 CrL 15

This question, posed to an arrestee while on the way to jail, as to whether the arrestee had any drugs in his possession, was not a routine booking question and should have been preceded by *Miranda* warnings. Although "couched in terms of a routine warning" against taking contraband into jail, the questioning amounted to interrogation for *Miranda* purposes.

In *Rhode Island v. Innis*, 446 U.S. 291 (1980), the U.S. Supreme Court held that "interrogation" under *Miranda* includes any words or actions by a police officer, except for those normally incident to arrest and custody, that are reasonably likely to elicit an incriminating statement from the suspect. The Court later clarified *Innis'* exception in *Pennsylvania v. Muniz*, 496 U.S. 582 (1990), by ruling that routine booking questions do not implicate *Miranda*.

The exception carved out in *Innis* and explained in *Muniz* does not apply here. The officer's question about drugs was not a normal inquiry incident to arrest but was designed to induce an incriminating response and, absent *Miranda* warnings, violated the defendant's privilege against self-incrimination.

The state argued that the inquiry was a harmless error because it enabled the defendant to avoid a charge of bringing a prohibited item into jail. That fact is irrelevant to a harmless error analysis. Rather, an error in admitting evidence is harmless only if the remaining undisputed evidence "in the prosecution at issue" overwhelmingly proves the defendant's guilt. In this case, there was no remaining evidence of the defendant's cocaine possession once his statement and its fruits were suppressed. The error in admitting the evidence was not harmless.

13.13   BALL v. STATE (MD.CT.APP. 1997)
(*Admissions and Confessions: Voluntariness*)

Defendant Wallace Ball was convicted and sentenced to death for the murder of Debra Goodwich. Goodwich was shot to death when she came home while her parents' home was being burglarized. Goodwich's father formerly employed the defendant's wife, Sharon, who terminated her employment in the wake of allegations of embezzlement.

Following his arrest, the defendant waived his rights under *Miranda* and agreed to speak with Detective Bollinger. The detective asked the defendant to review two documents that the detective had previously prepared. One of the documents read as follows: "On September 30, 1994, Debbie Goodwich was brutally killed in her parents' home. Wallace Ball 1) Is a cold blooded killer. 2) Has no regard for human life. 3) Killed Debbie Goodwich for fun. 4) Has been looking to kill someone for a long while. 5) Would kill again because he liked it. 6) Killed Debbie Goodwich because he hates Walter Goodwich."

In contrast, the other document stated: "On September 30, 1994, Debbie Goodwich was accidentally killed in her parent's home. Wallace Ball 1) Has had a tough life. 2) Loves his son, Dillon. 3) Was trying to support his family, which is why he broke into the Goodwich home. 4) Unfortunately became hooked on drugs. 5) Walter Goodwich was an unreasonable man in dealing with Wallace and Sharon Ball. 6) Is sorry in his heart for killing Debbie Goodwich. 7) Wishes he could change what happened. 8) Debbie struggled with him causing him to shoot her which he didn't want to do."

Detective Bollinger testified that the defendant read the documents, placed them on a table and "asked what they do for me." Bollinger explained to Ball that they were two ways of characterizing him. After some additional discussion, the defendant confessed to killing Debbie Goodwich.

On appeal, the defendant assailed the method of interrogation employed by Detective Bollinger. Characterizing the interrogation technique as a "classic example" of psychological coercion, he claimed his subsequent statements were involuntary.

- *Analyze this case. Is the confession voluntary? Explain why.*

Ball v. State (Md.Ct.App. 1997): 61 CrL 1551

"A confession clearly is not voluntary if it is the product of physical or psychological coercion. However, police officers are permitted to use a certain amount of subterfuge when questioning an individual about his or her suspected involvement in a crime. An appeal to '[t]he inner psychological pressure of conscience to tell the truth does not constitute coercion in the legal sense [*].' It is only where police conduct 'overbears [the accused's] will to resist and bring[s] about confessions not freely self-determined' that the confession will be suppressed [*]. Simply stated, police officers are not permitted to employ coercive tactics in order to compel an individual to confess, but they are permitted to 'trick' the suspect into making an inculpatory statement."

In [*], the court held that the police did not improperly induce the suspect to confess where the interrogating officer feigned loathing of the victim and admiration for the perpetrator. "The officer stated that he wanted to shake the hand of the person who killed the victim; in response, the suspect offered the officer his hand. Holding that the officer's deception did not amount to an overbearing inducement, the court explained: 'The words used ... are certainly not such as to automatically render that which follows inadmissible. It is barely conceivable that *anyone* could have interpreted the officer's comment as anything more than an effort to 'soft soap' the appellant'" [emphasis in original].

The court reached a similar conclusion in [*], in which the suspect complained that he was deceived by the interrogating officer's smile, "coddling words," and "sympathetic sounds." The court acknowledged that although this interrogation technique was "somewhat unique," it did not "coerce the appellant into making an incriminating statement."

"The same reason applies to the interrogation technique employed by Detective Bollinger in this case. There is no indication that Appellant's will was overborne by the use of this interrogation method. Nor does the record support Appellant's assertion that the police took advantage of Appellant's ignorance that the two different scenarios both amounted to first degree murder. Detective Bollinger testified that after Appellant read the two documents, he asked 'what do they do for me.' Appellant apparently recognized, therefore, that under either scenario he would be admitting to the murder of Debra Goodwich. We find no merit in Appellant's contention that this interrogation technique rendered his subsequent statements involuntary."

13.14   SABO v. COMMONWEALTH (VA.CT.APP. 2002)
(*Admissions and Confessions: Voluntariness*)

The defendant and the victim were romantically involved until the victim ended the relationship. Following the breakup, the victim began receiving anonymous telephone calls, and her car's brake lines were cut, causing her to crash. During the course of a criminal investigation into the harassing telephone calls and the sabotage, a police detective hooked a cassette recorder to her telephone and gave her a half-dozen blank cassettes "for any phone calls that she might receive." However, the detective specifically asked her several times not to call the defendant, but to wait for the defendant to call her.

Despite the officer's advice, the victim called the defendant repeatedly to "discuss" the frightening phone calls and her auto accident. Eventually, she captured on tape statements in which he admitted guilt. Because she had only six cassettes, she used and reused them, recording only portions of their conversations. She delivered one incriminating tape to the detective, who again advised her to let the police investigation take its course; nevertheless, she made another tape and delivered it the next day. After listening to the victim's tapes, the detective got a search warrant.

Testimony at trial included statements by the victim that she threatened to have the defendant prosecuted and promised to forego prosecution if he admitted his guilt to her.

The defendant was prosecuted for attempted malicious wounding. Over his objections, the tapes were admitted into evidence at his jury trial.

The defendant objected that the victim was acting as an agent of the government.

He also objected that any admissions he might have made were involuntary because the victim threatened to have him prosecuted and promised to forego prosecution if he admitted his guilt to her.

- *Was the victim acting as an agent of the government? Explain fully.*
- *Were the statements made by the defendant involuntary? Explain.*

Sabo v. Commonwealth (Va.Ct.App. 2002): 71 CrL 102

A crime victim who used equipment provided by the police to tape record, for her own purposes, a telephone conversation with her former boyfriend was not acting as an agent for law enforcement. Therefore, her use of trickery and threats to elicit the defendant's statements could not render the statements coerced in violation of the due process protections of the 5th and 14th Amendments.

The defendant in this case argued that the victim "was acting as an agent for the Commonwealth" and that his statements to her were involuntary. The involuntariness argument was based on statements by the victim in which she threatened to have him prosecuted and promised to forego prosecution if he admitted his guilt to her. The court concluded that her primary purpose was not to assist law enforcement, but to further her own ends and goals. The court found no prior case to give guidance, so it drew on search and seizure cases by analogy. A private search, no matter how unreasonable, is not a constitutional violation warranting suppression of the evidence. The majority applied the same logic here.

For an agency relationship to exist between a private citizen and the police, both parties must manifest their consent to the relationship, either expressly or by implication from their conduct; the government's awareness of the private party's conduct is not enough. A lower court case prescribed a two-part test, under which the trial court must look at "(1) whether the government knew of and acquiesced in the search, and (2) whether the search was conducted for the purpose of furthering the private party's ends."

In this case, the victim testified in detail about the state of fear in which she lived and the steps she took to protect herself from a real, but unknown, threat. She testified that the detective told her not to call the defendant but she ignored his advice. The majority concluded that her testimony "clearly reveal[ed] her desire to find out who was terrorizing her and to put an end to it and regain a sense of peace."

The majority concluded that the detective did not supervise the victim's private investigation or offer her any reward, and that the detective and the victim did not share a common purpose or plan. Accordingly, the majority concluded that the victim was not acting as the state's agent.

Because only state action can violate a criminal defendant's due process rights, "coercive police activity is a necessary predicate to the finding that a confession is not 'voluntary'" for due process purposes. If police are not actively involved, a confession obtained by a private party is deemed voluntary under due process, obviating the need for voluntariness analysis. Having found that the victim acted on her own in obtaining the defendant's incriminating statements, the court saw no due process impediment to their admission into evidence.

One judge dissented, arguing that the victim was acting as the state's agent. She was not pursuing her own interests in making the recordings; on the contrary, police were using her as their surrogate to carry out their investigation. In her opinion, the threats and promises the victim made amounted to police coercion.

13.15   WHITTINGTON v. STATE (MD.CT.SPEC.APP. 2002)
(*Admissions and Confessions: Voluntariness*)

Three days after the defendant's husband was shot to death, the defendant came to a police station at the request of police. There, she was warned of her rights, agreed to talk, and gave an oral statement denying involvement in the crime. The interrogator gave her a pen to use in writing out her statement. Unbeknownst to the defendant, the pen had been dusted with a fingerprint powder visible only under a neon or infrared light source.

Besides questioning the defendant about "inconsistencies" in the written statement, the detective asked her to consent to a test he said would show whether she had "blow back" on her hands from recent handgun use. In fact, the test was bogus. The defendant consented. During the purported test, a technician examined the defendant's hands under an infrared light. The powder glowed orange, and the technician falsely told the defendant that the powder was residue from a gun.

Subsequent to the bogus test, the defendant repeated the consent she had earlier given to a voice stress test, consented to a search of her home, and was subjected to further questioning by police. Finally, 18 hours after her arrival at the police station, she confessed to murdering her husband.

On appeal, the defendant argued that her confession was involuntary. She focused primarily on the deceptive conduct of the police regarding the phony gunpowder residue test, but the argument for involuntariness also cited use of the voice stress test, which the defendant was told she had failed, and the length of the interrogation.

- *The police lied. Does that render the confession unconstitutional? Why?*

- *What about the fact that she was held at the station 18 hours? Does that render the confession unconstitutional?*

- *Do these elements, in combination, render the confession unconstitutional?*

Whittington v. State (Md.Ct.Spec.App. 2002): 72 CrL 139

Interrogators' use of a bogus test to induce a defendant to confess did not render the defendant's confession involuntary. The court distinguished the interrogators' conduct in this case from interrogators' preparation and use of false documents, which a few courts have said invalidates an ensuring confession.

The defense relied on a Florida case, [*], in which police showed a teenage rape-murder suspect two phony scientific reports purporting to demonstrate that his semen had been found on the victim's underwear. The Florida court acknowledged that deception by police does not automatically invalidate a confession, but it distinguished between verbal "artifices" and the fabrication of phony documents. The same distinction was drawn in a West Virginia case [*].

This court distinguished the Florida case and saw nothing in the type of deception used in this case that makes it more coercive than deceptive tactics the courts have approved. The Florida case reasoned that suspects and the public probably expect the police to use some oral deception, given the confrontational or adversarial atmosphere of police interrogations, but that they do not expect the deception to include fabrication of documents. The Florida court said that documents, unlike oral lies, have the facial appearance of authenticity, and it worried that false documents could wind up in official files or as courtroom evidence.

The effort of the defendant in this case to equate the phony test with the documents in the Florida case failed, the Maryland court said. For one thing, it was clear from the course of events in the Florida case that the confession in that case was induced by the documents. This case is different, in that the defendant did not confess immediately after being told of the supposed test results; instead, the confession came 15 hours later. Furthermore, the bogus test produced no potentially permanent record, so the Florida court's concerns about the potential for later misuse of such a memorialization were not implicated.

"We reject [the defendant's] contention that police deception with regard to the use of bogus scientific procedures is inherently more coercive than other forms of deception," the court said. The court noted that its prior cases approved such trickery as falsely telling a suspect that he failed a polygraph and falsely saying that a suspect's fingerprints were found at the crime scene. Such ploys are constitutionally equivalent to the approved tactic of telling a suspect that his accomplice confessed. Courts in other states have approved such tactics as falsely asserting matches of tire and shoe prints, the court added.

The bright line drawn in the Florida case, the court said, is inconsistent with case law, holding that determining a confession's voluntariness requires examination of the totality of the circumstances. Applying that standard, the court concluded that the confession was voluntary.

13.16 UNITED STATES v. SYSLO (EIGHTH CIR. 2002)
(Admissions and Confessions: Voluntariness)

The defendants, husband and wife, were suspects in the theft of approximately $100,000 from a bank. Investigators asked the husband to come to the station for the purpose of giving a handwriting exemplar in connection with an unrelated forgery case. The district court found that he was told he would be questioned about the forgery but was not informed that the detectives intended to question him about the bank burglary. He was read his *Miranda* rights. When he asked whether he needed an attorney to be present for a handwriting exemplar, an investigator said no and that reading the rights in this situation was "just a formality." The defendant waived his *Miranda* rights and began the handwriting exemplar.

Meanwhile, other officers executed a search warrant at the defendants' home and found a box filled with cash. The police asked the wife to come to the station. There was no one to stay at home with the defendants' young children; therefore, they were also taken to the station, and a caretaker was obtained for them during their mother's interrogation. The police read the wife her *Miranda* rights, which she waived, and put her in an interview room separate from her husband.

The husband was informed of his family's presence, but he expressed disbelief and continued to deny involvement in the bank burglary. Nevertheless, the wife was informed that her husband was talking and telling the truth. She then began to make statements acknowledging that her husband had robbed the bank. During this part of the questioning session, she was told that she would not go to jail if she refrained from lying. She responded by indicating that she was motivated to be truthful by concern about who would care for her children if her husband were imprisoned.

The police returned to the husband and told him that his wife was telling the truth and that it was now his turn to do so. When he continued to deny his involvement, he was shown notes from his wife and, later, a Polaroid photo of his children with the caretaker. When he saw the photo, he admitted his involvement in the burglary, saying that he needed the photo as proof that his wife was at the station because he believed his crime could not have been proved without a confession.

The defendants entered conditional guilty pleas and sought suppression of their statements. The trial court suppressed only the statements the wife made after she learned that the children she had voluntarily brought to the police station would not be allowed to leave.

- *What constitutional arguments are available to the mother in support of suppression of her statements?*
- *What constitutional arguments are available to the state in support of using the mother's statements against her?*
- *What is the result? Should any of the other's statements be used against her? If so, which ones? Why? If not, why not?*
- *The father complained that police withheld critical information from him about what they planned to do during the interrogation session (specifically, they did not tell him before he waived his rights that they intended to question him about the bank burglary). Does that police practice invalidate his waiver of rights? Explain.*
- *Police told the father that signing the waiver forms was just a formality. Does that police practice invalidate his waiver of rights? Explain.*

United States v. Syslo (Eighth Cir. 2002); 71 CrL 676

Presence of the suspects' children at the police station during their mother's questioning was not coercive. Beyond that, interrogators did not run afoul of *Miranda* by switching the topic of questioning of the father to a crime other than the one they indicated would be covered in the interview.

The court began its analysis with the father's claim that the interrogators undermined the validity of his waiver of rights by withholding critical information about what they planned to do during the session and by minimizing the significance of the *Miranda* advisement. Contrary to the defendant's contention, the court credited the trial judge's finding that the defendant knew he would be questioned about the forgery, and the majority said it did not matter that the robbery was actually the first topic broached by the interrogators.

Under *Colorado v. Spring,* 479 U.S. 564 (1987), police need not give notice before changing the topic of interrogation. Nor has investigators' silence about the subject matter of interrogation been held to be "trickery" sufficient to invalidate a waiver.

Responding to a complaint about the investigators' statements that signing the waiver forms was a mere formality, the majority pointed out that the defendants went to the police station voluntarily, were told they would be questioned, and agreed to answer. Furthermore, the father's statements and demeanor showed that he was not susceptible to police pressure and that his will was not overborne.

Turning to the mother's arguments, the majority agreed with the trial court that her statements were initially uncoerced. According to the findings of the trial judge, the children were taken to the police station as a matter of expediency and with the agreement of the defendant, and there was no finding that the children were kept there to coerce the wife to confess. Furthermore, it was the wife, not the police, who introduced the issue of the children's welfare during the questioning.

Under these circumstances, it was reasonable for the trial judge to conclude that the wife's statements became involuntary only when she realized her children would not be released to the custody of a relative. The statements the mother made up to that time were admissible.

One judge dissented, arguing that the father's statements were induced by police trickery, and that the mother's statements were coerced by fear for her children.

The investigators' statements suggesting that the husband was wanted only for a handwriting exemplar and that the *Miranda* warning was a mere formality constituted the sort of "affirmative misrepresentations" that the Supreme Court indicated could invalidate a waiver. Contrary to what the father was told, *Miranda* rights would have an "enormous difference" to the defendant.

The dissenting judge also contended that at no point was the children's presence at the police station voluntary on the mother's part, and that they were kept there for the purpose of coercing her to confess.

13.17   MITCHELL v. COMMONWEALTH (VA.CT.APP. 1999)
(*Admissions and Confessions: Waiver*)

The defendant was taken into custody after stolen property was found in his girlfriend's home. After receiving *Miranda* warnings, the defendant agreed to answer an officer's questions about a burglary but refused to sign a written waiver. The next day, another investigator interviewed the defendant and advised him again of his *Miranda* rights. The defendant refused to sign a written waiver and told the investigator, "I ain't got shit to say to y'all." The defendant, however, continued to converse generally with the investigator about his prior incarceration and his concern for his girlfriend. A few minutes later, a sheriff arrived. The sheriff confirmed that the defendant understood his *Miranda* rights and said that he wanted to offer the defendant an opportunity to tell his side of the story. The defendant replied that there was nothing he could say that the police did not already know. Nevertheless, he later asked if there was a way he could help his girlfriend or himself and was told that he could talk to police about property that had been stolen in the county. The defendant eventually confessed to stealing a tractor.

- *Is the defendant's confession constitutional? Explain fully.*

Mitchell v. Commonwealth (Va.Ct.App. 1999): 65 CrL 608

The court upheld the admissibility of the confession. Even after the defendant made the remark at issue, he continued to volunteer information to the officers. In these circumstances, the defendant's statement did not amount to the unambiguous invocation of the right to silence that is required before police must cease their questioning under *Miranda v. Arizona*, 384 U.S. 436 (1966). The court found further support in a Seventh Circuit case [*] in which a defendant's statement, "I don't got nothing to say," was held not to constitute an invocation of the right to remain silent. In this case, the defendant's statement that "I ain't got shit to say to y'all" was not an unambiguous invocation of his right to remain silent.

13.18   JACKSON v. LITSCHER (E.D.WIS. 2002)
(*Admissions and Confessions: Waiver*)

The defendant was arrested and held for several days. He was then brought to an interview room at the jail, where he was interviewed by a Milwaukee police detective. He was advised of his *Miranda* rights and, in response, he asked for "a lawyer right now." He also asked whether the police officer could arrange for that. Wisconsin law provides that the Public Defender's Office is available to provide counsel to people in custody on an emergency basis. Nonetheless, the detective told the defendant that he could not obtain an attorney for him and that a public defender would be assigned when he was formally charged in court.

The defendant said again that he wanted a lawyer but that he also wanted to talk to the detective. The detective testified that he told the defendant that he could not talk to the defendant because of the request for counsel. The detective also testified that, rather than leaving the room, he paused for a few minutes and that the defendant then "reinitiated conversation with me, and at that point is when he replied to me that he wished to talk to me now, and that's when I reinitiated whether or not he was going to waive his right to an attorney and that's when he replied yes he would." The defendant then confessed to a cocaine offense.

- *Was the detective's false claim that he could not obtain an attorney for the defendant permissible? Explain.*
- *Did the defendant reinitiate conversation with the detective for purposes of allowing the detective to further question the defendant? Explain.*
- *Is the defendant's confession admissible, or was it obtained in violation of his constitutional rights? Why?*

Jackson v. Litscher (E.D.Wis. 2002): 71 CrL 41

The detective's false statement cannot be used to obtain a waiver of the defendant's *Miranda* rights. Misinformation or trickery that distorts the meaning of the interrogation warnings prescribed by *Miranda v. Arizona,* 384 U.S. 436 (1966), cannot induce a valid waiver of those rights. It is the defendant's state of mind (not the detective's state of mind) that determines whether a valid waiver of *Miranda* has occurred; given that, it does not matter whether the misinformation was provided intentionally or unintentionally.

The court distinguished between using trickery to get a confession and using trickery to get a waiver of *Miranda.* The court quoted *Miranda's* assertion that "any evidence that the accused was threatened, tricked, or cajoled into a waiver will, of course, show that the defendant did not voluntarily waive his privilege." There was evidence of that in this case because "the officer's misinformation about when an appointed lawyer could be made available to [the defendant] influenced his decision to confess."

The court discussed the public policy reasons supporting this conclusion, explaining the purpose of the *Miranda* warnings is to reduce the coercion inherent in a custodial interrogation by giving some power to a suspect in a police-controlled environment. Tricking the suspect into waiving his rights defeats this goal by denying the suspect any real power to control the situation. Beyond that, *Miranda* was designed to create a bright line to prevent police from using coercive tactics. Allowing some trickery in the inducement of confessions has produced a fuzzy line that creates difficulties for courts and gives police little guidance. A bright line prohibiting false and misleading statements to secure a waiver is easier for courts to administer and police to follow than some system of evaluating "big lies" from "little lies" as part of totalities of the circumstances analysis.

In this case, the defendant had initially invoked the right to counsel. Given that, his subsequent waiver should be viewed with skepticism. The "critical factor" was that the waiver was precipitated by the detective's "patently false" statement about whether a lawyer could be provided at the interrogation. It is immaterial whether the detective intentionally misinformed the defendant or whether he actually believed a lawyer could only be appointed after the court appearance. The analysis must focus on the state of mind of the suspect and not of the police.

The defendant's decision to waive counsel was based on the false impression that it might be days before he could have counsel. If the defendant had known that a lawyer might be minutes or hours away, he might have insisted that the detective call the public defender or allow him to do so. Therefore, the court concluded the waiver was involuntary.

The detective here technically complied with the rule that a suspect who has invoked his right to counsel cannot be reapproached for interrogation without counsel unless he reinitiates contact with the police. However, the court accused the detective of violating the "spirit" of that rule by failing to leave the interrogation room quickly.

13.19   ROEHLING v. STATE (IND.CT.APP. 2002)
(*Admissions and Confessions/Consent/Automobile Exception*)

The defendant was at the residence of another individual when police officers arrived with a warrant to search the residence. The defendant and two others were handcuffed and given the warnings required by *Miranda v. Arizona,* 384 U.S. 436 (1966). Before the search began, an officer announced that his warrant to search the house covered all vehicles on the premises; that was not true–the warrant did not extend to vehicles. The officer asked the defendant and the others "if they had anything on them" that the police needed to know about. The defendant stated that he had an unlicensed handgun in his vehicle. The officer retrieved the handgun and also found marijuana in the ashtray.

The trial court denied the defendant's motion to suppress.

- *Did the officer misrepresent his authority? If so, how?*
- *Was the search of the automobile constitutional? Explain fully.*
- *Can the evidence found in the car be used against the defendant? Explain.*

Roehling v. State (Ind.Ct.App. 2002): 72 CrL 89

Police officers' false statement to a defendant about the scope of a warrant they were executing vitiated the voluntariness of the defendant's admission, following a warning of his rights, that he had an unlicensed handgun in a place the officers said they could search.

The court said that absent presentation by the state of evidence that the warrant authorized the search of vehicles, the search of the defendant's car had to be treated as a warrantless one. The state attempted to justify the search under the automobile exception to the 4th Amendment's warrant requirement, arguing that the officer had probable cause to search after the defendant provided information about the handgun. However, the state did not contest the defendant's testimony that probable cause was obtained by police deception. The question thus was whether the defendant's postwarnings admission was voluntary.

The voluntariness of a defendant's admission is determined by the totality of the circumstances, with police deception, although not conclusive, weighing heavily against a finding of voluntariness. The court noted that in the context of consent, the U.S. Supreme Court indicated in *Bumper v. North Carolina,* 391 U.S. 543 (1968), that police misrepresentation about the existence of a search warrant is particularly egregious. Although the instant search was not based on consent, the court observed that the definition of voluntariness that applies to consent searches is the same as that for confessions. "[A]t this intersection of 4th Amendment law on searches and seizures and 5th Amendment law on confessions, we hold that police deception concerning the existence of a search warrant vitiates the voluntariness of an admission, given in response to police questioning, regarding evidence that might be found in the place falsely represented to be covered by the warrant."

Pretrial Identification

Pretrial identification presents something of an anomaly in criminal procedure: In the face of some of the most persuasive evidence for jurors (eyewitness identification), we find some of the weakest constitutional protections. There are good reasons for why the law has developed as it has in this area; nonetheless, the protections are not strong.

There are two major constitutional protections that come into play to govern pretrial identification. The U.S. Supreme Court made it clear in *United States v. Wade,* 388 U.S. 218 (1967), that the accused is entitled to have counsel present at any postindictment lineup or show-up because, especially in light of the inherent unreliability of eyewitness identification, this is a "critical stage" of the prosecution, one in which the absence of counsel might jeopardize a fair trial. That 6th Amendment right to counsel at a postindictment identification at which the accused is present is useful, but its utility is clearly limited because it comes into play so late, and it only applies to postindictment lineups and show-ups, not to the use of photo arrays. By the time of the indictment, frankly, the need for pretrial identification has generally passed. To the extent the police want to use pretrial identification to determine who the defendant in the case should be, that has been done.

Notwithstanding the general tardiness of the 6th Amendment as a protective tool in pretrial identification, *Wade* is nonetheless very valuable because it set out the Court's appreciation of the fact that eyewitness identification is very fragile and suspect, and because it set out considerations that should be taken into account to assure that the pretrial identification is fair.

When the appellate court has cited and relied upon a U.S. Supreme Court opinion in reaching its decision, those citations are set out in full so you will know what Supreme Court authority the court relied upon. When you see an asterisk [*] in the court's opinion, that means the appellate court has referenced and relied upon a lower court case in reaching its decision. Those case citations are not included here.

The constitutional protection that might be more useful to the defendant is a due process protection. We are talking basic fairness here and the due process questions focus on whether the pretrial identification techniques were too suggestive. Due process is operative at all times, including during initial police investigation before any "criminal proceedings" have begun. Due process also applies to the use of photo arrays as well as to traditional lineups and show-ups.

Indeed, the due process analysis was clearly set out in a show-up case, *Stovall v. Denno,* 388 U.S. 293 (1967), a companion case to *Wade.* The defendant there was the subject of a show-up (a one-person lineup). His challenge to that procedure prompted the Court to consider the totality of the circumstances to determine whether the confrontation was "so unnecessarily suggestive and conducive to irreparable mistaken identification" that the defendant was denied due process of law. The Court recognized that a pretrial identification procedure might be suggestive. It is only unconstitutionally so if it is unnecessarily suggestive under the totality of the circumstances and, as the Court further explained in *Simmons v. United States,* 390 U.S. 377 (1968), if the procedure creates a very substantial likelihood of irreparable misidentification. The defendant has the burden to establish the due process violation; it is a heavy burden.

The gap, indeed the great divide, between a lay juror's understanding of the reliability of eyewitness identification and the literature on the subject that has been produced by social scientists is enormous. The student interested in the social science aspects of this question might be interested in reading a fairly recent polygraph opinion, *United States v. Scheffer,* 523 U.S. 303 (1997), in which the Court, especially in the dissent, examined some of the empirical evidence on the reliability of eyewitness evidence.

14.1 STATE v. MCMORRIS (WIS. 1997)
(*Pretrial Identification: Right to Counsel/Pretrial Identification: Due Process*)

Patricia Jordan, a 67-year-old White woman, was robbed by an African-American male at knifepoint as she was working alone at a grocery store. A store surveillance camera taped the robbery in its entirety. According to the tape, the robbery lasted approximately 25 seconds. Officers viewed the videotape and concluded that the defendant was the robber. The eyewitness was shown a photographic array that included a photograph of the defendant, but she did not identify the defendant as the robber.

A month later, the defendant was charged with armed robbery and a public defender was appointed. Five days later, a lineup was staged, and the eyewitness identified the defendant as the robber. The police failed to notify the defendant's counsel about the lineup, the defendant's counsel did not attend the lineup, and at no time did the defendant waive his right to have his counsel present. The officers did not photograph the lineup, either by video or still camera.

The eyewitness subsequently identified the defendant in court at the preliminary hearing.

There are other facts from the record you might or might not find useful:

- The eyewitness had never seen the robber prior to the robbery.

- She gave a general description of the robber.

- There was a discrepancy between her description of the robber immediately after the robbery and the defendant's actual physical appearance.

- There was a lapse of 5 weeks between the robbery and the lineup identification.

- The witness said at the suppression hearing that she was positive the defendant was the robber and she would be able to identify him even if he had not been in the lineup.

- *Does this pretrial identification violate the defendant's 6th Amendment right to counsel? Explain.*

- *Does this pretrial identification violate the defendant's 5th Amendment due process right? Explain your thinking.*

State v. McMorris (Wis. 1997): 62 CrL 1132

The court held that *United States v. Wade,* 388 U.S. 218 (1967), controls this case. *Wade* held that an in-court identification subsequent to a constitutionally defective lineup in violation of an accused's 6th Amendment right to counsel is not per se inadmissible. Instead, the in-court identification is admissible if the state carries the burden of showing by clear and convincing evidence that the in-court identification was based on observations of the suspect other than the lineup identification. The in-court identification is admissible if made "by means sufficiently distinguishable to be purged of the primary taint." The *Wade* test has been referred to as the "independent origin" test and the "independent source" test.

To determine whether the in-court identification is sufficiently distinguishable to be purged of the primary taint, a court should consider, as *Wade* suggested, various factors including the following: (1) the prior opportunity the witness had to observe the alleged criminal activity, (2) the existence of any discrepancy between any prelineup description and the accused's actual description, (3) any identification of another person prior to the lineup, (4) any identification by picture of the accused prior to the lineup, (5) failure to identify the accused on a prior occasion, (6) the lapse of time between the alleged crime and the lineup identification, and (7) the facts disclosed concerning the conduct of the lineup.

After examining these factors, the court concluded that the state had not demonstrated by clear and convincing evidence, as *Wade* requires, that the in-court identification had an origin independent of the lineup or was "sufficiently distinguishable to be purged of the primary taint." The eyewitness's opportunity to observe the robber was limited to 25 seconds; she had never seen the robber prior to the robbery; she gave a general description of the robber; there was a discrepancy between her description of the robber immediately after the robbery and the defendant's actual physical appearance; and there was a lapse of 5 weeks between the robbery and the lineup identification.

The state argued that the court should consider another factor—the witness's level of certainty in making the in-court identification. The eyewitness in this case said at the suppression hearing that she was positive the defendant was the robber and that she would be able to identify him even if he had not been in the lineup and she had seen him on the street.

This "certainty" factor is not mentioned in *Wade,* but is set forth in *Neil v. Biggers,* 409 U.S. 188 (1972). The *Biggers* court promulgated a "totality of the circumstances" test that includes five factors: (1) the opportunity of the witness to view the criminal at the time of the crime, (2) the witness's degree of attention, (3) the accuracy of the witness's prior description of the criminal, (4) the level of certainty demonstrated by the witness at the confrontation, and (5) the length of time between the crime and the confrontation.

The court conceded that judges disagree on whether the *Wade* and *Biggers* tests are functionally equivalent (as argued earlier in this section). This court determined that they are not functionally equivalent and the *Biggers* "certainty" factor should not be included in the *Wade* test. The *Wade* and *Biggers* tests are derived from different constitutional amendments and are intended to achieve different purposes. The *Wade* test focuses on the 6th Amendment right to counsel at postindictment lineups and on the exclusionary remedy for a constitutional violation of the 6th Amendment. The *Wade* test is used to exclude evidence tainted by an unconstitutional lineup. Exclusion of derivative evidence is intended to deter unlawful police conduct and preserve judicial integrity.

The inquiry in *Biggers,* on the other hand, evaluated the reliability of a pretrial identification when it is claimed that the pretrial identification was made under impermissibly suggestive circumstances. *Biggers* uses a witness's certainty as a suggestive pretrial identification procedure to measure the reliability of the witness's identification in that procedure. *Biggers* is based on due process considerations, not on a 6th Amendment violation or the *Wong Sun v. United States,* 371 U.S. 471 (1963), exception to the fruit-of-the-poisonous-tree doctrine. Under *Biggers,* the totality of the circumstances test is applied to determine whether a pretrial out-of-court identification was unreliable as a matter of law.

The case at bar is a *Wade* case. The issue is not whether a witness's observation of a perpetrator of a crime or an in-court identification of an accused was reliable. The issue is whether a witness's observation of a perpetrator of a crime constitutes an independent source for that witness's in-court identification of the accused.

The primary concern in a *Wade* case is whether an unconstitutional lineup tainted a subsequent in-court identification. In a *Wade* case, the degree of certainty displayed by a witness at an in-court identification is independent of a tainted lineup. As the *Wade* court stated, "It is a matter of common experience that, once a witness has picked out the accused at the lineup, he is not likely to go back on his word later on, so that in practice the issue of identity may (in the absence of other relevant evidence) for all practical purposes be determined there and then, before the trial."

Three judges dissented, arguing that the state had shown by clear and convincing evidence that the in-court identification was based on observations of the eyewitness that were independent of the lineup identification and he would allow consideration of the certainty of the witness in a *Wade* analysis. "Although *Wade's* 'independent basis' test and *Biggers'* 'totality of the circumstances' are derived from different constitutional amendments, they are both premised on concerns of accurate and reliable witness identification.... The majority emphasizes the unreliable nature of eyewitness identification; however, the *Wade* test is utilized to remedy such concerns and combat any inherent unreliability. The language of *Wade* indicates the factors enumerated were proffered as a guideline—not an all-inclusive list. The extent of the witness's certainty would not be dispositive in *Wade* analysis. Rather, it would merely be a factor to be considered in addition to those outlined in *Wade*. Eyewitness identification is relevant and extremely valuable to criminal convictions."

14.2   STATE V. WILLIAMS (IOWA CT.APP. 2000)
(Pretrial Identification: Due Process)

The witness reported that a man known to him as "Sug" was one of three men who assaulted the witness and murdered his father. Police knew that the nickname referred to the defendant and placed his picture in a photo array from which the witness identified him. Prior to showing the array to the witness, an officer told the witness that "Sug" was one of the men pictured. The witness quickly identified the defendant's picture.

- *What constitutional challenge(s) should the defendant make to this procedure?*
- *Analyze each challenge you identify and explain whether the challenge would succeed.*

State v. Williams (Iowa Ct.App. 2000): 67 CrL 723

The court rejected the defendant's due process challenge to the identification. The defendant was unable to show that the identification procedures made misidentification substantially likely. The photo array contained five other men who closely resembled the defendant in terms of race, skin tone, hairstyle, facial hair, and clothing, the court pointed out. It also noted that none of the pictures was placed so as to give it more or less prominence among the group.

14.3   PEOPLE V. ORTIZ (N.Y.CT.APP. 1997)
(Pretrial Identification: Due Process)

Two officers were fired on the outside of an apartment building. The defendant was apprehended in the building by other officers; some 2 hours later, the original officers came back to the building from the hospital and identified the defendant.

- *Specifically, should the burden fall on the state to show that the procedure here was constitutional, or should the burden fall on the defendant to show that it was not? Why?*

People v. Ortiz (N.Y.Ct.App. 1997): 62 CrL 1099

Presentation of evidence demonstrating that an identification of a defendant was a show-up identification conducted in temporal and geographical proximity to the crime is not enough to shift to the defendant the burden of showing that the identification was invalid.

Instead, the prosecution must also present some evidence to demonstrate that the identification procedure was not unduly suggestive. The state's initial burden of demonstrating the reasonableness of an identification procedure is satisfied by evidence that a show-up identification was conducted close in time and place to the crime. However, the people also have the burden of producing some evidence relating to the show-up itself, to demonstrate that the procedure was not unduly suggestive [*]. In many cases a defendant simply does not know the facts surrounding a pretrial identification; therefore, defendants would be unduly prejudiced in their efforts to establish whether an identification was unduly suggestive if the state were relieved of its burden to produce evidence of the way the identification was conducted. Before reversing the defendant's convictions, the court pointed out that it could not tell from the record whether the identification was a show-up or an impromptu lineup.

Effective Assistance of Counsel

The 6th Amendment guarantees that in all criminal proceedings the accused shall enjoy the right to have the assistance of counsel for his or her defense. It says we are entitled to a lawyer; it does not say how good that lawyer has to be. In this section, we focus on the effective assistance of counsel.

The U.S. Supreme Court has recognized that assistance of counsel must mean the assistance of effective counsel. The test for effective assistance of counsel is set out in *Strickland v. Washington,* 466 U.S. 668 (1984). It is a two-pronged test, in which the defendant complaining of ineffective assistance of counsel has the burden of proof. The defendant, to establish ineffective assistance of counsel, must prove that the attorney was deficient and that this deficiency prejudiced the defense. In trying to establish deficiency, it is not enough for the defendant to show that counsel proceeded in a manner the defendant did not approve; tactical decisions, reasonably made, are not deficient performance. Proof of prejudice requires proof that, but for the deficiency, the outcome would have been different. Proof of either deficiency or prejudice will not suffice; both must be present to provide relief. Further, the Court has made it clear that there is a strong presumption of competence. The burden is not an easy one.

The cases included here are selected to illustrate how the test for ineffective assistance of counsel works.

When the appellate court has cited and relied upon a U.S. Supreme Court opinion in reaching its decision, those citations are set out in full so you will know what Supreme Court authority the court relied upon. When you see an asterisk [*] in the court's opinion, that means the appellate court has referenced and relied upon a lower court case in reaching its decision. Those case citations are not included here.

15.1   UNITED STATES v. MULLINS (FIFTH CIR. 2002)
(Effective Assistance of Counsel)

The defendant was indicted on firearms charges. His counsel made a strategic decision to prevent him from testifying to keep his past convictions for drug-related crimes and bad check writing from the jury. The defendant was convicted.

Four years later, the defendant filed a petition asserting that his counsel had interfered with his constitutional right to testify. At the evidentiary hearing, his counsel testified that the defendant initially went along with her trial strategy, but during the trial he changed his mind. Counsel said that the defendant told her several times he wanted to testify but that, against his wishes, she "prevented" him from doing so.

- *What is the test for determining ineffective assistance of counsel?*
  - *Make the argument that this is ineffective assistance of counsel. Be specific.*
  - *Make the argument that this is not ineffective assistance of counsel. Be specific.*
    - *What do you conclude?*

United States v. Mullins (Fifth Cir. 2002): 72 CrL 258

A defense attorney renders deficient performance under the test set out in *Strickland v. Washington*, 466 U.S. 668 (1984), by barring testimony from a client who wishes to take the stand. The court further ruled that a defendant does not waive the right to testify by failing to complain to the trial court that his wish to testify is being overridden by counsel. The court went on to conclude, however, that the defendant in this case was not prejudiced by counsel's deficient performance.

With Respect to Whether Defense Counsel's Performance Was Deficient

In these cases, the courts are highly deferential to counsel's trial strategy, but even an otherwise meritorious strategy "cannot be permissible" if it involves overriding a defendant's decision to testify, the court said. The constitutionally protected decision as to whether to testify belongs to the defendant, and his attorney cannot waive it over his objection. If the attorney believes that testifying is bad strategy, he or she is obligated to communicate and explain that view to the defendant. Nevertheless, if counsel is unsuccessful in persuading the defendant to forgo testifying for strategic purposes, counsel must accede to the client's wishes, however unsound he or she believes that approach to be.

The court distinguished cases in which the defendant reluctantly acquiesced in a strategy he did not favor. It is proper to infer such acquiescence, the court said, when the record shows only that the defendant knew of and wished to exercise his right to testify, that counsel took the opposite view, and that the defendant ultimately did not take the stand. Here, the record showed that the defendant repeatedly told his counsel he wanted to testify and that he was prevented from doing so solely by his counsel. Under the circumstances, the court refused to infer from the defendant's silence at trial that he acquiesced.

The court rejected the government's argument that a defendant must directly address the trial judge to assert his right to testify, or else lose his right to complain later. Although that rule would avoid posttrial swearing contests, it would be inconsistent with the way trials are run, the court said. "Careful defense counsel" routinely advise the judge out of the jury's hearing as to whether the defendant will or will not testify contrary to their advice, and judges usually ask the defendant if he understands his right to testify. Moreover, the court pointed out, defendants are generally instructed to address the judge only when asked to do so and must otherwise speak through their counsel. Accordingly, no waiver should be assumed from a defendant's silence.

With Respect to Whether Defendant Was Prejudiced

The court found defense counsel's strategy to be sound. Defense counsel used other witnesses to present essentially the same testimony that the defendant would have given. Noting that the defendant's extensive criminal record and history of drug use would come out if he were to testify, the court pronounced counsel's strategy sound and concluded that the defendant could not show prejudice. The jury was unlikely to credit the testimony of a felon against the testimony of a police officer, which was supported by a statement the defendant had signed, the court said.

15.2   UNITED STATES v. HOLMAN (SEVENTH CIR. 2002) (*Effective Assistance of Counsel*)

The defendant was indicted on one count of cocaine possession and three counts of firearms violations. Unlike the weapons charges, the drug charge did not carry a mandatory minimum sentence. At trial, counsel conceded the defendant's guilt on the possession charge in both his opening and closing statements, but vigorously defended on the weapons charges. There was no evidence in the trial or sentencing transcripts to show whether the defendant consented to that strategy.

    The defendant was convicted. He appealed, claiming that his lawyer rendered ineffective assistance of counsel.

- *Can the lawyer concede a client's guilt without a showing that the client consented?*
- *How do we determine if that is ineffective assistance of counsel? That is, what is the test? Apply it here. What do you conclude?*

United States v. Holman (Seventh Cir. 2002): 72 CrL 235

Conceding a client's guilt on one count of a multicount indictment amounts to a deficient performance by counsel. However, in this case, the defendant was not prejudiced by his lawyer's error.

With Respect to Deficient Performance of Counsel

There are cases in which conceding guilt on one count of a multicount indictment has been approved under the performance prong of *Strickland v. Washington,* 466 U.S. 668 (1984). Those are cases where, for example, the lawyer concedes guilt on a lesser count to build credibility with the jury, and that could be a valid trial strategy. In most cases in which that kind of performance is approved, however, there is evidence that the client consented to it. The lawyer is required by the 6th Amendment and by ethical considerations to consult with the client on important decisions such as this.

The court distinguished this case from those in which the concession is made at the very end of a trial when defense counsel, evaluating the prosecution's strong presentation, determines that the only hope for saving the defendant's credibility is to concede one count. Here, because the concession was made at the start of trial, the defendant lost the constitutional rights he would have relinquished in a guilty plea before trial—the privilege against self-incrimination, the right to trial by jury, and the right to confront his accusers. Before those rights can be extinguished, the defendant's agreement must be shown. "[T]o think otherwise would leave open a side door that would allow attorneys to abandon their clients."

With Respect to Whether Defendant Was Prejudiced

The court saw no way counsel could have mounted a successful defense to the drug charge. The court concluded that the concession strategy did not have a reasonable probability of affecting the trial's outcome.

The conviction was affirmed.

15.3   PAYNE v. STATE (S.C. 2003) (*Effective Assistance of Counsel*)

The defendant and his co-defendant were tried together on charges of murder and criminal conspiracy. They presented antagonistic defenses in which each blamed the other for murdering the victim. In closing argument to the jury, the co-defendant's counsel said:

> [Y]esterday you heard nothing but [co-defendant] Joe Kelsey because Joe wanted and was willing to sit right there and look y'all in your eyes and tell you the answer to the only questions that matter, not whether he remembered seeing blood when he talked about it at one point and didn't remember it another time or whether, you know, there is a two-inch difference in the size of the pipe bomb.

The defendant's counsel made no objection to this statement. The defendant was convicted. He applied for postconviction relief on the grounds that his counsel was ineffective for failing to object. At the postconviction relief trial, the attorney who represented the defendant at trial testified that the reason he had not objected was because he believed highlighting the co-defendant's testimony was favorable to the defendant's case, insofar as the co-defendant admitted acts that might have been the cause of the victim's death.

As you analyze this case, keep in mind that a defendant has a 5th Amendment right to remain silent and is not required to testify at trial. Further, it is improper to comment on that silence or to ask the jury to draw inferences from it. Of course, in this case, the comment was not made by the prosecutor, but by counsel for the co-defendant. Does that matter? Should it matter?

- *What is the test for determining ineffectiveness of counsel?*
- *Applying that test to these facts, do you conclude that this effort by defense counsel was deficient? Why?*

Payne v. State (S.C. 2003): 74 CrL 6

It was improper for the co-defendant's counsel to comment on the defendant's failure to testify. Remarking on the defendant's exercise of his right to remain silent is no less improper when done by counsel than it is when done by the prosecutor or the judge.

It was improper for the co-defendant's counsel to argue that the only reason the jury had heard from the co-defendant was because "he was willing to sit right there and look y'all in your eyes and tell you the answer." Because that was constitutionally improper, the failure of the defendant's attorney to object to it amounted to deficient performance for purposes of the defendant's 6th Amendment protection against ineffective assistance of counsel.

In [*] the South Carolina Supreme Court held that a co-defendant's counsel is held to the same standard as the prosecutor in the prohibition of direct or indirect comment on the defendant's decision not to testify. This protection is required, the court said, because of the effect a comment could have on the jury regardless of whose counsel made the comment. Here, the co-defendant's counsel's statement did indirectly refer to the fact that the defendant elected to remain silent; accordingly, the reference was an inappropriate comment on the defendant's constitutional right not to testify.

The test for ineffectiveness of counsel set out in *Strickland v. Washington,* 466 U.S. 668 (1984), has two prongs: The defendant must prove, first, that his counsel's performance was deficient and, second, that the deficiency prejudiced the outcome of the trial.

The attorney's failure to object to the improper comment satisfied the deficiency prong here. The court concluded, however, that the prejudice prong was not satisfied because overwhelming evidence proved that the defendant murdered the victim.

Two justices concurred in the result but for different reasons: In this case, the co-defendants' defenses were antagonistic to one another. In this situation, each lawyer must be given leeway to zealously represent his or her own client. They thought that the test should be one that focuses on whether the comment actually or implicitly invited the jury to infer the defendant's guilt from his silence. Cases in the Eighth and Eleventh Circuits support this position.

15.4   OUBER v. GUARINO (FIRST CIR. 2002) (*Effective Assistance of Counsel*)

The petitioner filed a habeas action; trial on the habeas was her third trial on a charge of selling cocaine from her car. The main testimony against her came from an undercover officer. The undercover officer claimed to have discussed the quality and weight of the cocaine with the petitioner and to have opened the envelopes containing the drug in her presence. During the petitioner's first two trials, she testified that she was only running an errand for her brother, did not know what was in the envelopes, and did not discuss drugs with the officer. Both those trials ended in jury deadlock.

During defense counsel's opening statement at the third trial, he promised the jury four times that the defendant would testify. He told the jury that they would "have to decide on truth and veracity of those two witnesses; and that will be your ultimate decision in this case." After the prosecution rested its case, counsel changed his mind about calling his client and persuaded her not to take the stand. He did call 24 character witnesses on her behalf to testify as to her reputation for veracity. Defense counsel also argued that some of the officer's testimony, along with testimony by a defense witness, supported a claim that the petitioner did not know what was in the envelopes.

After deliberating for parts of two days, the jury, like its predecessors, said it was deadlocked. The judge gave a "dynamite" instruction and the jury returned a verdict of guilty.

The petitioner claimed ineffective assistance of counsel.

- *What argument(s) can the petitioner make in support of that claim?*
- *What is the standard for determining ineffective assistance of counsel?*
- *What should the result be here? Why?*

Ouber v. Guarino (First Cir. 2002): 71 CrL 453

Failure to call the defendant after emphatically promising the jury in his opening statement that his client would testify in her own defense was constitutionally ineffective assistance of counsel.

The court observed that when a jury is promised that it will hear the defendant's story from the defendant's own lips, but the defendant does not take the stand, common sense suggests that the course of the trial can be profoundly altered. A broken promise of that magnitude taints both the lawyer who made it and the client on whose behalf it was made.

The state argued that defense counsel's midtrial decision should be excused as a justified reaction to unfolding events. Among other things, the state contended that the undercover officer's testimony was stronger and more consistent than it had been at the previous trials.

The court responded that, to the contrary, nothing occurred during the third trial that could have blindsided a reasonably competent attorney or justified a retreat from the promise. Anyway, it said, having the petitioner testify was the defense's only shot at controverting the undercover officer's account. The court also noted that the presentation of numerous witnesses to testify to the petitioner's veracity likely backfired when the jury did not hear from her.

The court concluded that counsel's performance fell below the minimum constitutional standard set out in *Strickland v. Washington*, 466 U.S. 668 (1984). "There is simply no record [to] support ... the finding that the attorney's conduct constituted a reasonable strategic choice. To the contrary, the only sensible conclusion that can be drawn from this record is that the attorney's performance was constitutionally deficient under *Strickland*—and severely so."

The court was equally skeptical of the argument that defense counsel's performance, even if constitutionally deficient, did not prejudice the petitioner. The court acknowledged that the situation did not call for a presumption of prejudice. However, it said a "unique circumstance" in this case made it relatively easy to find a strong possibility that counsel's error affected the outcome of the trial and was therefore prejudicial under *Strickland*. That circumstance was the fact that "the only substantial difference" among the petitioner's three trials "relates to the omission of her testimony at the third trial." After noting the critical differences between the stories of the petitioner and the undercover officer as to how the drug deal occurred, the court said:

> Because these contradictions were not introduced into evidence, the jury never had an opportunity to assess the conflicting testimony or to weigh the petitioner's credibility against [the officer's]. What is worse, counsel's belated decision not to present the petitioner's testimony sabotaged the bulk of his efforts prior to that time (and, in the process, undermined his own standing with the jury, thereby further diminishing the petitioner's chances of success). Because the error was egregious, we are fully persuaded that, but for its commission, a different outcome might well have eventuated.

The state court had found counsel's performance in this case in compliance with constitutional standards. It had opined that defense counsel's opening promises were not "dramatic" or "memorable." The First Circuit declared this conclusion difficult to understand in light of the lawyer's explicit and repeated promises to present the petitioner's testimony and his stress on the importance of her credibility.

The state court had also implied that the jury's initial report of deadlock showed that it was not immediately overborne by the detrimental effect of the broken promises, and that the error was therefore inconsequential. Saying that this argument "effectively assumes that because a blunder did not lead to a summary conviction, it was of negligible effect," the First Circuit declared that argument unreasonable.

15.5   STATE v. ROBINSON (WASH. 1999) (*Effective Assistance of Counsel*)

The defendant's problems stemmed from friction between his counsel and the trial judge. The judge held counsel in contempt twice during the defendant's trial and fined him for making disrespectful comments to the court. The second time the court held him in contempt, counsel left the courtroom and told the bailiff that he was not coming back. Counsel returned only after being ordered by the court to do so. It was apparent at this time, after the defense rested but before closing arguments, that the defendant told counsel that he wanted to testify. The evidence showed that defendant demanded of counsel to be allowed to take the stand and the lawyer conceded that the defendant "pleaded" with him to be allowed to testify. However, counsel did not move to reopen the evidence to allow the defendant to testify.

Counsel later testified that the reason he refused to move to reopen was that he was upset and wanted to end the case as soon as possible.

The defendant was convicted and claimed on appeal that he was deprived of his right to testify on his own behalf by the actions of his lawyer. The defendant argued that counsel rendered ineffective assistance of counsel, hence the defendant should get a new trial.

Note: The defendant could prevail in this case if he could show that his lawyer actually prevented him from testifying.

- *Was this ineffective assistance of counsel? Explain.*

State v. Robinson (Wash. 1999): 65 CrL 560

The court began with a discussion of the availability of an evidentiary hearing when it was alleged that counsel infringed the right to testify. Under case law in Washington and elsewhere, a defendant is entitled to such a hearing if he alleges that his lawyer "actually prevented him from testifying" and backs up the claim with factual allegations that are specific and credible.

Fleshing out the meaning of "actually prevented," the majority rejected the state's argument that the defendant must show that counsel coerced him into remaining silent. Such a showing would suffice, as would a showing that counsel misinformed the defendant of the consequences of testifying or made other misrepresentations to induce him to remain silent. However, the court made it clear that coercion and misrepresentation are not the only ways counsel can actually prevent a client from taking the stand. Counsel's refusal to call the defendant as a witness, after the defendant has unequivocally made his desire to testify known to counsel, also amounts to preventing the client from testifying.

The majority acknowledged that it is counsel's job to advise the client on the tactical implications of the decision of whether to testify, and that for counsel to persuade the defendant to change his mind is not an infringement of the defendant's right. Distinguishing that situation from one in which the lawyer ignored the client's wishes can be difficult. Nevertheless, the majority said it was unwilling to require that a defendant speak up in open court in order to assert the right.

Here, the defendant provided the necessary factual allegations. He submitted affidavits and other evidence indicating that he demanded of counsel to be allowed to take the stand; furthermore, the lawyer himself conceded that the defendant "pleaded" with him to be allowed to testify. The defendant was therefore entitled to an evidentiary hearing, at which he would have the burden of showing by a preponderance of the evidence that counsel actually prevented him from testifying.

The question of ineffective assistance of counsel is governed by *Strickland v. Washington*, 466 U.S. 668 (1984). *Strickland's* two-pronged inquiry provides the appropriate framework for the evidentiary hearing. Under the first or "performance" prong of *Strickland,* counsel falls below the objective standard of reasonable conduct for trial counsel preventing a client from testifying against the client's wishes.

Strickland's second, or "prejudice," prong requires proof of a reasonable probability that, but for counsel's errors, the result of the proceeding would have been different. The defendant argued that prejudice should be presumed when counsel has prevented the defendant from testifying, but the majority disagreed. It indicated that such conduct does not fall into the small class of circumstances, such as the complete denial of counsel at a critical stage or counsel's total failure to subject the state's case to adversarial testing, that are so likely to prejudice the defendant as to call for a presumption. Other courts that apply a *Strickland* analysis in this context have rejected a per se reversal rule, the majority added. Accordingly, the defendant must prove not only that he was prevented from testifying but also that his testimony would have a reasonable probability of producing a different outcome.

Four judges dissented. They contended that a defendant who was prevented by counsel from testifying should not have to show prejudice to obtain a new trial.

15.6   LETTLEY v. STATE (MD. 2000)
(*Effective Assistance of Counsel: Deficient Performance*)

Should a lawyer be allowed to withdraw from the representation of a criminal defendant after another client confidentially confessed to the crime of which the defendant was accused?

The lawyer's problem surfaced at a hearing the day before the start of the defendant's trial on charges arising from a nonfatal shooting. The lawyer told the trial court that an existing client, whom she represented on an unrelated matter, had come to her in confidence and confessed to the shooting. The trial court refused to allow the lawyer to withdraw. One of its reasons was that no other lawyer would have access to the confidential communication, so substituting a new lawyer would not improve the defendant's position. The court also expressed doubt about the credibility of the confessing client. Finally, the court feared that permitting withdrawal would be an "open invitation" to abuse. With self-representation the only other option, the defendant chose to stay with his current attorney. He was convicted of attempted murder and related crimes.

The defendant appealed his conviction, complaining that the trial court should have allowed the lawyer to withdraw and failure to do so violated his 6th Amendment right to conflict-free counsel. The defendant argued that the lawyer had an interest in staving off any renewed investigation of the crime, so as to benefit the confessing client. That interest limited both the extent to which counsel could investigate the crime and the way she could cross-examine witnesses.

The state argued that although it was true that the lawyer was ethically barred from using the other client's confession to help the defendant, a new attorney would have no way of learning about the confession. As a result, new counsel would be unable to provide better representation. This meant, according to the state, that there was no conflict of interest.

- *What result? Why?*

Lettley v. State (Md. 2000): 66 CrL 476

The lawyer should have been allowed to withdraw. Counsel faced a conflict of interest that adversely affected her representation, and that conflict was not dissipated by the fact that no other lawyer would have had the information that the defendant's lawyer could not use. Counsel suffered from "an actual conflict of interest which endangered [the defendant's] right to undivided loyalty and assistance. In order to properly defend [the defendant], counsel had, by implication, to incriminate her other client."

The lawyer had information that was relevant to cross-examination, but her ethical obligation to the source of that information, a client, prevented her from using that information. On the other hand, not to use the information would violate her duty to represent the defendant zealously.

The fact that new counsel would not be privy to the confidential information was immaterial. Counsel's fear of misusing the confidences of another client can create the risk that counsel might overcompensate and fail to cross-examine witnesses fully [*].

The trial court's fear of abuse was that a defendant could postpone a trial at will by having another person retain the defendant's counsel and give the lawyer a false confession. The appellate court responded that a defense lawyer's professionalism acts as a buffer against such abuse. Trial courts "should give credence to defense counsel's judgment that a confidential statement by a client should be taken seriously. Defense counsel is in the best position to make this judgment, and will often be ethically barred from giving the court sufficient information to make it independently" [*].

15.7   PEOPLE v. BERROA (N.Y. 2002)
(*Effective Assistance of Counsel: Deficient Performance*)

The defendant was accused of a fatal shooting on a Bronx street. Although several eyewitnesses identified the defendant as the perpetrator, the defense attempted to establish mistaken identity. To that end, it called three witnesses to testify that, at the time of the crime, the defendant did not have dark hair as described by the state's eyewitnesses, but had his hair dyed an orange-yellow color.

However, two of the witnesses went beyond their expected testimony and attempted to provide an alibi for the defendant, saying that he had been with them in Philadelphia on the day of the crime. After direct examination of the first witness, the trial court inquired of defense counsel why no notice of alibi had been filed before trial. Counsel indicated that she had elicited all the witnesses knew and none of them had been able to pinpoint the defendant's whereabouts on the day of the shooting. The court expressed concern that defense counsel might be called as a witness to impeach the false testimony. The court suggested that counsel could stipulate that the witnesses had not told her of the alibi information prior to trial, and counsel indicated agreement with this course.

When the trial resumed, both witnesses testified that they had told defense counsel of their alibi testimony. The defendant took the stand and testified both to his hair color and to being in Philadelphia on the day of the shooting.

After the defense rested, the court read to the jury a statement in which defense counsel stipulated that in meetings prior to the trial, neither of the witnesses had told counsel where the defendant was on the day of the crime. In her summation, counsel argued that the only issue was misidentification and that the jurors could either "disregard" or "look at" the alibi testimony.

The defendant was convicted and he appealed. The intermediate appellate court held, over one member's dissent, that the stipulation was a reasonable trial strategy.

This is an appeal from that decision.

- *Is this ineffective assistance of counsel or reasonable trial strategy? Explain your reasoning.*

People v. Berroa (N.Y. 2002): 72 CrL 173, reversing 733 N.Y.S.2d 52, 70 CrL 233

A defense lawyer rendered ineffective assistance by stipulating to facts that were facially adverse to the defendant to avoid having to testify herself. Entering the stipulation, which concerned what defense witnesses had told the lawyer prior to trial, was no different than the step counsel was trying to avoid—taking the stand and putting her credibility against that of the defense witnesses.

One issue that divided the intermediate appellate court was defense counsel's motivation for revealing to the trial judge what the witnesses had told her before trial. The majority here said she was fulfilling her ethical duties, whereas the dissenter accused her of acting to protect her reputation.

This court made clear that defense counsel's reason for disclosing the witnesses' statements to the trial judge is not the crux of this case. Instead, the proper focus on inquiry is the attempt to remedy the dilemma that unfolded once the witnesses testified. "Under the unusual facts of this case," the court agreed with the defendant that defense counsel's attempt to cure the problem with the stipulation "transformed" counsel "into an adverse witness whose credibility was pitted against his other witnesses."

Defense counsel faced a conflict of interest as a result of her trial preparation and her knowledge that the witnesses' testimony deviated from their pretrial statements. The court emphasized that the trial judge could have excluded the alibi testimony but did not do so. As a result, a dilemma arose when the trial judge suggested, and counsel did not dispute, that defense counsel was the only source who could impeach two of the defendant's key witnesses and thus stood to be called as a witness. The stipulation was meant to avert this prospect, but far from doing so, "it exacerbated the conflict by eviscerating the credibility" of the defense witnesses and the entire defense, the court said.

The court distinguished this case from another [*] in which it held that a defendant was not deprived of effective assistance of counsel, even though his counsel testified and contradicted the defendant's testimony. The lawyer in that case testified voluntarily in an attempt to further an insanity defense. The decision was a strategic one.

Here, by contrast, counsel was faced with being compelled to testify against her client in violation of the traditional advocate–witness rule. Thus, it was not trial strategy that motivated counsel to impeach her own witnesses via the stipulation. Another distinguishing feature noted by the court is that the counsel here, but not in the prior case, was the only course of the impeachment evidence.

In other cases [*] in which stipulations by defense counsel have been allowed, the defense lawyers' conduct supported the best defense or softened damaging evidence. That was not the case here. Defense counsel's stipulation "crystallized rather than cured the conflict of interest." The court pointed out that although counsel had a duty to disclose the witnesses' potential perjury to the trial judge, she was not automatically required to provide testimony to rebut the perjury.

15.8　SCAPA v. DUBOIS (FIRST CIR. 1994)
(*Effective Assistance of Counsel: Prejudice*)

The defendant was convicted of drug trafficking and unlawful distribution of cocaine. At trial, the state's two principal witnesses were a DEA agent and a Boston police detective. The DEA agent testified that the defendant passed cocaine to a third party who handed it to the DEA agent in exchange for $1,500 in cash. The defendant's trial counsel did not attempt to impeach the agent's testimony. Counsel offered no witnesses for the defense. During closing argument, counsel told the jury that the state's witnesses were credible and had no motive to lie. The defense argument was essentially a plea that the defendant was a "mere conduit" for the contraband.

The trial court found that this strategy effectively conceded the only disputed elements of the charged crimes and relieved the prosecution of its burden of proof. Being a "conduit" denotes acting as an agent or intermediary. Persons who knowingly serve as agents or intermediaries in narcotics transactions are punishable as principals under Massachusetts law.

- ■ *Is the defendant entitled to relief on his claim of ineffective assistance of counsel? Defend your answer.*

Scapa v. DuBois (First Cir. 1994): 56 CrL 1128

Substandard performance, in the nature of particular attorney errors, cannot be conclusively presumed to have been prejudicial. "Put bluntly, because [the attorney's] errors are more an example of maladroit performance than of nonperformance, *Strickland v. Washington,* 466 U.S. 668 (1984), necessitates an inquiry into the existence of actual prejudice."

The appellate court's review of the record convinced the judges that the defendant suffered no prejudice from counsel's ill-advised request that the jury credit the government's witnesses; that was minimized by the one-sidedness of the evidence. There was no contradictory version of the critical events that a skeptical jury otherwise might have chosen to believe.

15.9　STATE v. HUNT, 254 NEB. 865 (1998)
(*Effective Assistance of Counsel: Prejudice*)

The defendant was convicted of first-degree murder. On appeal, he complained that his counsel was ineffective because of statements the attorney made about the defendant in closing arguments to the jury. In part, the attorney said about the defendant that "he is a creepy, slimy, sexual degenerate. I don't think there is anyone in the courtroom who could call him anything else. He took the life of a beautiful young girl who died during the administration of events for his own sexual gratification. He's a creep. If you put ooze on the door, he would ooze into the door."

The defendant said the trial court should have presumed prejudice on the grounds that the attorney's comments and concessions were essentially a failure to subject the prosecution's case to meaningful adversarial testing.

The defendant said this couldn't possibly be attributed to tactics!

- *What result? And why?*

State v. Hunt, 254 Neb. 865 (1998)

The court found that the district court did not err in refusing to presume prejudice on the ground that the attorney's comments and concessions equaled a failure to subject the prosecution's case to meaningful adversarial testing.

The Nebraska Supreme Court also said, assuming arguendo, that the attorney's comments could be considered deficient, because the comments (in light of the evidence before the jury) did not prejudice the defendant. "Although he could have been more tactful in gaining credibility with the jury and showing that the prosecution's case relied on sympathy," said the court, it was a tactical decision, and because of the overwhelming evidence, there was no prejudice.

References

Brennan, William J., Jr. (1977). State constitutions and the protection of individual rights. *Harvard Law Review* 90:489.

Dressler, Joshua, and George C. Thomas, III. (1999). *Criminal Procedure: Principles, Policies, and Perspectives*. St. Paul, MN: West Group.

LaFave, Wayne R., and Jerold H. Isreal. (1985). *Criminal Procedure*. St. Paul, MN: West Publishing.

Index